STORIES OF
CRICKET'S
FINEST PAINTING
KENT v LANCASHIRE 1906

STORIES OF
CRICKET'S
FINEST PAINTING

KENT v LANCASHIRE 1906

JONATHAN RICE

First published by Pitch Publishing, 2019

Pitch Publishing
A2 Yeoman Gate
Yeoman Way
Worthing
Sussex
BN13 3QZ
www.pitchpublishing.co.uk
info@pitchpublishing.co.uk

ISBN 978 1 78531 505 3

Typesetting and origination by Pitch Publishing
Printed and bound in India by Replika Press Pvt. Ltd.

Contents

Acknowledgements

I HAVE had a great deal of help in researching the stories connected to *Kent v Lancashire 1906*, but in particular I would like to thank Adam Chadwick, Neil Robinson and Robert Curphey at MCC for letting me browse through their archives and minutes; Howard Milton and David Robertson at the Kent Cricket Heritage Trust for advice and access to the county archive; as well as Chris Beetles, Barrington Bramley, Andrew Brownsword, Nicholas Burrows, Derek Carlaw, Peter Cattrall, Barrie Dyer, Peter Francis, David Frith, Bill Gordon, Liam Knight, Tony Martin, Carl Openshaw, Catherine Reeve, Tim Rice, Tom Rice, Becca Smith, Simon Storey, Derek Ufton, Margaret Woodall and Henry Wyndham for their help, memories and comments.

I would also specially acknowledge the help of Chris Lane and Claire Weatherhead of Bloomsbury Publishing for permission to quote many passages from many different editions of *Wisden Cricketers' Almanack*. All material quoted from *Wisden* is © John Wisden & Co Ltd, used by kind permission of Bloomsbury Publishing Plc.

Thanks also to everybody at Pitch Publishing, without whom there wouldn't be a book. Finally, I would like to thank my wife Jan, who continues to tolerate me shutting myself away with my laptop and piles of books and magazines while suspecting no doubt that I am really just playing solitaire rather than doing any useful work. Without her, I would have to make my own coffee.

Canterbury Cricket Week

THE painting by Albert Chevallier Tayler, entitled *Kent v Lancashire 1906*, shows Colin Blythe, the Kent left-arm spin bowler universally known as 'Charlie', bowling to J.T. 'Johnny' Tyldesley of Lancashire, on a sunny August day at the St Lawrence Ground in Canterbury, the headquarters of Kent County Cricket Club. The painting clearly shows all 11 Kent players who took part in that match, as well as two Lancashire batsmen and one of the two umpires officiating that day. It shows flags flying and marquees crowded with spectators, as well as the bell tower of Canterbury Cathedral in the distance. Most importantly, at least to the man who commissioned it and to the members of the committee of the Kent County Cricket Club that paid for it, it shows that season's champion county in action at the height of their powers. It shows them showing off their skills among the large friendly crowds who flocked to Canterbury for Cricket Week, the oldest and most fashionable cricket festival of them all. As *The Times* leader writer put it a few years later in 1919, after the long bleak years of the First World War, 'Originally the property of Kent alone, the Week is now the property of all who love the game.'

Canterbury Cricket Week is still, well over a century after the picture was painted, the oldest continuing cricket festival on the planet. It dates back to 1842, only five years after Queen Victoria ascended to the throne and six years before W.G. Grace was born. There was no Kent County Cricket Club in those days, but the most important club in East Kent was the Beverley Club, which played its matches in St Stephen's Field, a little north of the cathedral on the other side of the River Stour, which runs through the city. Although St Stephen's Field is long gone, built over as the city expanded, there is still a Beverley Meadow in the same vicinity, no doubt the meadow which gave the club its name.

On Monday, 15 July 1839, the Beverley Club played a match against the Chilston Club, based near Maidstone. Only one day had been set aside for the game, which somewhat inevitably ended in a draw, but the crowds flocked to see the first appearance in Kent of two major figures of Kent and English cricket, Nicholas Wanostrocht, known as Felix, and Alfred Mynn, later to be renowned as the Lion of Kent. Felix played for the Beverley Club and Mynn for the Chilston XI, and such was their fame that some 4,000 spectators came along to enjoy the day. The committee of the Beverley Club, which had struggled to keep financially afloat since its founding in 1835, must have wondered why they did not charge admission for the game, and it must have occurred to them that if the right players could be assembled in the right place at the right time, there was money to be made. And the right place was obviously the Beverley Club ground.

A return match was played at Chilston Park later in the season, but that too was inconclusive, so in 1840 the two teams arranged a further pair of fixtures. The first was scheduled for two days in July 1840, at Chilston Park, and resulted in a clear six-wicket win for the Beverley Club. The return match was played over three days later that same month, at a new Beverley Ground, which was near to the Cavalry Barracks in Canterbury. It was here that the club for the first time charged admission, and with crowds of between 1,500 and 2,000 each day, the takings would have been very healthy – certainly enough to pay for the band of the 13th Dragoons based at the barracks to play every day, and still have plenty left over. The Chilston Club won the return match, thanks mainly to Norfolk-born Fuller Pilch, who scored 108 runs for once out, out of a total of 208 runs off the bat. Felix did his best for the Beverley Club, but it was not enough as they collapsed to defeat by 53 runs.

Of course, it was not just the Beverley Club that saw the earning potential of great matches played in festive surroundings. Gamblers loved cricket almost as much as they loved horse racing, and it was just as easy a sport to bet on. In 1841, a 'Grand Cricket Match For One Thousand Guineas' took place at Lord's, presumably with the tacit agreement of MCC, between Kent and England. The Kent team was made up of leading cricketers from all around the county, but the direction clearly came from Canterbury. Kent won the first game by 70 runs, largely thanks to the bowling of Alfred Mynn and William Hillyer. A return match was fixed for Canterbury, beginning on 10 August 1841.

This was the match that created the atmosphere and public fervour which allowed Canterbury Cricket Week to develop. On the first day as many as 4,000 people came to watch the match, including, as the local journals noted, the leading county families. A 'large booth' was set up for some 300 of these pillars of Kent society to sit down to lunch, and although England won the match easily enough, the success of the day on every level – sporting, financial and social – was enough to encourage the Beverley Club committee to make bigger plans for 1842.

That first Canterbury Cricket Week in 1842 was defined in an official history published in 1865 as 'the first occasion when the two great matches, Kent v England and Gentlemen of England v Gentlemen of Kent, were played in Canterbury'. The point of Canterbury Cricket Week from the very outset was not just to play games of cricket, but also to give the leading county families (and, in passing, the other citizens of Canterbury) a thoroughly entertaining week at the height of summer, a week which would also serve to fill the coffers of the Beverley Club.

However, to ensure that the Canterbury Week would be socially acceptable, it needed the active support of some of the great names of the county. Men such as the Earl of Thanet and J. Stoddart Douglas, the owner of Chilston Park, were always visible in the crowds from the beginning, as was one of the best and most controversial cricketers of his era, the Rev. Lord Frederick Beauclerk, who had been the president of MCC in 1826. Also a regular visitor was the MP for Dover, Edward Rice, who had in 1829 enjoyed the rare distinction of being blackballed when applying for membership of MCC. We have no idea what his misdemeanours might have been, but given that the foul-mouthed and universally loathed Frederick Beauclerk had achieved membership, it is hard to imagine that anything less than being a member of the wrong political party could have been the cause. His proposer for MCC had been Benjamin Aislabie, secretary and a former president of MCC, which makes it all the odder, but at least Rice was not blackballed from the festivities of Canterbury Week. Aislabie himself attended in 1841, the year before he died, further strengthening the link between Kent and London cricket. This link was essential to the continuing success of the festival week, and in the darker years it could be argued that the link was the only reason the Week was able to keep going.

It seems that arranging for the best cricketers to come down to Canterbury for a week was not an insurmountable problem, provided that the city could also offer entertainment in the evening that did not necessarily merely involve the many public houses frequented by the Dragoons, most of which were not known either for their sophistication or for their standards of cleanliness and hospitality. It was felt, therefore, that some kind of evening entertainment should also be arranged for those of higher social standing, and after much consideration, although a Grand Fancy Dress Ball was also planned, the centrepiece of the social week was to be an amateur theatrical performance. As the publications of the day put it, 'The first of a series of Amateur Performances was given, in the old and time-honoured Temple of the Drama in Orange Street'. From that time until very recently, Canterbury Cricket Week has been closely linked with the performances of the troupe that became known as The Old Stagers, and Kent society loved it.

The driving force behind the Beverley Club's efforts in the early years was Mr John Baker, the secretary of the club, but the men who did more than anybody else to establish the Week on the social calendar as more than just a couple of good games of cricket were Frederick Ponsonby and Charles Taylor. Ponsonby, the eldest son of the Earl of Bessborough, whose title he would inherit in 1880, was the leading man, along with his brother Spencer and John Loraine Baldwin, both behind the formation of The Old Stagers and in front of the footlights. Charles Taylor, a Londoner who had become firm friends with the Ponsonby brothers during their undergraduate days at Cambridge, was a great cricketer and a great eccentric. He was described as 'the finest Gentleman batsman of the time', playing mainly for Sussex and for the Gentlemen against the Players. In the 1843 match, he was recorded as being given out 'hat knocked on wicket, b Hillyer 89'. He also was reputed to have learnt to play the piano in six weeks, but to what level we do not know. He certainly loved to perform and be the centre of attention. He played cricket occasionally during the Week, but was a tower of strength at the Orange Theatre. In 1842, the troupe came down from London by sea to Ramsgate, and from there by coach to Canterbury, and despite the rigours of the journey and the fact that he had badly injured his arm playing cricket a few weeks before, Taylor insisted on playing the part of 'Desdemona (a striking beauty)' with his arm in splints and a sling. The prologue, a 46-line piece of rhyming couplets, which gave new meaning to the word 'doggerel', included the lines:

> And though our best man's arm be out of joint
> Despite his splints, he'll try and make a point.

It must have been a distressing sight.

The 'amateur band', which gave musical accompaniment to the splintered Mr Taylor's performance, was conducted by Nicholas Wanostrocht, and included two notable cricketers of the day in Herbert Jenner and Charles Baldock. The first rehearsals of the band were reported to have proved that 'mirth and music

14

did combine'. Whether either mirth or music was felt by the audience is another matter. Nevertheless, the success of The Old Stagers' amateur theatricals and the Grand Fancy Dress Ball, held at the Assembly Rooms on the Wednesday evening, laid down a prototype for the Week which was built on over the next few years.

That first Canterbury Week in 1842 produced two excellent matches, in the first of which Kent were thoroughly beaten by England (beginning a tradition that over the years has shown that the Kent county side has frequently performed remarkably poorly during Canterbury Week), and in the second of which the Gentlemen of Kent restored the county's honour by beating the Gentlemen of England by 173 runs. The leading families of Kent continued to support the whole Week, enjoying not only the cricket but also the balls and the theatrical offerings in the evening. It quickly became the major annual event at which all of Kent society could gather and the Week established a reputation for being where the well-heeled young of the county could meet, talk, dance and, frequently, fall in love. The *Kentish Gazette*, albeit an interested party for whom the success of the Week was important, told of 'bouquets of flowers and evergreens, which contrasted with the verdant lawn, and the varied coloured dresses of the ladies produced a very animated and picturesque scene'. The writer, reporting early in the Week, was sure that 'the remainder of the week, if the weather continues favourable, will draw a greater number of visitors to the city than has been known for many years past'. This was a big claim to make, but it shows how rapidly and strongly the Canterbury Week festival had captured the imagination of the local populace, as well as the wider cricket community.

The success of the Grand Week, as it was described, produced a 'cricket fervour' in Canterbury, and after the end of the week several 'Citizens' Matches' were played in and around the city, and financially the risks of staging cricket on such a grand scale seemed to have paid off for the Beverley Club: the balance sheet was reportedly in fine shape.

For the 1843 season, the Beverley Club changed its name to the East Kent Cricket Club, and subsequently to the Beverley Kent Club, perhaps to reflect the wider range of its cricketing authority, and the second Cricket Week was as successful as the first, despite rather poor weather towards the end of the week. The matches were the same as the previous season – Kent v England, and Gentlemen of Kent v Gentlemen of England. These were not just matches of local interest: Kent were acknowledged as one of the strongest teams in the country and the England side was a very strong representation of what the rest of the country had to offer. For those in Kent who loved their cricket, these were matches not to be missed. Kent beat England very easily, by nine wickets, thanks largely to the batting of Fuller Pilch (57 not out), and the all-round strength of the county's bowling attack, consisting of the Mynn brothers, as well as Martingell and Hillyer. The Gentlemen of Kent also had the best of their game, winning by 31 runs despite frequent stops for rain. In this game, Alfred Mynn, the Lion of Kent, took ten wickets.

The 'Private Theatricals' also played their part in the success of the Week. The main production was Sheridan's *The Critic*, in which most of the parts were taken by members of the cricket teams, but some performers were obviously more professional. The part of Miss Dangle, for instance, was played by 'Miss Sidney' (of the theatres York and Cambridge), and Tilburina by 'Mrs Walter Lucy' (of the theatres Royal Covent Garden and Drury Lane). Other productions of *Othello (Travestie)*, *Bombastes Furioso!*, *A Roland For An Oliver* and *High Life Below Stairs* were also performed by the troupe, who must have put at least as much time and effort into their acting as into their cricket. The accent was always on farce, with men playing some of the female roles, to the obvious delight of the audience. A certain Michael Bruce was particularly fond of the female roles, clambering into women's clothing year after year for the amusement of his audience.

In 1844 the connection between the Beverley Kent Club and MCC was further strengthened by the president of the Beverley Club, Sir John Bayley, being elected president of MCC. Bayley was a remarkable man for his era, a baronet with some sense of social awareness. His two passions were cricket and horse racing, and in 1823 he resolved that his newborn son would be named after the winner of that year's Derby. The two favourites were apparently called Emilius and Lollipop. Fortunately for the boy, who was to become a successful cricketer in his own right, Emilius won and the child became Emilius Bayley. As Arthur Duke Coleridge wrote in his book, *Eton In The Forties*, 'Lollipop out of Sweetmeat would have been a very trying name for an Eton boy'.

Despite the leadership that Bayley gave to the Beverley Club, and to MCC, he was far more interested in cricket than the social scene. His time at MCC included overseeing a 12 per cent increase in membership, from 417 to 465, and a greater interest in the welfare of the professional cricketers, who until this time had no real champion at MCC or in the counties. He was instrumental in setting up, in 1847, the Cricketers' Fund, which was to help professional cricketers 'in case of sickness or accident'.

Sir John attended Canterbury Week in 1844, despite his obligations at Lord's, but it was a year in which the weather once again played its part, rather more forcefully and decisively than the year before. As a contemporary report noted, on the first day, 13 August, 'the wind blew the booths down, broke the supports and did sad havoc'. The storms continued all week and the Kent v England match had to be played 'at intervals between the showers'. However, the storms abated for the Friday which gave the ground 'for the first time during the week, an appearance of animation and enjoyment'. Canterbury Week has always needed to be a time of enjoyment, even if on occasions over the years there has been little sign of animation on the cricket pitch.

A scandal hit the 1844 production of *Esmeralda*, a burlesque written for Canterbury Week and performed by The Old Stagers, which was accused of political bias by a local journal. The production, it was claimed, criticised 'domestic policy of the existing government, of which some slashing hits at Peel and others ... were loudly applauded by the audience in all parts of the theatre'. So despite its popularity, *Esmeralda* was cut from the programme for the rest of the week. William Bolland, another of the original Old Stagers who played a fair amount of cricket, explained to the audience that it had been suggested to the management of the theatre that 'a few words had, by a distortion of their meaning, given offence to some of the firmest supporters of the Cricket Week', and so the management immediately withdrew the play 'to the regret of many'. Then Sir John Tylden, a strong supporter of the Week and all that went with it, responded by thanking the cast and disassociating himself from the 'foolish and wicked attack which had been made, expressing a hope that they would be spared another year'. From this distance it is hard to understand what the fuss might have been about, and certainly the criticism of the domestic policy of Peel's government would be seen as lightweight in comparison with some of the political comment today. But it was severe enough to create concern that they might not be spared another year.

Whether the *Esmeralda* scandal had anything to do with it or not, by the end of 1844 the Beverley Club's finances were not in good shape. They had an overdraft of £250, equivalent to at least £30,000 today, which they managed to keep under control by public and private subscriptions. But it was not a situation that could last. In July 1845, the wandering cricket club I Zingari was formed by the Ponsonby brothers and John Baldwin, with other Canterbury stalwarts such as William Bolland, Charles Taylor and many others being elected members of the new club, so their attention was to an extent diverted from Canterbury Week. They did not desert completely – the Gentlemen of England team that played against the Gentlemen of Kent that summer included six IZ players in their side – but they did not do as much work behind the scenes as before. This did not help the Beverley Club's finances.

Over the winter of 1846–47, the club moved to a new and final home at St Lawrence at the eastern edge of Canterbury. The great batsman Fuller Pilch was appointed as groundsman, and he managed to create a playable surface by mid-May 1847, when the first match at the St Lawrence Ground took place. The Cricket Week began on 2 August, but once again the fates were against the organising committee, who had to report at the end of the Week that although the weather was beautiful, 'the general election which was taking place at the time prevented so large an assemblage of the leading families and visitors as on other occasions'. The election was a fiercely argued and closely fought one, being the first since the repeal of the Corn Laws the year before, so it was not surprising that the leading families of the county should have been more occupied by politics than cricket. It was won by the Whig Party led by Lord John Russell, who captured a majority of the popular vote but a minority of the seats. The repeal of the Corn Laws had brought into sharp focus the deep split in the Conservative Party between the trade protectionists, led by Lord Stanley, and the free traders, led by Robert Peel. The party was so disunited that the Whigs were able to remain in power for another five years. The lessons of 1847 were obviously not studied by the modern Conservative Party before the 2016 referendum on EU membership. Politics and sport always seem to find a way to trip each other up.

By 1849, despite the establishment of Canterbury Cricket Week as a mainstay of Kent's summer social season, the Cricket Club was in dire financial straits. A meeting on 17 March that year was called to decide whether to carry on or wind up the club. The meeting was poorly attended and the 'apathy evinced for the future welfare of the Club by its members was so truly disheartening' that the committee resigned en bloc, and effectively turned off the club's life support machine. However, reports of its death proved to be premature, as when word of this meeting got out, other citizens of Canterbury resolved to make sure that the Cricket Week, at least, would carry on. With backing from the Earl of Winchilsea, who was the son of one of the founders of the Marylebone Cricket Club as well as being a major landowner at Eastwell, near Ashford, the club secured enough money to carry on, and the eighth Canterbury Week was saved.

Throughout the 1850s and 1860s, while Canterbury Week was establishing itself ever more securely in the social calendar, the club that organised and hosted the cricket matches was limping from crisis to crisis. There was always a reason why the crowds were never large enough to cover the bills – the 1851 Great Exhibition 'took away many who would otherwise have assembled at the favourite August trysting place for Kentish lasses and lads', for example – but in 1859 a greater threat to the financial well-being of the club appeared. A meeting was held in Maidstone, chaired by the Earl of Darnley, proposing the formation of a Kent County Cricket Club, not in opposition to the organisers of Canterbury Week, as they were at pains to point out, but simply to have the opportunity of taking the increasingly popular game of cricket to other parts of the county. The meeting enthusiastically approved the new venture. The new Kent County Cricket Club based itself in West Kent, a long and arduous ride from Canterbury, and started slowly, playing only ten matches in its first two seasons. Throughout the 1860s it played county matches at places as far afield as Chatham and Tonbridge, as well as at Canterbury. By the early 1860s, matches between 'Kent' and other counties such as Sussex, Surrey, Nottinghamshire and Middlesex were being played under the auspices of the Kent County Club, at Margate, Faversham, Maidstone, Crystal Palace and Gravesend, but the climax of the season was still Canterbury Week, when Kent played England and MCC.

In 1862, the great hero of the Week, as far as the spectators were concerned, was E.M. Grace, who played for MCC against the Gentlemen of Kent, and scored 192 not out, of his side's total of 344. In this 12-a-side match, the 20-year-old Grace also took five wickets in the first innings and ten wickets for 69 in the second, which were all the wickets to fall, as the last man was recorded as absent. The match was, however, played under protest, and might have caused lasting damage to Canterbury Week, had tempers not cooled in time. Two matches were scheduled for the week, the first being a comparatively friendly fixture between England and Fourteen of Kent. Hon. Spencer Ponsonby, who was running the fixtures on behalf of MCC, was having great difficulty in raising an England team, and just when he thought he had 11 men, Tom Hayward had to drop out through illness. E.M. Grace was immediately contacted, and he said that he would come and play, on condition that he was also allowed to play in the second match of the Week, MCC v Gentlemen of Kent. The manager of the Week, William de Chair Baker, agreed to this request, and so E.M. came to play both games. In the first game he scored a duck in the first innings, but did rather better in the second, making 56. When it came to the second match, the captain of the Kent side, William South Norton, knowing nothing of Baker's promise to Ponsonby and Grace, objected to Grace playing for MCC when he was not a member of the club. This is described as 'a little friction' in the club history, but the truth of the matter seems to have been that Norton was adamant that neither Grace nor E.W. Burnett, a bowler who was listed in the MCC XI despite also not being a member of the club, should play for MCC. While all this discussion was going on, Spencer Ponsonby was in rehearsals for The Old Stagers' programme that evening.

As there were several other MCC members at the ground, it was suggested that E.M. be elected by them there and then, but this proved to be not possible under MCC rules. Luckily this was 1862 when the waiting list for MCC membership was rather less than the 20+ years it takes these days, but it still proved impossible to elect him or Mr Burnett to the club. Norton then declared that the Kent team would refuse to play, but when it was pointed out to him that if they did not play, all the gate money would have to be returned to the thousands who had turned up to watch, but also it was quite possible that MCC would not wish to take part in future Canterbury Weeks, he relented. Baker also added that he had given his word to Ponsonby that Grace would be allowed to play, so if the game were to be cancelled, he would have to resign his position. The match went ahead, but as one Kent Gentleman later said, 'we, unwillingly, I must say, and under protest, played the match. We all thought that, as there were competent cricketer members of MCC on the ground, it was somewhat out of place to play two men, neither of whom was a member of the club.'

By 1866, W.G. Grace had joined his elder brother at Canterbury, playing for 'South Of The Thames' against 'North Of The Thames', W.G.'s birthplace of Downend near Bristol being 0.016 degrees of latitude (just over one mile) south of Tower Bridge. W.G. also played for 'Gentlemen Of The South' against I Zingari in that Canterbury Week, both of which games, along with the third match of that week, Gentlemen of Kent v MCC, are listed under 'MCC matches' in the 1867 *Wisden*. This was a sign that control over Canterbury Week was slipping away from the ever-weakening Beverley Club. Matters did not improve in the next two years, although the profile of cricket all around the country was being raised by the astonishing exploits of the young W.G. Grace, and this had a positive effect on Canterbury Week spectator numbers.

By the last decades of the 19th century, Canterbury Week was one of the highlights of the county's holiday season. The first railway line in Kent, the Canterbury and Whitstable Railway, locally known as the 'Crab and Winkle', had opened in 1830, with the world's first season tickets sold for that line a year later. By the 1850s railways were criss-crossing the county, allowing people from London, both from high society and from the East End, to enjoy summer sunshine in Kent. People came down from London for the hop-picking, to build sandcastles and sunbathe on the sands at Margate and Folkestone, and to watch the cricket at Canterbury. St Lawrence during Canterbury Week would be a sea of tents stretching halfway around the ground (but never obscuring the lime tree), tents hosted by wandering cricket clubs such as I Zingari and the Band of Brothers, by the President of Kent CCC, by the Mayor of Canterbury, by military units like the Buffs and the East Kent Yeomanry, by The Old Stagers and by several smaller private tents for rich members of the crowd who had not been invited into any other tent. Each tent flew a flag which added to the colour and pomp of the occasion. One day of each Week was set aside as 'Ladies' Day', when the fashions of the ladies were displayed even more prominently, it seemed, than the cricket. What might seem somewhat condescending and sexist to modern eyes was a joyous highlight of every Week for over a century, and in the latter part of the 19th century and the early 1900s the fashion highlights were as eagerly reported on as any cover drive or smart stumping.

The St Lawrence ground during Canterbury Week showed Britain at play, all classes in what was still a very stratified society enjoying the experience in their own ways. In many seasons, the only first-class games played in Canterbury were the two in Canterbury Week, so it was not surprising that the cricket lovers of the city should be so enthusiastic during their Festival Week.

A certain Lt Col Newnham-Davis, writing in 1907, describes Canterbury Week as 'the Goodwood of cricket, and the first sight of the great half hoop of tents, the flags, the carriages, and the moving crowd does suggest a racecourse'. He lists many of the tents that reappear every year, and many of the names still ring with a Kent connection over a century later. 'There is no merrier tent at teatime,' he writes, 'than Mrs Neame's pavilion, set back from the main line of tents and screened by little trees and flowering shrubs.' Shepherd Neame, the Faversham brewers, are still the main sponsors of the county club, and the ground is now named the 'Spitfire Ground' after their most famous brand of beer. Several Mrs Neames throughout the generations have entertained merrily down the years.

In 1876, *Wisden* described Canterbury Cricket Week as 'the most famous yet played', partly because W.G. Grace scored 344 playing for Gentlemen of MCC against Kent, the first triple century ever made in first-class cricket and still the highest score ever made on the St Lawrence Ground, but also because of the 'large and brilliant assemblages on the cricket ground', including the 'maids, matrons and magnates of the county'. The first day, Monday, was the August Bank Holiday and the sun shone. The game was an odd one – Kent and Gloucestershire against the Rest of England – but that did not stop a huge crowd of people coming to the ground. 'Kent and Gloucestershire' was little more than a ruse to fit two of the Grace brothers, W.G. and G.F., and their cousin William Gilbert into the home side, and the match petered out into a draw. Even the next match, in which W.G. made his record score, was drawn and the third match of the Week, against I Zingari, was not even begun. However, the character of Canterbury Cricket Week is not affected by the results of the games played: it is a celebration of cricket, of summer and of the county of Kent. As a journalist wrote in 1908,

'How very poor cricket would be without these Kentish festivals. All the glories of a great game are crowded in them. Kent cricket belongs exclusively to Kent. It is always a rich sporting carnival. Such cricket is not possible outside of Kent and I am glad that the people of the county are so jealous of it all.'

* * * *

There had always been one potential problem which could have spelt the end of this particular Kentish festival at any time. This was the fact that the county club, now firmly established, did not own the St Lawrence ground. In the first half-century of Canterbury Week, the ground was owned by George Milles, Lord Sondes, whose family home was at Lees Court near Faversham, very close to the Harris estate at Belmont House. Milles, a politician, began life as the heir to a barony, but in 1880 was promoted to the rank of earl, but whichever way you look at it, he was still a lord. The club rented the ground at £40 a year from Lord Sondes's tenant, at Winter's Farm in Nackington, but in 1890 the rent was raised to £50 a year. There was always the theoretical possibility that Lord Sondes, who was a cricket lover and had been Kent's club president in both 1873 and 1887, might nevertheless wish to sell the land or use it for some other purpose, which would have forced Canterbury Week to come to an end. In 1894, the first Earl Sondes died and his son, who as Viscount Throwley had been president in 1891, decided he wished to sell the St Lawrence Ground. Throwley had played half a dozen games for the county in 1882 and 1884, although oddly enough none of them had been at his own ground in Canterbury. Fortunately, he was willing to give the club first refusal when it came to selling. Lord Harris knew that for the club to buy the ground was the only sensible course if the Canterbury Week, and with it the club, were to be safe, and so negotiations began. Sondes wanted £5,500 for the 13-acre site, a little over £500,000 in today's money, but Harris's valuers put it at only £4,000. In the end, Sondes proved his commitment to the club by agreeing to a figure of £4,500 for the unencumbered freehold, a price that today we would consider a wonderful bargain, even allowing for inflation. The parcels of land sold off by the club for housing in the early 2000s fetched several millions of pounds. In the 1890s the club struggled to meet the price, but achieved their target through a mix of donations by subscribers, the sale of government Consols and a transfer from the club savings. Now the club owned its headquarters and Canterbury Week was safe indefinitely. However, the two main instigators of the purchase, Lord Harris and George Marsham, a long-serving committee member and cousin of Slug Marsham, were clear that this would not mean that Kent would be playing more first team matches at Canterbury. As *Wisden* reported, 'there does not seem any idea of the county committee arranging matches at Canterbury, outside the time-honoured week at the beginning of August'. The Kent eleven would remain peripatetic despite now having a permanent home.

By the turn of the century, cricket was entering what is now seen as a golden age, and Canterbury Cricket Week was its seasonal high point. It was this, as much as Kent's cricketing success, that Lord Harris wanted to celebrate in 1906.

Kent County Cricket Club

In the 1860s, relations between the two big Kent cricket clubs were cordial, but it soon became clear that there was not room for two major clubs, both claiming in some way to be in charge of cricket in the county. In 1865, the secretary of the Kent County Club, William South Norton, wrote to his counterpart at the Beverley Club, William de Chair Baker, stating his committee's view that 'the cricket of the county might be much improved in the future if an amalgamation … could be obtained without interference in the maintenance of the Canterbury Week in its integrity'. Baker wrote back, rejecting the Kent County Club's overtures and suggesting that any amalgamation would be harmful to the Beverley Club, who had the one jewel in the county's cricketing crown, Canterbury Week.

Both clubs struggled on, short of money and short of any major success on the cricket field, until by 1870 matters had reached a crisis. The Beverley Kent Club was still officially hosting an outwardly thriving Canterbury Cricket Week every August, so famous and socially important that it was able to attract the biggest names in cricket, but behind the painted smile was a weeping accountant or two.

The figures quoted by Lord Harris in his 1907 publication *The History of Kent County Cricket* show that in 1864, the club made a loss of £68 on an income of £162 from the Week; in 1865, when Baker turned down the first overtures from the Kent County Club, the loss was £44; and in 1866 and 1867, the loss each year was over £100. In 1868 there was another year of loss, and despite small profits in 1869 and 1870, the total losses over the most recent seven years before the amalgamation meeting in 1870 totalled £362 on gate receipts of £1,211. Running a Week that cost 30 per cent more than it earned could not continue for long. It seemed inevitable that the Beverley Kent Club should look to amalgamate with the Kent Cricket Club at last.

It was not only in Kent that changes were in the air. From 1864, an informal system of declaring a champion county had been in place, which was widely if not universally recognised as conferring the laurels fairly. In the absence of any organised international cricket, this was the ultimate prize that any county cricket club could aim for. Surrey, Nottinghamshire, Middlesex and Yorkshire dominated those early seasons, and Kentish pride was dented. Kent was a cradle of cricket as old as any other county, and it hosted the biggest and most fashionable cricket festival in England, so why could it not organise itself to win the County Championship? Yorkshire, Lancashire, Surrey, Sussex, Worcestershire and Middlesex had already formed county-wide cricket clubs, and Derbyshire and Gloucestershire both established themselves in 1870. Because there was no club that had a clear mandate to organise county cricket in Kent, and because the Canterbury Week had become such a fashionable cricketing success, many of the best amateur players had little interest in playing for their county, but preferred to play country house cricket, of which there was plenty in Kent, with only occasional forays into county cricket. This left the county side rather weak, which in turn further discouraged the better amateurs from playing. Which was the chicken and which was the egg in this problem is hard to determine, but if Kent had a well organised county side to take on the bigger counties, especially the northern powerhouses of Yorkshire, Lancashire and Nottinghamshire, then the best players could be persuaded to play for the county more often.

On 13 October 1870, the committee of the Kent County Club met and passed a motion that 'this meeting is of the same opinion with regard to an amalgamation with the Beverley Club as that expressed in a report issued in 1865'. It was suggested that rather than risk writing to Mr Baker again, a personal approach might work better. The task of persuading the Beverley Club to consider amalgamation was given to Herbert Knatchbull-Hugessen, a member of a grand cricket-loving Kent family who were based at Mersham, near Ashford. It was always likely to be a difficult task, requiring a great deal of tact and diplomacy. As Knatchbull-Hugessen himself wrote a few years later, the Kent County Club 'was regarded as a West Kent club by many East Kent people and, perhaps not unnaturally, there was a kind of antagonistic feeling between the two divisions, and a little jealousy. I am bound, in passing, to state that this feeling was stronger in East Kent, because it was suspected by some that there was a desire on the part of West Kent to interfere with the Canterbury Week, and have the matches at Maidstone'.

Despite the overdose of suspicion from the Beverley Club, Knatchbull-Hugessen's approach was successful, and thus it was that on 6 December 1870, a meeting was held of members of both the Kent County Club and the Beverley Kent Club, at the Bull Hotel in Rochester. The Bull, an old staging inn, had been carefully chosen as the venue for the meeting which was to unite the two clubs, one based in Tonbridge in the deepest western recesses of Kent, and the other in Canterbury, a long way to the east. Rochester is on the River Medway, which traditionally marks the dividing line between East and West Kent, but the Bull is just on the east side of the river, an inn fit for a Man (or Maid) of Kent. On the other side of the river are the Kentish Men and Kentish Maids, and although the distinction these days is now more a matter of idle banter than anything else, in past times the distinction was clear. Kent is a big county, and it is still difficult to travel smoothly from, say, Tunbridge Wells to Canterbury despite the presence of motorways and railways. For railway travellers, the loudspeaker message 'Change at Tonbridge for Tunbridge Wells and High Brooms' strikes like an icicle through the heart, and road travellers who have to make the choice between using the M2, M20 and M25, or the country lanes through Biddenden, Tenterden and Goudhurst, will know better than to expect to arrive at the appointed time. Kent is still really two counties. Uniting the two halves into one cricket club might not have been an easy project. So it was a clever piece of political flattery that caused the County Club to suggest a meeting place just within East Kent, the home turf of the Beverley Club.

The evening chosen for the first meeting was cursed with weather that was described as 'inclement' even for December, which meant that many supporters of the amalgamation could not get to the meeting. However, there was still a good number of keen Kent cricket supporters who braved that December night in horse-drawn coaches and railway carriages, and even on foot, to debate the resolution 'that the Kent County Club and the Beverley Kent Cricket Club be amalgamated in one club, to be called the Kent County Cricket Club, and that the St Lawrence Cricket Ground, Canterbury, be the County Cricket Ground'. This may have been another sop to the Beverley Club, but in truth St Lawrence, which by now had hosted many major matches, was by far the best ground in the county and it would have made no sense to have tried to base the club anywhere else. Nevertheless, the new club always intended to play on as many grounds around the county as it could, and in this it certainly succeeded. First-class cricket continued to be played all around the county as much after 1870 as before, which only served to emphasise the excitement when Kent played at Canterbury during Canterbury Week. A final resolution was included as a counterbalance for the western element: 'That a President be chosen alternately from East and West Kent, and a Committee consisting of ten gentlemen from East Kent, and ten from West Kent, be formed to conduct the business of the club.' Given the time it had taken to get to this point, it was surprising but nevertheless gratifying that the resolutions were carried with enthusiasm. The second resolution did much to put the East Kent contingent's minds at rest: 'That the entire management of Canterbury Cricket Week be retained by Mr W de Chair Baker, the amalgamation being effected upon the basis that no change whatever take place in this Annual Meeting at Canterbury.'

The man chairing this meeting was George Francis Robert Harris, 3rd Lord Harris, a man of frail health who had nevertheless been Governor of Trinidad from 1846 to 1854, and Governor of Madras from 1854 to 1859. His grandfather, the 1st Lord Harris, was the soldier son of the rector of Brasted, a village just west of Sevenoaks in Kent. He had fought successfully in America and India and had been rewarded with the title of Baron Harris of Seringapatam and Mysore, and of Belmont in the County of Kent, in 1815. The Harris family were long-established in the county, but comparative newcomers among its nobility.

The 3rd Lord Harris's son, also George, had been born in Trinidad while his father was governor there. He soon grew to love cricket and eagerly accompanied his father to the founding meeting of the Kent County Cricket Club. Lord Harris was duly nominated as president in the club's founding year, and the 18-year-old George Harris, fresh out of Eton and beginning his time at Oxford University, was invited to join the committee.

Young George, a slim youth, slightly on the tall side and with the beginnings of a moustache which was to grow more luxurious with the years, had played for Eton for three seasons from 1868 to 1870, and would win his cricket Blue at Oxford in 1871, 1872 and 1874. One of the most famous photographs of him shows him posing at the wicket with bat, pads and gloves and a high starched collar and bow tie, as well as his ubiquitous panama hat. That image may seem a caricature of a country house cricketer to us today, but there is no doubt that young George Harris was a very good cricketer, a fine batsman, a bowler who strove to bowl as fast as he could, with varying degrees of success, and a fielder of the highest calibre. He merited the place that he would go on to win in both the Kent and England sides through pure cricketing skills, and not because of his social connections. But the social connections certainly helped in his Kent committee work.

Despite the geographical imbalance, and the fact that the wealthier citizens of the county were generally Kentishmen rather than Men of Kent, the new club based in Canterbury seemed to work. There was good will on all sides. Much of the organisational skill came from the West Kent contingent, but the administration of Canterbury Cricket Week remained in the hands of the man who had been running it for several years, William de Chair Baker. William South Norton, who had captained and acted as honorary secretary of the old Kent County Club since its formation in 1859, was appointed honorary secretary of the new club, but within a year stood down in favour of Mr Baker, who combined the job of running Canterbury Week with that of running the county club. At first there was no officially appointed chairman, and yet a committee of 20 people, drawn from all over the county, managed to keep the club running, and indeed growing, in a way that would confuse any organisational management expert today.

In 1872, the 3rd Lord Harris died, and young George, still studying at Christ Church Oxford while playing countless cricket matches and even going on a cricket tour to Canada, found himself the inheritor of the title and the family seat at Belmont House, near Faversham, which is definitely in East Kent. From this time, rather than busying himself with matters concerning the estate that he had so unexpectedly inherited at an early age, he immersed himself in Kent cricket. He had played once for Kent in 1870, before the amalgamation of the two clubs, but it was from 1873 onwards that he began to personify Kent cricket.

Although Lord Harris played half a dozen matches for the county side in the first couple of years of its existence, his playing career for Kent really only got under way in 1873. Lord Harris related the story of how on 10 July that year he was 'going up to London to see Eton v Harrow and, on the day before, to play for Lords and Commons v I Zingari, a regular match in those years, and so had my cricket bag with me. At the Faversham station was Mr Knatchbull-Hugessen on his way to see Kent v Lancashire at Gravesend. Seeing my bag, he was delighted, supposing I was also on my way there.' Despite Lord Harris protesting all the way to Strood, the persuasive arguments of Knatchbull-Hugessen won the day. The two men got off the train at Strood and after Harris had telegraphed to Lord's to explain his defection, they made their way to the Bat and Ball ground at Gravesend, where one unfortunate and unnamed professional had to stand aside to allow Lord Harris to play. Harris scored 26 and 6, and Kent won the match against Lancashire by three wickets, but it shows how much times have changed. Such meddling in the selection of the side, even by a committee member as Knatchbull-Hugessen was, would not be tolerated today. Having said that, a county that operated with 37 vice presidents, all 'noblemen and gentlemen of the county' and a committee of 20 was unlikely to be able to keep track of everybody's actions all through the summer. But from then on, Lord Harris became a firm fixture in the county XI.

It is probable that no county cricket team has ever been quite so completely dominated by one man as Kent was in the latter part of the 19th century. In the winter of 1874, he accepted an invitation to become honorary secretary of the club, and in 1875 he was invited to captain the county side. In that year too, he was nominated as president, and accepted the honour with alacrity. He was then 24 years old, and still completing his degree at Oxford, which unsurprisingly finished that summer without much distinction – a pass degree in 'Arts', which is about as low as it gets without actually being sent down.

But nobody would ever accuse Lord Harris of being an academic. He was a cricketer, and a man of Kent (or possibly a Kentishman: his birthplace in Trinidad is definitely west of the Medway). As *Wisden* put it in their review of Kent's season in 1875, 'Lord Harris, as President, Hon. Secretary, Captain of the County Team, greatest aggregate and highest average scorer for the County, must have been head and hands full of Kent cricket in 1875.' There was a sting in the next sentence, however. 'It is to be regretted that such influential energy and very fine and successful batting displayed by his lordship should have resulted in so unsuccessful a campaign.' There was no doubting his devotion to the cause, however. 'If there be one man more than another whose position, influence, earnest devotion to, and practical knowledge of, the glorious game, can, in due time, work Kent up to its old position among the cricketing counties, that man is Lord Harris.' *Wisden*'s words were prophetic, although the due time was well into the future. It would take another 30 years for the dreams of Lord Harris to be fulfilled.

Sir Pelham Warner, in his book *Lord's 1787–1945*, describes Lord Harris as being 'interested in every aspect of the game – the actual playing of it; the laws; the organising and financial sides; and the general welfare of the professional cricketer. He was an admirable Chairman of a committee … he was deferential to the opinions of others, did not force his own views, and was fair and balanced. He inspired confidence.' This all sounds a bit too good to be true, but Warner went on to add that Harris was 'occasionally a little testy, some thought it was as well to agree with him, but he was ready to listen to the other side. I have heard it said that he was a little difficult to play under, being apt to be somewhat cantankerous and abrupt in his manner.' The fact that he remained a power in cricket, both at Canterbury and Lord's, until his death in 1932 is a testament to the value he gave to the administration of cricket, and how much he was appreciated by his colleagues, even if occasionally he was 'somewhat cantankerous'.

Lord Harris also, as secretary, did much to revive the county's financial status. Membership subscriptions rose from £338 in 1874 to £520 the following year, and by putting up the entrance fee to the ground during Canterbury Week from sixpence to one shilling, the take at the gate virtually doubled within two years. None of the Canterbury Week matches that summer were against county sides, and all of Kent's home county matches were played at Catford Bridge, the home of the Private Banks Cricket Club. The decision to play at Catford was in order to save money, but financially it did not prove to be worth doing, and both players and spectators missed seeing the county side playing at different grounds through the summer. The experiment was not repeated, and in 1876 they played at Gravesend, Faversham, Tunbridge Wells and Maidstone, but not at Catford. Again, no County Championship matches were played at Canterbury.

Harris only held the presidency for one year, but remained as secretary until 1880, and as captain until 1889. He became chairman of the club in 1886, a position he held until 1931, the year before he died, and he was also chairman of the Young Players Sub-Committee from 1897 until his death. For 48 years he took at least one leading role in the management of Kent County Cricket Club, while at the same time being a deputy lieutenant of the county (from 1884), Under-Secretary of State for India (in 1885), Under-Secretary of State for War (from 1886 to 1890), Governor of Bombay (1890 to 1895), Lord in Waiting to Queen Victoria (1895 to 1901) and aide-de-camp to the next two monarchs, Edward VII and George V, among other lesser duties. He was a busy man, but cricket and Kent were always closest to his heart.

Lord Harris gave up the captaincy of the county side when he was 39 years old, by no means a veteran in that era, but his appointment as Governor of Bombay meant that not even he could find time to play for Kent and govern a large part of western India at the same time. His final game for the county at Canterbury took place during Cricket Week, with all the flags fluttering and the tents brimming over with the cream of Kent society, on 8, 9 and 10 August in 1889, against Gloucestershire, for whom W.G. Grace, three years Lord Harris's senior, was opening the batting. Harris made 33 as Kent just failed to force a victory, and he probably guessed then that this would be his last innings for Kent on his favourite ground. After his final game for Kent that summer, against Nottinghamshire at Beckenham, he told his team at dinner that 'the umpire has called last over, gentlemen', but he was not entirely correct. There would still be a handful of games to play for the county before the umpire finally called time.

In the light of the enthusiastic reviews given in the local newspapers over the years to Canterbury Week and the efforts of The Old Stagers, it is refreshing to read *Wisden*'s views on Canterbury Week in the final season of Lord Harris's captaincy. 'It is almost too much to hope, but in the Jubilee Year of Canterbury Week, The Old Stagers may possibly give us an epilogue with a little real fun and a little real poetry instead of the dreary productions, only half rehearsed and not half sung, which have been put on to close the season for years past. One of the many clever dramatists now writing for the stage could surely find time to send the management something that was worth hearing and worth remembering.' A heartfelt plea, but barely heeded.

Lord Harris's five-year term of governorship of Bombay was not a political success, but he did a great deal to popularise even further the game of cricket in the subcontinent, at least among the British in India. This was a small plus in an otherwise very undistinguished gubernatorial career. On his return to England, at the age of 45, he played three games for Kent in 1896, including a match against Somerset at Taunton in which he scored a brilliant 119 and put on 220 in partnership with W.H. Patterson, but apart from that he did little. He played one more game in 1897 and a final game for the county in 1906, their triumphal year. That match was against the touring West Indian side, who were then well short of Test class, and probably only up to county second eleven standard. The match was at Catford Bridge, where Kent had played all their home matches in 1875, and the 55-year-old Harris made 33, the same score that he had made in his final game at Canterbury, as Kent eased to an innings victory.

During the 1870s and 1880s, when the County Championship was still finding its feet and the champion county was decided by general agreement in the press and among the cricketing public, Kent did not manage to claim the title. These were the years when the title was awarded to Nottinghamshire, either outright or shared, ten times, Lancashire four times and Gloucestershire, full of Graces, three times. Derbyshire, Middlesex and Surrey also took the laurels in these decades, but neither Yorkshire nor Kent could claim the crown. From 1890, when Lord Harris left for Bombay and the championship was regulated by MCC whose points system produced a winner each year, Yorkshire (seven titles) and Surrey (six titles) were generally well ahead of all the other counties, although before Kent's unexpected championship in 1906, Lancashire (twice) and Middlesex (once) had also taken the title. Kent had never been placed higher than third, a position they achieved in 1890, 1900 and 1904.

Chevallier Tayler and the Art of Cricket

CRICKET has for a very long time been a subject that artists have liked to portray. Perhaps the earliest work of cricketing art is on a stained-glass window in the north-east transept of Canterbury Cathedral, which dates back to around 1180, only a few years after the murder of Thomas Becket there. The window shows a boy with a curved bat and ball, representing 'boyhood' in a series of windows representing the ages of man. It is of course possible that this is the first representation of hockey or even golf, rather than cricket, in art, but there are several other similar works, one in Gloucester Cathedral in a window that was erected to celebrate the victory of the English army at Crecy in 1346, and in a number of medieval illuminated manuscripts now safely stored in the Bodleian and British Libraries. Whether these can truly be described as representations of cricket or some other rudimentary bat and ball game is clearly a matter of debate, but the preponderance of the images shows that ball games were not considered sinful or wrong by the Church of the time. That would have encouraged their spread, even if the local authorities would have preferred the people to have been spending their free time practising archery and other military pursuits.

There is a natural bucolic charm to the sport and from the early 18th century, when cricket was beginning to become more widespread and organised, and a recognisable sport in its own right, artists have been drawn to its alluring mixture of peace and activity. The earliest cricket picture which has a date attached to it is generally agreed to be an engraving in the style of Hubert-François Gravelot, a French Huguenot engraver who fled to London in 1732. The work is called *The Second Part of Youthful Diversions – Youth Playing At Cricket*, by one J. Cole, and dated 7 May 1739. Gravelot had become a very highly regarded artist and engraver during his short stay in London – he worked with William Hogarth, and included Thomas Gainsborough among his pupils. It seems unlikely that as a Frenchman he became an aficionado of cricket, but his disciples obviously included those who were.

His colleagues William Hogarth and Thomas Rowlandson, among other famous artists, featured cricket sometimes, either centrally or peripherally, in their work in the middle of the 18th century. Another associate of Gravelot was Francis Hayman (1708–76), whose *Cricket In Marylebone Fields* from around 1748 is the first known depiction of cricket in the place where 70 years later Thomas Lord built his third ground for the Marylebone Club. There is also a painting in the MCC collection depicting a game of cricket on Thomas Lord's first ground at Dorset Fields, now built over as Dorset Square, which was used as the home ground for MCC from its establishment in 1787 until 1810. It shows two top-hatted batsmen, with curved bats, and a two-stump wicket, surrounded by equally top-hatted fieldsmen as the bowler prepares to bowl – underarm of course. Two umpires control the game and two scorers look on from a bench in the foreground. But none of the players are identified: the engraving is simply a representation of a typical match played at Dorset Fields rather than an attempt at a true portrait of an actual moment on the cricket square. The painting was subsequently engraved by the London-based French engraver Charles Grignion, and his engraving was published in 1748 in an issue of the *General Advertiser*. The popularity of this engraving was such that it was copied many times for many purposes, so that the image became well recognised by very many people from all walks of life. In the MCC collection there is even a linen handkerchief dating from the same period which shows a scene based on Hayman's painting. Cricket art began to excite general interest from then on.

The MCC collection, by far the most comprehensive collection of cricket art in the world, has a wide range of paintings from the early years of organised cricket which tend either to have a game of cricket as part of a painting of a country estate, for example, or else feature a cricket match as the focus of the work. There are several portraits from the late 18th and early 19th centuries of notable persons holding a cricket bat, or involving themselves in other ways in cricket, but these are meant to be portraits of the individual rather than a painting of cricket, but they show that cricket was becoming as obvious a shorthand to signify a well-to-do sportsman as a painting of a person holding the reins of a racehorse, or out hunting with his dogs.

From around this time there are two paintings which have strong Canterbury connections. An oil painting by the Irish artist Henry Hodgins, showing a game of cricket at Canterbury, dates from some time after 1762, when Hodgins arrived in England, and with Canterbury Cathedral visible in the background, its location is clear. There is an organised match in play, with 11 fielders, two batsmen with curved bats defending a two-stump wicket, and two umpires, each holding a spare bat. At the boundary's edge, a tent has been set up for the gentry, who are eating a hearty meal. Clearly Hodgins, who lived in Kent after his arrival from Dublin, was very familiar with cricket in the county. But it should really be considered as a landscape painting, rather than an intrinsically cricket painting. The second painting dates from a similar time, or perhaps a decade later. It is by the German-born neoclassical artist, Johann Zoffany, and it shows three children standing by a large tree in a typically idyllic rural scene of the time. The two boys and their toddler sister are the children of the first Baron Sondes, the eldest of whom, a boy of about ten years old, is holding a cricket bat and ball, and there is another bat lying on the ground. This is a family portrait rather than a cricket painting, the bats and ball being merely props to help set the scene. There is no evidence that Zoffany himself knew much about cricket, if anything, but he was probably the most fashionable portraitist of the time, and anybody who considered themselves important and rich enough to commission him, especially if they were a newly ennobled baron, wanted a Zoffany portrait of their offspring. The Sondes family went on to play a crucial part in the history of Kent cricket, as the original owners of the fields that became the St Lawrence Ground.

The well-known portrait of Thomas Hope of Amsterdam, by the Swiss artist Jacques Sablet, shows how far the symbolism of cricket as a sign of wealth had spread. Thomas Hope was the son of an Englishman and his Dutch wife, and the portrait was painted in Rome while he was making his grand tour of Europe. He holds a cricket bat, but the stumps behind him are pitifully small (although there are three of them) and the man behind the stumps seems to be holding a large black cape to catch the ball. A thoughtful umpire stands at square leg, while Hope himself, leaning on his bat as though it were his sole means of support, is staring at the artist, not the bowler. But at least there is cricket in the painting. The 1814 portrait by William Novice of Benjamin Aislabie shows him sitting on his horse with his dog behind him. Despite the fact that Aislabie was secretary of MCC for 20 years from 1822, and president of the club in 1823, there is no cricket reference at all in the portrait.

Most cricket art of the 19th century consists of engravings and lithographs. The most popular of all was – and still is – *A Cricket Match Between the Counties of Sussex and Kent, at Brighton*, which was first published in 1849 by the Brighton cricketer and publisher, W.H. Mason. It shows a cricket match taking place, although it is not a record of a real game as all 22 players portrayed never played together in one game, although all of them did play in the fixture between 1849 and 1851. It was designed to be a collective portrait of the 71 named people in the painting, all important names in cricket of the time, and Mason planned to make his money through subscription, especially from those 71 people. However, the painting was pirated and copied several times over the first years of its popularity, and although you may well find reproductions of the painting in some form or other in club pavilions and bars around the world, very few indeed will be Mason originals.

In 1851, a coloured lithograph from a painting of *Cricket at Tonbridge School*, by the local artist Charles Tattershall Dodd

(1815–78), became popular, especially in Kent. Tonbridge School, later to be known as the alma mater of the Cowdrey family among other fine cricketers, laid its cricket square in 1838, using soil from the construction work on the South Eastern Railway which ran past the school. Even today, from the train, the playing fields of Tonbridge School can be clearly seen, with what seems like hundreds of boys playing cricket on a sunny summer afternoon.

The widely known lithographs by G.F. Watts of cricket instructional drawings, such as *The Draw* or *The Bowler* and *The Batsman* (Kent's Alfred Mynn and Fuller Pilch, respectively), while excellent in every way, do not show a match in progress, whether real or imagined, and it was not until the final two decades of the 19th century, when cricket had become much more modern with the spread of the game around the world and the appearance of the cricketing phenomenon that was W.G. Grace, that artists began to paint cricketers in a cricket setting. There were still many portraits of the great players on their own, seated or standing, but almost never actually playing, but occasionally an artist would find himself lured into painting a cricket scene.

* * * *

It helped if the artist himself was a keen cricketer. Albert Chevallier Tayler certainly fitted that description. Born in Leytonstone in Essex in 1862, the seventh and youngest son of a local solicitor, William Moseley Tayler, he was educated at Bloxham School, near Banbury in Oxfordshire. On leaving that school, with a sigh of relief, he studied art at the Heatherley School of Fine Art in London, and the Royal Academy School,

45

from where he won a scholarship to the Slade in 1879. There he met many students who became lifelong friends and who would go on to become successful and highly regarded artists, including Stanhope Forbes, Thomas Cooper Gotch and Henry Scott Tuke. After his time at the Slade, Tayler, a lively and restless soul in his youth, followed Gotch to Paris, where he studied under many of the painters who were then considered very avant-garde. After two years in France, he brought back to England an enthusiasm for the 'en plain air' style of painting, which simply means painting in the open air, dispensing with the studio and its often artificial light. Painting outdoors may always have had appeal for artists, but until the first half of the 19th century, it was not an easy thing to do logistically. Painters like John Constable (1776–1837) and J.M.W. Turner (1775–1851) were determined to break away from the shackles of the studio, but until the invention of paint in tubes in the 1840s, allowing artists to move further away from their mixing pots in the studio, most artists stayed indoors to paint, perhaps having first sketched an outline in pencil and ink outdoors. At around the same time, the artist's box easel was developed. With easel and paints able to be carried without difficulty in a box no bigger than a standard briefcase, artists were able to venture farther afield, and work on a much wider range of subjects.

Turner painted four works featuring cricket, as far as we can tell. This is not a large number when you remember how many paintings of his are known today, but they prove that cricket was an intrinsic part of the English landscape at the turn of the 19th century. In each of the paintings, cricket is an incidental part of the composition rather than the central feature, and in the case of one of them, *The Lake, Petworth: Sunset, Fighting Bucks*

(1829), the cricketers were added quite late into the painting, as the original version does not include them. The focus is on the deer rather than the cricketers playing beneath some large trees, and of course these days the umpires would have stopped play for bad light – although nobody should describe a Turner sunset as 'bad light'.

On his return to England at the end of the summer of 1884, Chevallier Tayler moved to the small fishing village of Newlyn, near Penzance in west Cornwall, where his friends, inspired by what they saw in France and by the determination of the French impressionist artists to move away from Paris, had set up an artists' colony. The founders of what became known as the Newlyn School were his friends Harry Tuke, Tom Gotch and Stanhope Forbes among others, and Tayler spent several happy and productive years based in Cornwall, developing his talents as an artist and portraitist. One critic, on seeing his work in the early 1890s, wrote of 'all his cleverness and his frankly scrutinising – but not idealising – observation brought to bear' on his work. 'He paints a clever and full portrait.'

The Newlyn artists carried on the English Pre-Raphaelite and French naturalist traditions of using local people as models and setting their compositions in recognisable sites. Their Cornwall is lively, clean and harking back to earlier days, qualities that suited the taste of art lovers of the late 19th century. They had come to Newlyn in the first place because of its strong natural light, its mild climate and its glorious scenery, not to mention the fact that it was a very cheap part of Britain for impoverished artists to live. The best Newlyn paintings, whether genre paintings or landscapes, feature elements of social realism created with a subdued and subtle palette, often experimenting with natural or artificial light effects, and brushwork techniques that the artists brought back with them from their years in France, in particular what was known as the square brush technique.

In November 1893, *The Sketch* published an article about Newlyn which included an encounter with Chevallier Tayler.

"'Well, Mr Tayler,' I asked, 'tell me, what is your definition of the Newlyn School of Art?'

"'My dear sir,' he replied, 'I have read of it and heard of it, but I never knew what it was, and no one who lives here is any wiser than I on this subject. The critics say they can identify Newlyn work. Perhaps they can; perhaps we who see so much of one another and so much of one another's work have subconsciously adopted smatterings of one another's style.'"

That is probably as good a definition as we can hope to get. The response not only shows Tayler's charm and wit, but also the fact that probably the only common feature that the Newlyn School of artists recognised in themselves was that they were all based at Newlyn.

Albert Chevallier Tayler lived in Newlyn in a house with fellow artists Stanhope Forbes and William Blandford Fletcher, which made for a noisy lodging at times. Tayler was a popular and highly sociable member of the group: Forbes called him 'a ray of sunshine in the house', and Frank Bourdillon, another Newlyn artist who was to become a Christian missionary to India a few years later, noted, 'Tayler is much occupied in Penzance and has the faculty of making himself so popular that he is out nearly every evening.' He was a restless artist, perhaps because his paintings did not always find a market as readily as those of some of his friends, and he would often spend time away from Newlyn. But his convivial personality and sense of fun, which remained with him throughout his life, meant that he was always a popular member of the community when he came down to Cornwall. He came and went in Newlyn over much of the next ten years, with Forbes noting with sadness each departure, and greeting each return with excitement.

One art critic has said that a common theme of Tayler's works is what he called a 'peculiar chastity, a repulsion to painting unclad flesh'. Most of his scenes were quiet, calm and often religious in theme, perhaps in contrast to his outwardly lively social life. In 1896 he had married Elizabeth Cotes, by whom he had two sons, and this may have reduced his wanderlust somewhat. He was described as 'a burly looking gentleman, the beau ideal of a country squire', but was never so wealthy that he could afford to turn down commissions, and that is perhaps why in 1903 he took on the task of painting a panel at the Royal Exchange entitled *The Five Kings*, portraying Edward III of England, David of Scotland, Peter I of Cyprus, John of France and Waldemar IV of Denmark enjoying a bacchanalian feast hosted by the Master of the Society of Vintners in London in 1363, quite a contrast to his usual body of work.

When he began to take portrait painting seriously, after having left Newlyn for the last time in 1895, his portrait of the Countess of Annesley the next year brought this comment from the *Illustrated London News* about Tayler: 'One of the cleverest and most painstaking of the Newlyn School has hitherto been best known as a "subject" painter.... His appearance, therefore, among the portrait painters may be regarded as a new departure, and if we may judge from [this] specimen of his work, he is likely to take a front place among the "limners of ladies". He has a delicate touch and a fine sense of illumination and, above all, is an excellent draughtsman.' One suspects that being a 'limner of ladies' appealed both to Chevallier Tayler's gregarious personality and to his wallet.

Tayler was always a keen cricketer, even though there is little hard evidence of his style, or indeed his standard, of play. In 1890 Frank Richards, another member of the Newlyn colony but not the author of the Billy Bunter books, wrote to a friend about the annual Newlyn v St Ives cricket match. 'Frank Bramley is the captain, and with Forbes, Langley, Tayler, Harris, Rheam, Blackburn, Da Costa, myself, and with Gotch and Mackenzie as umpire and scorer, and with Fred Hall, caricaturist, we make up not so bad a team.' Henry Meynell Rheam, one of this Newlyn side, was a watercolour painter who moved to Newlyn not because of the light or the stunning landscape, but largely because of the cricket.

As Stanhope Forbes wrote, 'The annual cricket match between the artists of St Ives and Newlyn was one of the chief sporting events of the year, and about the time I speak of, St Ives had acquired two notable batsmen and Newlyn seemed likely to endure defeat. But in a fortunate moment the situation was saved, for Harry Rheam, that notable cricketer, was imported at great expense from Polperro.' Chevallier Tayler was at the heart of the cricketing in Newlyn and elsewhere – he was a member of the Artists' Cricket Club, which played matches across a wide area of England over many seasons – and after one match he left Newlyn for Venice in 'high glee, for he had played a cricket match in the afternoon and made top score'. In a speech at a Cornish painters' exhibition in Nottingham in 1894, Chevallier Tayler said that 'the painters of Cornwall adopted cricket as their hobby, which they practised with very limited success, but with a great deal of enjoyment'. Any amateur or village cricketer even today can identify with Chevallier Tayler, the cricketer.

We have the scorecards of several games in which Chevallier Tayler played for the Artists XI after he had moved from Newlyn, between 1900 and 1906, mainly against The Authors and mainly in Esher, but also at St Quintin's Park in Kensington, which is now part of the Wormwood Scrubs recreation area, and Denmark Hill. He played for the Artists XI against such famous authors as Arthur Conan Doyle, Gerald du Maurier, J.M. Barrie, P.G. Wodehouse, future knights all, and his good friend E.W. Hornung, Conan Doyle's brother-in-law and like Tayler destined to lose a son in the Great War. Among other men he met frequently on the cricket field was Gordon Guggisberg, a future Governor of Gold Coast and then of British Guiana. Chevallier Tayler and his artist friends played seriously smart social cricket. However, in all these games his highest score was only 43, and his batting average about 14. He took just one wicket, when an unsuspecting batsman lobbed a catch to the Liverpool artist Gerard Chowne, so we assume he was picked for his batting – or more likely for his energy and his happy disposition.

In 1886 Tayler painted the first of several works that are in the MCC collection. *Eton v Harrow at Lord's 1886* is a small work of oil on canvas, concentrating on the crowd rather than the game. Only one lonely and unidentifiable fielder on the boundary is shown, the main focus being the fashionable crowd who are seated in the old pavilion (which was to be demolished three years later) and the 'A' enclosure. The gentlemen in their morning suits, top hats and spats, and the ladies in their smart and voluminous but hardly colourful outfits are the focus of our attention, along with the union flag fluttering in the breeze and the great expanse of carefully tended outfield grass in the foreground. The cricket is not even a sideshow to this; who is to say that the lonely fellow at long-on is not just coming in for lunch, or even just back from a game of real tennis? But it is a fine painting all the same, and indicative of Chevallier Tayler's love for the home of cricket. It is now on display at Lord's because Tayler gave the painting to MCC.

There are other paintings produced at this time which show a little more of the action on the field, but even they seem more interested in the setting than the match. The wonderful 1878 work by the Scot John Robertson Reid, *A Country Cricket Match*, is typical of the time in that it is more interested in the social aspects of the game, the rural idyll represented by a game of cricket, than in the match itself. The players can be seen in the background, but the focus is on the table in the foreground where spectators and cricketers, of a wide social range, are talking, eating, playing and doing almost anything except watching the cricket. Tayler's colleague and friend Henry Scott Tuke also painted several cricketers, notably two fine head and shoulders portraits of W.G. Grace in 1905 and Fred Spofforth in 1906, but they were simple portraits – paintings of real people playing a real game were not part of his *oeuvre*.

The famous oil, also in the MCC collection, by George Barrable and Sir Robert Ponsonby Staples, purporting to show a moment in an England v Australia Test match at Lord's, is purely a fiction. The painting was completed in 1887, and is of more interest for the faces in the crowd than the action on the pitch. The Prince and Princess of Wales (later King Edward VII and Queen Alexandra) are shown sitting at the boundary edge, while one of the prince's mistresses, Lillie Langtry, is seated in the 'A' stand, with her back to the royal couple. There is some action on the pitch, at least, with the Australian T.W. Garrett bending to his right to field the ball before it reaches the cover boundary, having been hit there by W.G. Grace. There are also 22 head and shoulders portraits of English and Australian cricketers around the frame as part of the painting, one of whom is Lord Harris, but this combination of 22 players never met in a Test match. A painting from the same era, *The Players In The Field*, painted in 1895, shows 11 professional and two amateur cricketers standing on the pitch as though waiting for the drinks to arrive. There is no attempt at action in the painting, and again this particular combination of players never met in any first-class match, although the subtitle to the painting is *Lord's on a Gentlemen v Players Day.*

Although he very much enjoyed playing cricket with his artist friends in Newlyn, perhaps Chevallier Tayler's most significant friendship, as far as his later work was concerned, was with the photographer George Beldam. Beldam (1868–1937), a well-to-do Cambridge engineering graduate of Huguenot descent, played first-class cricket, mainly for London County, Middlesex and MCC between 1899 and 1907. He was a late starter, not playing his first first-class match until the age of 31, but by the time he retired from top level cricket he had played a total of 142 first-class matches, finishing with nine hundreds and a batting average of just over 30, to go with 107 wickets taken by his canny slow-medium bowling, also at an average of just over 30. In 1903 he played his part in Middlesex winning the County Championship for the first time. His cricket career may not have been out of the ordinary, but at the same time as scoring runs and taking wickets, he was experimenting with action photography, in an attempt to produce pictures of sportsmen in action that captured a real moment, rather than the stiff poses that had been the norm until then, largely because of the long exposure times required by the early cameras. In 1887, the British-born photographer Eadweard Muybridge (sic), who was at the time based in the United States, published a series of photographs under the title *Animal Locomotion*, which he had taken with the aid of tripwires and multiple cameras. His series of 18 photographs of a naked batsman, described only as 'the best all round cricketer in the University of Pennsylvania', playing an expansive off drive in the nets has been described by David Frith, the renowned cricket historian and writer, as 'the earliest of all genuine cricket action close-ups'.

Photographs such as these fired Beldam's imagination. In cricket and in photography, he was a great theorist, always wanting to learn the mechanics of how a stroke was played or how a camera could create the ideal picture. In cricket he consulted all the great cricketers, from W.G. Grace to C.B. Fry and Victor Trumper, but only Fry could really tell him anything useful. Grace and Trumper were just geniuses for whom theory was hardly needed. Beldam used his engineering background to experiment with different cameras, and by 1902, while still an active cricketer, he was using a camera with a maximum shutter speed of 1/1,000th of a second. His problem, however, was still how to get closer to the action, as long-distance shots from the boundary could not capture the glory of a fine shot or a great bowler's action. His first solution to this problem was to take photographs of other sports, where he could easily get closer to the action, and thus analyse more clearly the way the sport was played. Golf and tennis were his first two subjects. His action photographs of famous golfers of the day, notably the great J.H. Taylor, were published in a book called *Great Golfers: Their Methods At A Glance*, in 1904, and the next year he followed it up with *Lawn Tennis Players: Their Methods Illustrated*. Both books were well received, notably the golf book. Golf has always been a very theoretical sport – there should be nothing difficult about hitting a ball that is just sitting there waiting to be hit, but as golfers over the centuries have discovered, there's more to it than that. Golf instruction books, and more recently videos, DVDs and downloads, are more profitable for many a professional than winning a tournament or two. Even W.G. Grace, who was introduced to golf by his London County opening partner Beldam, needed instruction.

In 1905, Beldam set himself a target – to take the definitive photograph of the great Australian batsman Victor Trumper in action. In achieving this he was helped by two of his cricket-loving artist friends, Henry Scott Tuke and Albert Chevallier Tayler. The end result of his summer's efforts was a photograph which truly deserves the overworked adjective 'iconic'. It shows Trumper jumping out for a straight drive, taken at the Kennington Oval. Trumper was the man of whom Neville Cardus wrote (in 1929, before Bradman first came to England), 'God no doubt could create a better batsman than Victor Trumper had He wished, but so far He hasn't.' Beldam's photograph of the great Australian is one of the most exhilarating sporting images of all time, an image which has been used time and again, not only to promote cricketing items of all kinds but also, for example, to sell beer, to promote a pop concert and on the cover of a theatre programme. Beldam's photographs of Trumper and many other great batsmen of the golden age of cricket were included in a book, with copy by C.B. Fry, called *Great Batsmen: Their Methods At A Glance*, which was published in 1905 to great acclaim. For the book, and for its natural successor, *Great Bowlers and Fielders: Their Methods At A Glance*, Beldam took thousands of action photographs of many first-class cricketers, of which some 600 were used. Chevallier Tayler, who had often discussed with Beldam and his friend Harry Tuke the artistic merit of sportsmen in action, agreed with Beldam to use several of his photographs as the basis for an exhibition of his own, called *The Empire's Cricketers*.

What Tayler produced, at a time when he was one of the most successful and celebrated portrait artists of his time, was a collection of 48 pastel drawings, commissioned by the Art Society and based closely on Beldam's action photographs. They were not mere copies, and Tayler himself was keen to point out in his exhibition catalogue that the drawings were completed with Beldam's 'information and assistance' rather than his templates. As the distinguished portrait painter Jonathan Yeo has said, 'You are trying to do something that is different from a photograph. The camera is one eye rather than two, and a static and stationary one.' Painting a portrait, even one based on a photograph, takes a far longer time than the split second of a camera shutter, and the artist has time to learn about the person being painted, and to decide how best to reveal the character. The 48 drawings in his 1905 collection included 11 of the Australian tourists of that year, but Tayler did not always use the obvious shot to base his work on. His portrait of Trumper is elegant, showing him leaning into a cover drive, which perhaps reveals the man just as well, but it does not have the magnificent power of the *Jumping Out To Drive* photograph, which has become as much an image of cricket in the golden age as *Kent v Lancashire 1906*.

The *Pall Mall Gazette* in June 1905 gave a good idea of how Tayler worked to create these portraits. The magazine noted that the exhibition opened, fittingly enough, at the Fine Arts Society's premises on the first day of the Lord's Test that year, and described Tayler, who was then 43 years old, as 'an amateur wielder of the willow', who 'does not play as often as he would like'. 'Tayler's studies for his portraits', continued the *Pall Mall Gazette*, 'were made at Lord's, and at that Mecca of the cricketer, the artist spent nearly every day from the commencement of the season until the opening of the exhibition, watching the players and sketching them in a temporary studio placed at his disposal by MCC.... All the Australians gave their sittings at Lord's. Mr Tayler has portrayed his cricketers with coloured chalks on grey-brown paper, but it was with the brush that he made his reputation.' A few days later, *The Globe* reported that the exhibition was going well. 'Mr Tayler's drawings are spirited and lifelike, and Mr G.W. Beldam writes some capital little biographical sketches.' John Arlott 80 years later was more scathing. 'The drawings ... are not unpleasant but lack movement and character; nevertheless, they enjoyed a period of popularity.'

Beldam, incidentally, did not solve the problem of how to get close-up shots of cricketers actually playing a real game. All his shots were posed, on a cricket ground but not during a match, with bat, ball and fielders all moving as the shutter clicked, so as to capture the realities of physical movement and timing the ball. But it was not until the long focus lens was first developed during the Great War that cricket photographers at the boundary's edge were able to get close to the players in match action. Beldam, who was still photographing in the 1920s, nevertheless only published one photographic book after the war, and that was on golf. His reputation rests on his pioneering work in the first decade of the century.

One of the cricketers portrayed by Chevallier Tayler in 1905 in *The Empire's Cricketers* was the archetypical Empire cricketer, Lord Harris. The image of him, still slim at the age of 54, forced back in his crease and standing on his back leg as he tilts towards the off side in an attempt to steer the ball to leg, has become very well known and is now part of the National Portrait Gallery collection. His panama hat is of course undisturbed. More importantly, for both Lord Harris and Chevallier Tayler, it created the context for the two men to meet. Although the portrait, hardly more than a chalk sketch, was based on Beldam's photograph, Chevallier Tayler still needed Lord Harris to come to sit for him at Lord's so that the artist could relate more closely to his subject. Lord Harris was not an aesthete. One suspects that he was a 'I don't know much about art but I know what I like' kind of a man, and luckily he liked Beldam's photographs and he liked Tayler's art. Tayler was a realist and a portrait painter – no funny stuff for him – and that chimed with the Harris view of art. Luckily, Chevallier Tayler liked Lord Harris too, and the two men struck up a friendship. Tayler took his art very seriously, as seriously as Harris took his cricket, but both men knew that there was more to life than their particular obsessions.

A year later this friendship would bear fruit.

* * * *

After finishing third in 1904, the highest position they had so far reached in the championship, 1905 was a somewhat disappointing year. As *Wisden* noted, 'Kent, though they again won ten matches, did not play so well as in 1904, their defeats rising from four to seven.' However, *Wisden* also pointed out that 'allowing for the inequalities in their play, they were one of the most attractive county sides to watch, their cricket being marked by a refreshing sense of enjoyment of the game for its own sake, irrespective of the mere fact of winning or losing'. This, and the fact that after a disastrous start to the summer, from the last week in June they won nine and lost only three of their championship fixtures, showed that Kent had the potential to be a very good side indeed. It has often been suggested that Kent have hampered themselves over the years by playing at so many different grounds each season, and 1905 was no exception. Their championship home games that summer were at Gravesend (lost), Tonbridge (lost), Tonbridge again (lost again), Blackheath (won), Tunbridge Wells (two games, one lost and one drawn), Catford (won), Maidstone (won), Beckenham (won), and finally Canterbury for the Week (one drawn and one lost).

Five of their seven losses came in home games, which were spread across eight different grounds. Still, the resolve of the committee since the foundation of the club had always been to bring the game to all the people of the county, and not just those living within reach of Canterbury, and that resolve was not about to be broken.

1906 arrived without any great expectations from the Kent cricket-watching public. Hopes, maybe, but expectations, no. And once again they began badly. As *Wisden* reported, 'up to the middle of June there did not seem the least likelihood that Kent would have an exceptional record, and the chance of carrying off the championship was hardly thought of'.

But by the end of the season, the championship was secured. It was a close-run thing, as we shall see, but Kent won, and nobody begrudged them their triumph. Two innings victories out of two games during Canterbury Week were the apotheosis of Kent's season, with the sun shining, the crowds huge and excited and the cricket both joyful and ruthless. For Lord Harris it was the culmination of 36 years as a committee member of the club, into which he had poured his heart, his cricketing skills, his leadership and plenty of his money, too. No wonder he wanted to have the scene immortalised in oils.

It was not uncommon for the champion county to reward its players with a memento of their triumphal season. Silver salvers, snuff boxes and even pen and ink stands are among the items that previous champions had given to their players. Slug Marsham received his first 'handsome silver salver, suitably inscribed' of the year almost before he had taken off his white flannels for the last time, when his home village of Harrietsham presented him with one late in August. By that time he had already received 109 telegrams, 234 picture postcards and 60 letters of congratulations, enough to give any postman a bad back.

Within days he had more commemorative silverware. As the local paper reported at the end of August, 'By way of indicating the splendid sporting spirit that prevails in the Kent cricket team, a pleasing ceremony took place last Friday evening at the Fountain Hotel, Canterbury. The occasion was the customary dinner given by Lord Harris to the team on the second day of the third county match at the St Lawrence Ground, and advantage was taken of it to make a presentation to Mr C.H.B. Marsham, this being exclusively the act of the professionals, who had kept their secret well, and contrived to spring a complete surprise on their captain.' The professionals were represented by Fred Huish, the wicketkeeper, whose speech was an exercise in forelock-tugging to the socially higher placed amateurs. He said that his fellow professionals felt that it was a great honour to be in the Kent XI at the present time, and that the success of the team was largely due to the brilliance of the amateurs, 'about whom they always heard such nice things in every part of the country they played'. Huish also said that their current success 'was principally due to the tact, ability and influence of their captain, Mr C.H.B. Marsham, who was immensely popular with the professionals, and who had their supreme confidence'. He then presented Marsham with a silver cigar box, which bore the inscription: 'Canterbury Cricket Week, 1906. – Presented to C.H.B. Marsham, Esq., by the following, as a token of esteem and appreciation of his captaincy – Walter Hearne, Alec Hearne, F.H. Huish, A. Fielder, C. Blythe, J. Seymour, E. Humphreys, F. Woolley, W.J. Fairservice, W. Hardinge and J. Hubble'. It is interesting to note that several of the professionals who coughed up for Marsham's cigar box had been dropped to make way for the amateurs during Canterbury Week, and only Woolley was back in the side for the Worcestershire game which was taking place as they ate.

On 10 October 1906, a dinner was held in Maidstone, the county town, to celebrate the county's success. The Mayor of Maidstone, Councillor Day, presented each member of the team with a silver cigarette box, funds having been raised from the pockets of the ordinary folk of Maidstone. But Lord Harris had grander ideas than cigarette boxes all round.

The next evening there was an even more spectacular dinner held in London, at the Hotel Cecil on the Thames Embankment, then the largest hotel in Europe. Tickets for the evening cost 5/6d (27.5p) and over 500 people were present. The professional cricketers even had their rail fares, totalling £2/2/11d, paid by the club, to make sure that they turned up. Lord Harris was in the chair and in his element. There were no fewer than 14 speeches and while the guests were drawing breath between each of them, Lady Harris presented every member of the team with a pair of silver cufflinks, bearing the inscription 'Championship 1906', as well as the name of the player, the White Horse of Kent and the county motto 'Invicta' – 'undefeated' (not strictly true in 1906, but they did finish on top). The Earl of Darnley, who as Hon. Ivo Bligh had been presented with the Ashes urn when his England team beat Australia in Australia a quarter of a century earlier, regaled the diners in his after-dinner speech with his view that Kent had won the title by playing 'cricket of the brightest and best description'. But it was left to Lord Harris to make the grandest gesture in proposing that a painting be commissioned showing all the players who had helped win the title in action in the setting of the St Lawrence Ground. The idea was greeted warmly.

Meanwhile, the players munched on. On 1 November, the six Christopherson brothers, members of the Christopherson family eleven that had played several games around the county, and of whom two, Percy and Stanley, had played for the county, hosted another dinner at Blackheath. Five days later, the team were the guests of honour at the annual dinner of the Association of Men of Kent and Kentish Men at the Holborn Restaurant in London. There were other smaller and more local celebrations for individual players in their own villages and towns. By the time Christmas came around, the players must have felt that they had been feted at most of the restaurants in south-east England.

It is difficult at this distance to understand how remarkable Lord Harris's concept was in 1906. No club had ever immortalised its champions in such a way, and paintings of actual cricket matches were, as we have seen, very uncommon. There had, however, been one earlier lithograph of Canterbury Week, published in 1845, showing a moment from the Kent v All England match on 4 August that year. The engraving was 'respectfully dedicated' to the president and members of the Beverley and East Kent Cricket Club by 'your obedient servant, Henry Ward' who published the print, and as you might expect from such a dedication, the focus was on the spectators in the foreground, many of whom would have been recognisable as members of the club, and many of whom were not even facing the cricket in the background. Lord Harris wanted the focus to be on the players, not the spectators.

He remembered the experience of sitting for his cricketing portrait with Chevallier Tayler a year or so before, and clearly realised that this man had a facility for portraying cricketers realistically and sympathetically. He also must have been aware of the commercial success of his *Empire's Cricketers* project. He obviously felt that a large painting, almost on a Roman emperor's scale, would be a fair memorial to this unique triumph. So he made the announcement, and set the wheels in motion.

It seems likely that Chevallier Tayler was the only artist that Lord Harris had in mind when he made his proposal. It is even possible that he had already spoken to him about the commission, and that the painting was an idea that came from discussions between the two men. Quite probably the idea was as much Tayler's as Harris's. There were, of course, other artists who Harris might have considered if the idea were entirely his, notably Henry Weigall (1829–1925), a noted portrait painter whose son Gerald had played regularly for Kent between 1891 and 1903. Henry Weigall had painted portraits of many notable people, including Queen Alexandra and Benjamin Disraeli, as well as cricketers such as the doomed England captain Andrew

Stoddart and Lord Bessborough. He had also painted a widely reproduced full-length portrait of his mother's great-uncle, the Duke of Wellington. His fine portrait of another of his five sons, Evelyn Weigall, is still in the Kent CCC collection and hangs in the pavilion at Canterbury to this day. But Weigall was already almost 80 years old and anyway had no experience of painting cricketing action. Similarly, Hugh de Twenebrokes Glazebrook (1855–1937), another popular late Victorian portraitist, had painted George Marsham, a long-standing Kent committee colleague of Lord Harris and cousin of the Kent captain in 1906, but Glazebrook's strengths were also not in open scenes such as Lord Harris envisaged. So Chevallier Tayler it would be.

The next question was which match should be the subject of the painting. Harris had already decided that the scene would feature the Kent side in the field, so that all 11 men could be clearly portrayed, and it was an easy matter to set the scene at Canterbury. The only question was which match should be immortalised, and which stage of the game should be shown. That year, as in many years, only three home matches were played at Canterbury, the final three games of the season. The first game, against Sussex, beginning on 6 August, was the first match of Canterbury Week, and Kent won the game easily, by an innings and 131 runs. The second game was against Lancashire, also in Canterbury Week, beginning on 9 August, and again Kent won easily, by an innings and 195 runs. The third match at Canterbury was against Worcestershire, beginning on 23 August, and again Kent won, by seven wickets. In choosing which match to celebrate, it was an easy matter to eliminate the Worcester game, as Harris wanted a scene that showed Canterbury in all its glory, and that had to be during the Week. The choice between

Sussex and Lancashire was perhaps more difficult. Sussex were the local rivals, whom Kent had beaten both home and away during the summer, but there was already the famous and widely reproduced painting *A Cricket Match Between the Counties of Sussex and Kent*, dating from half a century earlier. The new painting needed to break new ground in every sense. Lancashire were one of the great sides, county champions only two years earlier, and what is more they had inflicted a ten-wicket defeat on Kent in the game at Manchester in June, not to mention an eight-wicket win for Lancashire in Canterbury Week the year before. A painting of victory over Lancashire would probably have been all the sweeter for Lord Harris.

It may be that here the voice of Chevallier Tayler is also heard, for he had already painted the Lancashire batsman Johnny Tyldesley in his series of the year before, so knew that portraying at least one of the Lancashire side would be straightforward. Harris also knew Tyldesley, one of the great batsmen in Lancashire's history, and had great respect for his batting. In that earlier game at Manchester, Tyldesley had made 295 not out, which is still in 2018 the record score against Kent in any county match, and Harris no doubt felt that no worthier opponent than the Lancashire batsman could be portrayed.

It is possible that Lord Harris had another reason for choosing the Lancashire match. In 1885, Harris had been at the centre of a dispute with Lancashire over the issue of throwing. Several players at the time had very dubious bowling actions, two of the most blatant being the Lancashire bowlers, George Nash and John Crossland.

Crossland had played for Lancashire since his debut in 1878, but although he was very successful, taking over 300 wickets at a cost of around 12.5 runs each, many critics thought he threw rather than bowled his fastest balls. George Nash, a slow left-arm bowler, had played for Lancashire since 1879 and was also a key member of the county's attack. Many people thought he threw every ball. Lord Harris was determined to stamp out throwing from the game, and before the game against Lancashire at Old Trafford in May 1885, Harris made his views clear that he felt both Nash and Crossland were chuckers. Nevertheless, Lancashire picked both players for the match, and duly won by 42 runs, Crossland taking seven wickets for 103 runs, including Lord Harris, bowled for a duck in the first innings and caught off Crossland's bowling in the second. Harris then wrote a letter to the newspapers saying that he was recommending to the Kent committee that they do not field a side for the return match, allowing Lancashire to win by default. This was eventually agreed by the committee, although not without a vigorous debate, and the return match did not take place. In its place, Kent organised a game between Gentlemen of Kent and Players of Kent, which was not deemed first class. For the record, the Players of Kent won by an innings and three runs.

Kent were not the only county to make a stand against throwing. Both Middlesex and Nottinghamshire had dropped out of fixtures against Lancashire in earlier years for the same reason, and by the end of the summer of 1885, the issue resolved itself. Nash dropped out of county cricket, the Lancashire committee having realised that his action was too blatant to be tolerated, and Crossland was removed by virtue of Nottinghamshire objecting to his qualification to play for Lancashire. Crossland had been born in Nottinghamshire, and Notts said he did not have the necessary residential qualification for Lancashire. MCC, the adjudicators in this little play, took the matter very seriously and took evidence from not only the two county clubs but also rent collectors, the local rates officers and even a village policeman. They reached the conclusion that Crossland was not qualified to play for Lancashire, and his career came to a halt. This was not the end of the throwing issue, and for at least another decade it rumbled on, but Harris had always said he held no ill feelings against the other Lancashire players, and by 1906, when his friend A.N. 'Monkey' Hornby was president of the Lancashire club, he may well have felt that it would be a good conciliatory gesture to feature Lancashire rather than Sussex in the painting. So the decision was made. Kent v Lancashire it would be.

Lord Harris also specified that the painting should show Colin Blythe, Kent's great left-arm bowler, bowling from the pavilion end. 'Charlie' Blythe, as he was known to all and sundry for no discernible reason, was one of the great Kent stars of the summer, and a man of whom nobody ever said a bad word. He was also a professional rather than an amateur, and one of Lord Harris's other cricketing values was to look after the interests of the professionals. His style may appear rather paternalistic and condescending to modern eyes, but the players of his day really appreciated his efforts on their behalf. Putting a professional in the centre of the painting was another little gesture that did not go unnoticed.

The minutes of Kent County Cricket Club Management Committee, chaired by Lord Harris and dated 5 November 1906, show the following decision:

Picture of the Kent Eleven: 'A suggestion by the Chairman that a picture of the Eleven in position in the field should be painted was approved, and it was decided to recommend to the

General Committee and the General Meeting of Members of the Club to sanction the expense.'

Three weeks later, another minute notes, under the item *Picture of the Eleven*, that, 'various ways of producing the picture of the Kent Eleven were discussed, and the Committee decided on photogravure, and to retain the copyright'.

On 10 December, the General Committee met. There were 23 members of the General Committee at this time, and the meetings were also attended by the club's secretary, its general manager and its treasurer, which made for a crowded room. Among the committee men were Lord Darnley, better known as Hon. Ivo Bligh, the man who first won the Ashes, and one of the players in the Lancashire game, Jack Mason. There was no disagreement with the chairman's proposal to the group, as the minute observes:

Picture of the Eleven: 'A suggestion was made by the Chairman that a picture of the Eleven should be painted by Mr Chevallier Tayler representing them in the field at Canterbury with Blythe bowling. It was proposed, seconded and carried that Mr Chevallier Tayler be commissioned to paint such a picture for the sum of 200 guineas with the prospect of sharing in the receipts from the sale of the print, after deducting the expense (if any) of the cost of producing the print, until he has received in all 350 guineas.'

In the notice of the Annual General Meeting of the club for 1907, the president's 'Report of the Season 1906' included the information that:

'The Committee propose to have a picture of the Eleven in the field at Canterbury painted by Mr Chevallier Tayler and arrangements will be made for a printed reproduction of it of about the size of that of the Kent and Sussex match at Brighton. A portion of the profits from the reproduction will go towards the cost of the painting, which will be the property of the Club.'

At the General Committee meeting on 10 December 1906, incidentally, it was proposed, seconded and carried that each player be given a payment of £10 'in appreciation of their services during the last season'. 'Player' meant professional player, of course, as the amateurs did well enough out of their match expenses not to need anything extra at the end of the year. But £10, worth about £1,200 in 2019, was a very generous Christmas bonus for the professionals.

From the end of the year, work could start on the picture, which, although not specifically mentioned in the minutes, was to be on a grand scale, a true panorama of Canterbury and its heroes as a fitting tribute to the team. The final painting measured 45 inches (115cm) high by 90 inches (230cm) wide, and 200 guineas (£210), the basic fee offered to Chevallier Tayler, was a fair if not massive fee for a man with a track record such as his, equivalent to about £25,000 in 2019. Tayler, who had not in the past been as successful as some of his contemporaries in actually selling his work, took the commission gladly.

His first task was to plan the painting, so that he could place all the Kent fielders recognisably and in realistic fielding positions. For Lord Harris, the important aspect was clearly that it must be Blythe bowling, so the point of view would have to be from somewhere backward of square, making Blythe's face and bowling action the focus of the painting. Equally, that would mean that the fielders behind square would be likely to have their backs to the artist, which was not a satisfactory outcome. Tayler largely solved this problem by taking the viewpoint of leg slip, which meant that only the wicketkeeper and first slip would not be full face portraits, and even Jack Mason at first slip is clearly recognisable in profile. The artist's eye is looking out towards the off side of the ground, where there are fielders lurking in wait for the ball to come their way, but the leg side is inevitably somewhat sparsely populated. Only Humphreys at silly mid-on and Ted Dillon positioned on the long-on boundary are there to guard the leg side, but with Blythe bowling as well as he did that day, it would be a rash batsman who risked a firm hit against the spin. Clearly Blythe would have to be bowling from the Pavilion End, as he usually did, to make the most of Canterbury's slope, which meant that the pavilion could be shown in its Festival Week glory, but this in turn meant that many of the tents, traditionally positioned along the Old Dover Road side of the ground, and those at the Nackington Road End, would not be visible. The famous lime tree, which was probably not within the playing area for this match, given the positioning of the wickets fairly well towards the top end of the ground, is also not visible, unless the tree that dominates the upper right background is that tree. If so, Tayler has used his artistic licence to move it several yards towards the city of Canterbury, just visible in the background.

The layout of the painting was thus decided. But in all this discussion and approval by Kent's well-populated committees, there was no mention of precisely which match it should be. Lord Harris had made up his mind, and the committee were no doubt aware of his proposal, but none of the official documents specify the Lancashire game. This is because permission had not yet been granted by Lancashire to feature any of their players in the painting. It was not until February that the minutes of the Managing Committee, under the chairmanship of Slug Marsham this time, were able to report that 'a letter had been received from Mr A.N. Hornby, giving his consent to the picture being a representation of the Kent v Lancashire match at Canterbury'. Marsham was also able to give the good news that 'orders had been received from 102 persons for 24 proofs on Japanese vellum, 40 on India paper and 62 plain prints worth altogether £242/11/-'. Already it seemed that Chevallier Tayler's fee had been covered before anybody had seen the painting or any sketches of it.

Tayler had by this time begun to work with the players to get likenesses of their faces for use in the finished painting. In a minute of Kent's Managing Committee dated 8 April 1907, when Tayler was already hard at work on the main painting, it was recorded that: 'The Artist had agreed to add a panel to the picture, on which he would paint portraits of Lord Harris, Mr George Marsham, Mr Patterson and Mr Marchant con amore [i.e. for free], also portraits of the seven members of the Eleven not represented in the picture. These seven would be charged at a rate of £7/10/- each.'

This panel is still in Kent's Chiesman Pavilion, and it features not only the four distinguished gentlemen mentioned in the minutes, but also Frank Woolley and Jack Hubble, both of whom were capped by Kent during the summer, as well as Bill Fairservice, Wally Hardinge and Alec Hearne, who between them played 51 matches for Kent in 1906. The brothers Arthur and Sammy Day, two more amateurs who played when they could, are on the panel, and so are Ken Hutchings and Ted Dillon, who also appear in the main painting. Their inclusion on the panel is probably because they are fielding so far from the bat in the main painting that their features are not clear, and Tayler, or Harris or both, wanted to make sure that they did not feel they were not being properly immortalised in oil. All five professionals were unlucky not to have been picked for the Canterbury Week games, but they have their consolation in their portraits on the panel. Lord Harris is there because it was his idea and he was chairman, while George Marsham, as probably the longest-serving committee man and an ex-president, earned his place. Messrs Marchant and Patterson were joint captains of the club in the 1890s, and still very much involved, but it is unclear why they should have been chosen to act as visual bookends to the panel. It is a very handsome set of head and shoulders portraits, with the coats of arms of Kent, Canterbury, Oxford and Cambridge among the heads. It is the only original Chevallier Tayler remaining in the possession of the club.

For Tayler, getting the likenesses of the Kent side was not a problem. Indeed, he had already portrayed Cuthbert Burnup in his series of cricketers from the previous year, and to come down to Canterbury, or to invite the players to his studio in Carlton Hill, St John's Wood, very close to Lord's in north London, to sit for their portraits was not a complicated logistical issue. However, the Lancashire players presented a little more of a problem. If, according to Lord Harris's dictum, Blythe had to be bowling and Tyldesley batting, then it meant that the batsman at the other end would have to be Harry Makepeace. In both innings, Reggie Spooner and Harry Makepeace opened the batting against Arthur Fielder and Colin Blythe, and in neither innings was there much of an opening partnership. Spooner was out for a duck in both innings, bringing Tyldesley in at number three. This was bad luck for Tayler, as his 1905 series had also included portraits of Spooner and Tyldesley, as well as MacLaren, and if any two of those players had been batting together in the match at any time, he could have used his previous year's work to create their likeness again. Spooner's early dismissal in both innings scuppered that plan.

Tyldesley's partnerships with Makepeace, however, were only worth 25 in the first innings, and 9 in the second, before they were parted, Tyldesley's scores of 19 and 4 being a poor return for a man who scored all but a triple century the previous time he faced the Kent attack.

Tayler nevertheless wanted Harry Makepeace in his painting. Tyldesley was easy to depict, as the angle of view meant that all that would be visible would be the backside of the batsman taking strike. Tayler knew Tyldesley's shape, size and stance at the wicket from his earlier portrait, so you would have thought that no new sitting would be required. However, there is an entry in the club minutes for 25 July 1907, which merely lists as an expense of creating the painting, 'Tyldesley's Expenses £3/14/6d'. Did he come down to London in order to have his rear view more accurately portrayed? Or was the expense connected with his offer, which the committee accepted in May, to sell engravings of the picture at his shop in Manchester?

Getting Makepeace to sit proved far more difficult. Harry Makepeace was a professional footballer as well as a professional cricketer. A half-back, he had been part of the Everton team that won the FA Cup in April 1906, and won his first cap for England that same month, playing against Scotland. He would go on to play in the Cup Final again in 1907, when Everton lost 2-1 to The Wednesday (now Sheffield Wednesday). It is highly unlikely that Everton would have allowed one of their star players to take time off in mid-season to sit for a cricket portrait, and he certainly would not have risked his career with Everton by going down to London without permission. Professional sportsmen at the time were poorly paid despite the large crowds of supporters they attracted to each game, and Makepeace would have realised how precarious his career was. Remarkably, he was not the only player in that Lancashire side who would go on to win England caps at both football and cricket – Jack Sharp, who batted at number five for Lancashire, also played for Everton on the right wing, and scored the only goal in their FA Cup Final defeat in 1907, having played alongside Makepeace in 1906 as well. He won two England caps for football between 1903 and 1905, and in 1909 won three for cricket.

If Tayler could not get Makepeace to pose for him, who could he get? None of the Lancashire players, even those who were not playing football professionally, were willing to come down to London for a sitting, and Tayler, apparently, did not feel inclined to take himself to Manchester. But as luck would have it, there was a substitute, William Findlay. Billy Findlay, an Old Etonian wicketkeeper who had captained his school XI in 1899, and had gone on to captain Oxford University, played a number of games for Lancashire as an amateur, including 19 during the 1906 season, but unfortunately he had not played in the game at Canterbury. At the end of the season, however, he retired from playing county cricket and during the winter moved to London to take up the post of club secretary at Surrey CCC, based at the Kennington Oval. He was well within reach of Chevallier Tayler, and so the approach was made. Findlay agreed promptly, and that is why his is the face of the non-striker, the only significant artificial element in the whole painting.

By the time of the next General Committee meeting, on 11 March 1907, Lord Harris was able to report that orders for the

Picture of the County Eleven 'had been received for 27 vellum proofs, 56 India proofs, and 74 plain proofs of the picture representing the Kent v Lancashire match at Canterbury. The value of these orders is £298/4/-, and the sum will be all but sufficient to pay all expenses of the picture and the reproduction'. This was excellent news. All that was needed was for the painting to be completed and the money would start rolling in.

Or not, as the case may be. By July, the picture had clearly been completed and unveiled, although the exact date of its presentation to the club has not been recorded. The verdict on the finished work was uniformly favourable, but not enough copies had yet been sold. Orders for 192 copies of the picture, from 156 members of the club, had been received, bringing in a theoretical revenue of £366/2/-, but this was not enough to cover the revised expenditure figure of £403/6/10d. In an attempt to promote the painting to Kent supporters who had not yet bought an engraving, Lord Harris ordered that 'six copies of the picture be framed and exhibited in the Pavilion Enclosure and Stands during the Canterbury Week, the men in charge to be provided with forms on which orders may be written'. Yet despite this attempt at a hard sell to Kent spectators, Lord Harris also decreed that an India proof copy would be given, as a thank you, to each of those who sat for their portrait. The India proofs are listed in the accounts at £21 per hundred, so the cost of giving away 14 copies (11 Kent players, two Lancastrians and an umpire) was only about £3.

The insurance of the painting, which would in the future become a major issue, one which in the end decided the fate of the painting, was also minuted. Together with the only other items of significant value owned by the club, Fuller Pilch's coffee pot and snuff box, the painting was valued at £300, and insured at 4/6d per cent.

There is very little evidence which can be gathered to show us the actual process that Chevallier Tayler followed in creating the painting. Its very size was a challenge, as was the need to depict an actual game in a realistic way, rather than merely painting an idealised version of a typical cricket match which had been the usual practice until then. Tayler was, if anything, a realistic romantic, if that is not a oxymoron. He believed in depicting real scenes as faithfully as he could, but these scenes were usually tinged with a romance, a sense of England at its purest and best, that marks him out from some of his contemporaries. So Kent v Lancashire, a real match and a paean to cricket and England at the height of Empire, was something he could put his heart and soul into.

Much of the painting was done at the artist's studio in Carlton Hill, just a few hundred yards from Lord's, but he also spent some time at the St Lawrence Ground in Canterbury, sketching the setting for his cricket match. It must have taken some feat of imagination in winter and early spring to conjure up the tents and crowds that would have lined the playing area at the height of summer the previous year, but as the painting was already on display by Canterbury Week in 1907, there was no question of Tayler using the reality of the next year's festivities to recreate 1906. The trees, too, are in full bloom in the painting, although Tayler must have studied them in February and March when their branches were bare. The flags are fluttering, and Canterbury Cathedral can be glimpsed, with a little bit of artistic licence, in the background, as can the cross timbers of the Bat and Ball pub across the Dover Road from the ground, a building which, like the cathedral, still stands. The I Zingari tent, under the big elm tree behind and beyond Cloudesley Marsham, its black, red and gold colours proudly flying from the top of the tent, is full of ladies in their colourful frocks. The pavilion is full of spectators both at ground level and in the upper area, and the clock, which reads 1.25pm, not to mention the shadows of the players, tell us it is late in the first session, just before the lunch break. Colin Blythe's left arm is just coming up in the instant before it brushes his ear and releases the ball towards the batsman, who is standing in his crease, prepared for whatever the great spinner bowls at him. The pose of Blythe's body is very similar to the action photograph taken by George Beldam of Blythe a year or two earlier, which seems clearly to have been the basis for Tayler's portrait. Blythe is framed within the main archway of the pavilion behind him, bringing the eye directly on to him as the instigator of the action. His teammates are all around, some crouched in close catching positions, some standing upright further away, but all generating a sense of anticipation as they wait for the batsman to play his shot.

The delicate colour of the tiles on the pavilion roof and the subtle mix of sunlight and shade on the pitch are such vivid elements in this portrait of the St Lawrence Ground that it is hard to believe that the painting was actually created in the winter months. If that were so, Tayler would have trudged around the outfield in December and January to get the geography of the ground right, but the sunshine, the summer clouds, the tents and the crowds around the boundary were all imagined.

Or were they? There is no evidence that Tayler was present at Canterbury during the 1906 Week, but there is no evidence that he was not. He was an avid cricket lover, with many friends, including Lord Harris, in the higher echelons of cricket. His most recent paintings, his series of *The Empire's Cricketers*, had been sufficiently successful for him perhaps to be thinking of more cricket paintings. He might have decided that a few days at the social centre of the cricket season would be an opportunity to look for more portrait commissions if nothing else. His name does not crop up in the lists of notable people at the ground or at the balls during Cricket Week in 1906, but as a mere artist, might he not have been of high enough social standing to warrant inclusion in the social diaries of the time? There was at Canterbury an exhibition by the East Kent Art Society during the Week, which might have been a further incentive to take the train down from London. Might he have brought down his sketchbook and made a few preliminary drawings while Kent wrapped up their victory over Lancashire? After all, he had worked on his sketches for *The Empire's Cricketers* at Lord's, so why would he not have considered sketching at Canterbury during the Festival Week? Could it be that the idea of the painting was his rather than Lord Harris's, and might he have suggested it to Harris as a suitable commemoration of the county's triumph once the season was over? This is pure speculation, but it seems no less likely than the notoriously philistine Lord Harris coming up with the idea unprompted.

At whatever time of year Chevallier Tayler painted it, there is possibly a small error in the painting in the time shown on the pavilion clock. According to the contemporary report in the *Whitstable Times*, the Lancashire innings began at 12.20pm, and the batsmen 'did none too well in the first hour' of their innings. Their reporter states that three wickets fell before 1.20pm, those of Spooner, out in Fielder's first over, Makepeace and 'after being unsuccessfully appealed against for lbw, Tyldesley was out to a splendid catch by Seymour at third slip'. So that would mean that when the clock showed 1.25pm, Tyldesley would already have been back in the pavilion. I suppose we have to assume that when the reporter from the *Whitstable Times* said 'the first hour' he could have meant 'the first hour or so', and equally he could have meant 'gully', which is where Seymour is portrayed, when he wrote 'third slip'. Or Tayler just thought 1.25pm on the clock looked good, but I cannot imagine that with so much detailed planning of the painting that he was not given guidance by his Lordship as to what the clock face should read. Let us be generous and suggest that not only was the *Whitstable Times* reporter's watch a little slow, but also that the ball that Blythe is about to release is the very delivery that accounted for Tyldesley, and that Seymour, in making his splendid catch, had to move from gully to third slip to grab hold of it.

Kent v Lancashire 1906 is a painting of Edwardian England at its most confident. Its brightest and best sportsmen are engaged in a vital but friendly struggle on a beautifully tended patch of grass in the garden of England. As the Sotheby's sale catalogue was to describe it a century later, 'the painting captures a masculine heroism and a glorification of national pride in an image of a sporting summer idyll. Gentlemen with rolled up sleeves battle in the summer sun before the expectant eyes of an encouraging crowd as the Union Jack flutters in the breeze' alongside the white horse flag of Kent. In the distance, the 400-year-old Bell Harry Tower at Canterbury Cathedral can be seen, the highest structure of the home of the established church, the very essence of all the values Britain's imperial class held so dear. The fact that the Bell Harry Tower is not exactly where Chevallier Tayler has put it, and cannot be seen particularly well from the St Lawrence Ground, unless you have a very tall ladder, adds to the symbolism of the painting: muscular Christianity, at the heart of an Edwardian Englishman's love of sporting contests, is on display. Everywhere we see *mens sana in corpore sano*, a healthy mind in a healthy body. The sun is shining, the skies are filled with fluffy, friendly clouds and the crowds in their best clothes and their best behaviour are sure that all is for the best in this best of all possible worlds. It was only a fleeting moment, but how wonderful to have it captured for all time. Within a dozen years, the two Kent players who did the most to win this game, Colin Blythe and Kenneth Hutchings, would both be killed in the Great War, Hutchings in September 1916 and Blythe in November 1917. Both of Chevallier Tayler's sons would also die in the conflict.

Tayler would have invited all the players to come to his studio to sit for the painting, although some may well have sat for him in Canterbury, especially if he was there during the 1906 Week. Tayler was a plein-air man, and so was used to setting up his sketchbooks, canvases and paints wherever the need arose. We know that Billy Findlay came to his studio, and probably several of the amateurs – Cuthbert Burnup, Ted Dillon, Jack Mason, Kenneth Hutchings, Dick Blaker and the captain Cloudesley Marsham – may have found it more convenient to meet in town rather than in Canterbury. In any case, Tayler set to his task enthusiastically and quickly, and within a few months the painting was complete.

Tayler favoured the square brush technique, which involves using the square edge of the brush to apply the paint to the canvas straight from the palette in a criss-cross or jigsaw pattern. This was a technique used by a number of French impressionist painters of the time, including Jules Bastien-Lepage, whom Chevallier Tayler much admired, and which many of Tayler's

Newlyn colleagues also used. This technique softened the edges of the strokes to give a vibrant impression of atmosphere and light. The Bloomsbury Group painter and art critic Roger Fry, who championed French artists of the turn of the 20th century, wrote that 'Bastien-Lepage … cleverly compromised between the truth and an accepted convention of what things looked like, to bring the world gradually around to admitting truths which a single walk in the country with purely unbiased vision would have established beyond doubt'. Chevallier Tayler had dealt with the compromise between truth and an accepted convention of what things looked like for all of his artistic life. That is how naturalist or impressionist artists worked.

According to conventional wisdom before the rise of the impressionists, the surface of any painting had to be smooth, and the brushstrokes should not be noticeable. By using a square or broken brushstroke method, the impressionists were able to give the impression of detail, of light and shade, of solidity or fragility, according to the needs of the composition. The size of the brushstroke squares means that non-essential details are eliminated. Anything smaller than one brushstroke would have to be very important to be included, and thus the painting is not cluttered up with what one might call visual background interference, allowing the eye to concentrate on the central images of the painting. As one artist has written, 'each stroke can be a slightly different colour and angle, which makes the painting appear to sing with more colour and detail than is actually there'. Broken brushwork fools the brain into seeing what it thinks should be there.

If you look closely at the painting, it quickly becomes clear that Tayler has created a detailed portrait of the day's cricket at

Canterbury, without actually putting in too much detail. The faces of the players are readily recognisable, and it would be quite wrong to suggest that the picture is no more than an impression of cricket at Canterbury. It is a true statement of how it felt to be at Canterbury on 10 August 1906. It is the truth and nothing but the truth (Billy Findlay, the height of Canterbury Cathedral's bell tower and perhaps some of the field placings always excepted!), but it is not the whole truth. The whole truth is not needed. As the musician Paul Weller said, when talking of The Kinks' brilliant album *Village Green Preservation Society*, another work that looks back at a nostalgic ideal of England, 'It's a great snapshot of England. Whether it's a real one or an imagined one doesn't matter too much, because it's art, so you can make of it whatever you want.' Substitute the word 'painting' for 'snapshot' and the same could be said of *Kent v Lancashire 1906*.

For the record, the players shown in the painting are, from left to right, Humphreys at silly mid-on; Dillon in the distance, fielding at long-on; Findlay, the non-striking batsman; umpire Atfield; Blythe, who is bowling in his county cap; the batsman Tyldesley; Blaker at mid-off; Huish, who is keeping wicket; Hutchings on the boundary near two flagpoles at deep extra cover; the Kent captain Marsham in the covers; Fielder at silly point; Mason at first slip; Burnup at point; and Seymour at gully. The square leg umpire, Titchmarsh, does not come into the picture.

The painting was completed in time for Canterbury Week in 1907, and, we think, hung in the pavilion in time for members to admire it, although there is no proof that the original was in place by then. Six copies of the painting were framed and exhibited in the pavilion enclosure and stands during the Week, and the men in charge, in a rush of commercial enthusiasm, were provided with forms on which orders could be written. The critical reception was uniformly excellent, but the financial viability of the project remained in doubt. In August, just before the start of the Week, the committee agreed to a suggestion from the Swan Engraving Company, who were making the prints for general sale, that 'complimentary copies of the artist's proofs should be sent to the most representative daily and sporting papers asking them for a review of the engraving'. All possible lines of promotion were being pursued.

It is clear that optimism over the commercial prospects of the painting still reigned as the season came to an end, because the committee decided on 30 September that year to order from the Swan Engraving Company a further 200 India proofs, at a cost of a further £42, and 'then to complete the order for 300 plain prints'. Two weeks later, the Managing Committee decided that India proofs should be sent to 'all dealers in London recommended by Mr Chevallier Tayler, and to write to all County Cricket Clubs and to clubs in Kent who have not taken copies'. Clearly they considered that the work was so important that all county clubs should have a copy, and that every cricket club in Kent should also feel obliged to buy one. They also suggested that letters should be sent to local regimental messes, asking them to subscribe to the 12 vellum proofs, one third of the original stock ordered, which had cost the club around 5/6d (27.5p) each.

However, it is possible that the decision made by Lord Harris that the painting should concentrate on the players rather than the spectators was proving expensive. If members could not see themselves in the picture, why would they buy it? Nearly all previous cricket prints had been sold by subscription to people who appeared in the picture, and attributed much of their financial success to this simple piece of marketing. Lord Harris may have instructed Chevallier Tayler to create a wonderful work of cricket art, but would it work financially?

By 9 December, there is a note of desperation creeping into the minutes. In 1907, also to celebrate the 1906 triumph, Eyre and Spottiswoode, 'His Majesty's Printers' as they proudly proclaim on the title page, had published a *History of Kent County Cricket*, edited by Lord Harris and subscribed to by many but not enough members of the club. A two for one discount was now being offered.

'The Print and the Book: Members are particularly requested to take copies of the print of the picture of the Kent Eleven of 1906, and the *History of Kent County Cricket*, and to assist in obtaining orders. Reproductions of the picture have been prepared on Japanese vellum at £4/10/- each, on India paper at £2/2/- each, and on ordinary paper at 10/6d each, and orders for these should be addressed to the Secretary.' As the minute book also notes, '*History of Kent County Cricket*: It was ordered that a circular be sent to all members of the club reminding them that copies of the *History* or of the picture would make acceptable Christmas presents.' Perhaps there was some irony in the quotation from Lord Harris on the title page of his *History*, which states that 'cricket is not only a game, but a school of the greatest social importance'. The school was teaching the Kent committee that selling is a difficult art.

By the beginning of the 1908 season, the financial state of Kent's efforts to market the painting in all its versions was becoming clear. In May, the committee was told the dismal news.

'Picture of Kent XI: An account of the picture was presented, showing a debit balance of £166/14/7d which would be reduced by £140 if all the subscribers would pay up. The stock of copies remaining in hand was worth £542/6/6d, and it was decided to exhibit the plain prints on all the home grounds; also to ask permission to exhibit an India proof in the Pavilion at Manchester, at Whitsuntide.'

'If all the subscribers would pay up' – the eternal problem for small businesses. Given that the total expenditure on producing and selling the painting, including Chevallier Tayler's fee, was scarcely over £500 in total, a debit balance of roughly one third of that amount was not good news. Even if all subscribers would pay up, there would still be a debit balance of £26, and yet they had a stock valued at £542. Clearly they had not only over-ordered, but were also overcharging. This was a sorry state of affairs for such a highly regarded painting, which would become known as the artist's masterpiece.

By the end of the summer, things had not improved. The minutes in August record that 'a cash account of the picture was presented showing that when the outstanding subscriptions, amounting to £32/5/-, had been collected, the debit balance on the account would be £143/13/7d; 392 copies remain in hand worth £539/3/6d'. Only £2/16/6d worth of prints had been sold over the summer, which is no more than five prints on ordinary paper, or one print on India paper and one and a bit on ordinary paper.

At the end of August, Lord Harris reported an offer from Mr Spottiswoode, the publisher of the *History of Kent County Cricket*, to advertise the painting by means of reproductions in The Sphere, an offer which was accepted with thanks, and a month later a request from Bolak's Electrotype Agency for permission to reproduce the painting in the *Illustrierte Zeitung* was granted on condition that they would advertise where copies could be obtained. Quite how many copies the club hoped to sell to a German-speaking audience is not clear.

By the end of 1908, 18 months after the completion of the painting, the committee were desperate to sell off their remaining stock. 'The Committee beg to remind members that it will help the club materially if they will take copies of the *History of Kent County Cricket* and of the print of the Picture of the Kent Eleven and will obtain orders from their friends.' They may have been hoping that the spirit of Christmas was still alive in their members' hearts, but the result was the same. Sales did not cover the outgoings, and there is no evidence that Albert Chevallier Tayler was ever paid any more than the original 200 guineas for the painting, and £52/10/- for the panel, that he had been paid as an advance.

1906

C HEVALLIER Tayler painted a scene showing Britain, or more specifically England, at the height of its imperial glory. King Edward VII was on the throne, hugely popular despite, or perhaps because of, his colourful private life which was in such contrast to his gloomy but long-lived mother Queen Victoria, who had died five years before. The new century was a mere half a dozen years old, and the spirit of hope and renewal that pervaded the world at that time had not dissipated. Advances in technology and engineering were making changes to ordinary people's lives in ways which could scarcely have been imagined a few years before – the motor car, the telephone, film, radio and even the possibility of flight were now part of real life and not just something imagined by H.G. Wells. The first public radio broadcast and the release of the first ever feature film, an Australian effort about the Ned Kelly gang, both happened in 1906. Agreed, the motor car was a German invention, film progress had been centred in France, Marconi was an Italian and Alexander Graham Bell and the Wright brothers were American, but Britain was still the leading power in the world. Was not half the world map painted red? Was the king not also Emperor of India and monarch of the largest empire the world had ever seen? Did it not have the newly launched *Dreadnought*, a battleship so powerful and so fast that it rendered all other battleships obsolete? Were the English not right to imagine that God was an Englishman, and that the greatest prize in the lottery of life was to be born an Englishman?

That would certainly have been the view of both Lord Harris and Albert Chevallier Tayler, but with the gift of hindsight, the year 1906 could be seen as the end of the calm and the beginning of the storm that would engulf the world in 1914. The vast advances in communication in the first decade of the 20th century, which affected everybody, not just the privileged few, brought the realities of the world to every home, through newspapers, magazines and personal experience in a way that had not been possible before. Newspapers and magazines could now print photographs of events around the world, people could travel more easily than ever before to distant lands and bring back tales of how life is lived in alien cultures, and of course, people could also learn more about their own country and their own way of life, and see the need to change many aspects of it. Transport within Britain was developing, with improvements to the railways and the roads: in 1906, two new London Underground lines were opened, the Baker Street and Waterloo Railway (the basis for today's Bakerloo line), as well as the Great Northern, Piccadilly and Brompton Railway (now a part of the Piccadilly Line), and the construction and resurfacing of roads continued rapidly as the motor car became more and more a fact of life. The world's largest ship, the *Lusitania*, was launched in Glasgow in June of that year, reinforcing the idea that Britannia rules the waves, both militarily with *Dreadnought*, and on a moral and social level. The first ship specifically designed to take passengers on cruises rather than journeys had been launched in 1900, and although foreign travel was still almost exclusively reserved for the rich, other ways of spending leisure hours than watching cricket under the lime tree at Canterbury were beginning to emerge.

Anyway, travelling to foreign parts was fraught with danger. On 7 April, Mount Vesuvius erupted, causing great damage and loss of life in Naples and surrounding areas. Five days later, on 12 April, just before the start of the cricket season in England, a huge earthquake destroyed much of San Francisco, and the fire that followed did even more damage. Over 3,000 people lost their lives. On 16 August, a few days after Kent's double triumph in Canterbury Week, another earthquake, this time in Valparaiso, Chile, caused upwards of 20,000 deaths, and in mid-September a typhoon and tsunami which battered Hong Kong left 10,000 people dead. Staying in England seemed definitely to be the safest option, even for those who were wealthy enough to have the choice.

In 1906 there were perhaps few signs of change visible on the surface of English society, especially at the higher levels, but there were straws in the wind, a wind that would prove to grow into a hurricane of change. There were all those troublesome women, for a start. The Women's Social and Political Union, created by the Pankhursts, Emmeline and her two daughters Christabel and Sylvia in 1903, was beginning to gain attention through its ways of agitating for votes for women, which were deliberately aimed at causing as much public outrage and notoriety as possible. The Liberal Party won the general election that had taken place in

January 1906 in a landslide under the leadership of Sir Henry Campbell-Bannerman, although despite what the rest of the country thought, Kent remained solidly Conservative.

The parallels with 2019, politically speaking, are remarkable. The ruling Conservatives were split: on the one side the liberal free-traders wished to continue the trade policies established by Robert Peel in the 1840s after the repeal of the Corn Laws, while on the other, the protectionist faction wanted to strengthen relations with the Empire by building tariff walls around Britain and its many dependencies and colonies. This split, on the issue of free trade, led the Tories to a massive defeat in the election, and they stayed out of power for almost two decades. The protectionists were led by a charismatic man who wanted to be prime minister, Joseph Chamberlain, but the internal party arguments meant that he never achieved that ambition, and instead the Liberal government that swept to power was the most left-wing that Britain had known to that time. It caused a huge change in the relationship between capital and labour, and between the landed gentry and their tenants. Kent still voted Conservative, however, and Lord Harris would hardly have noticed the changes on his estates until the war came along and created a different society.

The Liberal Party was not socially completely left-wing. It was not inclined to support the cause of women's suffrage, or at least it realised that there was no majority in parliament for the idea. Campbell-Bannerman's response to the suffragettes' agitation was to suggest they 'go on pestering', but he also advised them to be patient. This advice was not followed. The Pankhursts and their allies resorted to ever more extreme activities, ranging from persistent heckling and interrupting political leaders who disagreed with their cause, to breaking windows and arson. In 1906, many suffragettes, as they came to be known, were arrested and imprisoned for demonstrating and lobbying parliament, which only increased public awareness of their cause, while at the same time tending to alienate their moderate supporters.

Women's suffrage was just one issue that would change the cosy world that the crowds at Canterbury Cricket Week enjoyed in 1906. Campbell-Bannerman's administration, one of the most radical in Britain's history, introduced old age pensions, the first efforts at creating a minimum wage, the National Insurance Act and the Parliament Act which restricted the power of the House of Lords, among many other sweeping new laws. Campbell-Bannerman himself died in 1908, but his legacy was established, and by the time 1914 came around, and with it global conflict, Britain would be a very different place from what it had been in 1906. But nobody knew it then.

Leisure time was changing too. Not only were the new laws brought in by the Liberals allowing working men and women more free time away from work, but also new ways of spending that leisure time were beginning to appear. In August 1906, the first Victrola phonograph, a device that played cylinders of recorded music and speech, went on sale, and though it would be ridiculous to suggest that this turned people overnight into avid record buyers, it was the start of a technological progression that would lead to record players, 45s, CDs and downloads, streaming, top twenties, music videos and a multi-billion-dollar music industry that would give millions of people another way of spending their free time, either playing or listening. Hobbies such as hill walking, stamp collecting (a particular interest for the future King George V) and bicycling grew in popularity, along with newer team sports such as rugby, football and lawn tennis. These all represented a challenge to the prime position of cricket in the social hierarchy of sport in Britain, a position that was retained for the time being by the national fame and statistical brilliance of one man, W.G. Grace.

If you look up W.G. Grace in the record books, they will tell you that his playing career stretched from 1865 to 1908, but in reality, his career was all but over by 1906. He was then 58 years old, but he had one more success to celebrate that year. Captaining the Gentlemen against the Players at the Oval on his 58th birthday, 18 July, he made 74, 'his success being hugely appreciated by all', as *Wisden* reported. He not only captained the side, but was so much older than the rest of the players on both sides that he had first played in this annual fixture in 1865, before any of them had been born. As *Wisden* pointed out, 'he was, in fact, old enough to be the grandfather of half a dozen members of his own side'. 'His play while he was getting his first 50 runs', said *Wisden*, 'was good enough to give the younger people among the crowd an idea of what his batting was like in his prime'. Grace has become a controversial figure since his death in 1915, only a few years after he played his final first-class game, but in 1906 he was still a cricketing god, and gods can make their own rules. What we might now see as cheating, both on the field and in his expenses claims, were at the time merely considered peccadilloes of the mighty, if they were considered at all. Grace was a good friend of Lord Harris, and had played both for and against Kent teams in Canterbury Weeks over the years, and spent his retirement years living in Eltham, on the border between Kent and London. His was, inevitably, one of the portraits that Chevallier Tayler produced for his series of

The Empire's Cricketers, the Old Man looking rather portly as he leans into an off drive, his trousers straining to retain some sort of decency across his backside. His fame was such that probably only the king had a more recognisable face, and it was Grace, almost single-handed, who raised cricket up to its position as the supreme sport of the English in their heyday. 1906 was for the most part a glorious summer of hot weather, a high point of English cricket's golden age. The *Kent v Lancashire* painting reflects this.

* * * *

The cricket season of 1906 was a remarkable one. As Sydney Pardon, *Wisden*'s editor, stated in the first sentence of his notes, 'The cricket season of 1906 was, by general consent, one of the most brilliant of recent years.' There was only one touring team from abroad, the West Indians making their second tour of England, but they did not play Test cricket. However, this lack of Test matches in no way reduced the quality of the cricket on display throughout the country and all through the summer. Several records were set, some of which still stand over a century later. Nobody, for example, has matched the achievement of George Hirst of Yorkshire in scoring over 2,000 runs and taking over 200 wickets in the same summer, as Hirst did in 1906. It took another 41 years before anybody was able to match, and beat, Tom Hayward's record total of 3,518 runs in the season. That record stood until 1947, when both Denis Compton and Bill Edrich of Middlesex went past Hayward's record aggregate. Hayward also scored 13 hundreds in 1906, to equal the record set by Charles Fry five years earlier, but it was not until Jack Hobbs scored 16 hundreds in 1925 that anybody had scored more hundreds in a season than Hayward's tally in 1906.

There were two remarkable bowling feats that summer, too. Playing for Gloucestershire against Essex at Bristol just four days before the date of Chevallier Tayler's painting, the slow left-arm bowler George Dennett took all ten Essex wickets for just 40 runs, as Essex slumped to 84 all out, and by close of play on the first day had taken another three wickets as Essex slipped to 63 for 4 in their second innings. Slow left-arm bowlers opening the bowling was a routine tactic in first-class cricket in those days. Nowadays it seems to be limited to white ball cricket, if at all. Twenty-four wickets in a day (Gloucestershire were all out for 173 in the middle overs of the day's play) would bring the pitch inspectors running in the 21st century, but in 1906 such things were not uncommon, and, what's more, were considered entertaining and exciting.

The other remarkable bowling feat was achieved by Kent's Arthur Fielder, playing in July for the Players against the Gentlemen at Lord's. In the Gentlemen's first innings, Fielder also took all ten wickets, at the rather higher cost of 90 runs, against a batting line-up that included several of the great names of the time, such as Reggie Spooner, Stanley Jackson, B.J.T. Bosanquet, Gilbert Jessop and Fielder's teammate Kenneth Hutchings. In the long history of Gentlemen v Players matches, which continued for a century and a half from 1806 until 1962, this was the only time any bowler took all ten wickets in an innings. And the Players still lost, by 45 runs.

On the same day that Kent were playing against Lancashire in the pleasant August sunshine, five other county games were taking place. At Lord's Middlesex were playing Surrey, where Middlesex's captain, their 36-year-old wicketkeeper Gregor MacGregor, won the toss and decided to bat. Although Middlesex had a strong team on paper, with Pelham Warner to open the batting and Frank Tarrant and Albert Trott among others to come in lower down the order, they were no match for Surrey's fast bowler Neville Knox, who dismissed the openers Warner and Douglas with only 25 runs on the board. They were all out for 173 before the end of the first day. The second day was 10 August, and while Charlie Blythe was luring the Lancashire players to their doom in Canterbury, Jack Hobbs and Ernie Hayes were helping Surrey surge past the Middlesex total with only one wicket down. Hobbs made 69 and Hayes ended up with 155 out of 239 runs added in the three hours and 45 minutes that he was at the wicket. A further 70 from Jack Crawford, including one hit on to the top balcony of the Lord's pavilion, put Surrey into a dominant position, with a first innings lead of 246. The match did not last long into the third day, despite MacGregor promoting himself to open the batting, and Middlesex collapsed again for 154 to lose by an innings and 92 runs.

Down at Taunton, the ground where 11 years earlier Archie MacLaren had made the highest individual score ever by an Englishman – a record that still stands a century and a quarter later – Somerset were playing against their western rivals Worcestershire. The match was described by *Wisden* as 'a match of huge scoring', with 1,371 runs being scored for the loss of 28 wickets, and five batsmen hitting centuries. The highlight of the prolific batting was unquestionably Reginald 'Tip' Foster's 198 in Worcestershire's first innings. Foster, who two and a half years earlier had made 287 on his Test debut against Australia, 'played a magnificent innings, hitting all around in his finest style'. The last 98 of his runs came in barely an hour, and around 50 of them (the exact details of the fall of all of the wickets in that match being unknown) were made in partnership with William

Hutchings, elder brother of Kenneth, who was now playing for Worcestershire after a brief but unsuccessful couple of games for Kent in 1899. Hutchings, described in Lord Harris's *History of Kent County Cricket* as 'a free and attractive batsman, hitting well all round the wicket, and an energetic field', made 21 while at the same time 200 miles away his young brother was flaying the Lancashire attack to all parts of Canterbury, but William's second innings of 26 not out certainly helped Worcestershire to secure a draw. Worcestershire ended the game 145 runs adrift of Somerset's aggregate, with five wickets still standing.

William, the eldest, and Kenneth Hutchings, the youngest, had another brother, Frederick, who also played a handful of games for Kent. He, like his brothers, was educated at Tonbridge, and was described as 'a sound and correct batsman, and a fine field at cover point'. He played twice for Kent in 1901 and once in the previous summer, 1905. That game was against MCC at Lord's, and Frederick Hutchings's final entry on the scorecard records him as 'absent' in Kent's second innings. He never played for the county again.

At Leyton, Essex were playing host to Sussex, who had journeyed across the river from Canterbury after their heavy defeat at the hands of Kent. The sun was out in Essex just as it was south of the Thames estuary, and on winning the toss, Essex chose to bat. This was obviously the right decision, and by the end of the first day's play, Essex had made 435 for 7. This was the second consecutive game in which Sussex had fielded all through the first day, and conceded over 400 runs in the process. It was also a match of long names. The Essex innings was opened by the future England captain, John William Henry Tyler Douglas, the only England player to have had four

Christian names, affectionately known as 'Johnny Won't Hit Today' for his obdurate batting style. He made 66 that day, many of them off opening bowler for Sussex that day, listed on scorecards as E.B. Dwyer, but in reality rejoicing in the full name of John Elicius Benedict Bernard Placid Quirk Carrington Dwyer. The 30-year-old Dwyer, born in Australia, remains the only first-class cricketer outside Sri Lanka to have had seven forenames. He came to England in 1904 on the recommendation of Pelham Warner, and was spotted at Lord's by C.B. Fry, who persuaded him to qualify for Sussex. In his first home game for the county after the two-year residential qualifying period, against Derbyshire in May 1906, he took nine wickets for 35 runs in Derbyshire's second innings, to help his adoptive county win by 88 runs. In June, against Middlesex at Brighton, he took 7 for 56 in Middlesex's first innings and 9 for 44 in their second, as Sussex won by an innings and 101 runs inside two days. Dwyer was obviously a fast opening bowler, but erratic, a man who could be deadly on his day. 9 August was clearly not one of his days. As his career progressed, the erratic days tended to outnumber the deadly ones, and after three early season matches in 1909, he was dropped by Sussex and disappeared from the first-class game. Sadly, neither Dwyer nor Douglas would live to see old bones. Dwyer died in 1912, and Douglas was drowned in 1930.

The star of the second day's play for Essex was Bill Reeves, who had come in at number eight for Essex and was 73 not out overnight. On 10 August he carried on where he had left off the evening before and took his score to 104, made in just 95 minutes, with 14 fours and two sixes. This was one of only three centuries in his entire first-class career, which lasted from 1897 until 1921, and took in 280 first-class games. His career batting average was less than 17, so this innings was something special for him. With Claude Buckenham, Essex's opening bowler and a man with a career batting average of 14.50, he put on 163 for the eighth wicket, taking the game well and truly away from Sussex. When it came to Sussex's turn to bat, they fared reasonably well, against an attack led by the veteran Walter Mead, but were all out for 313, a deficit of 209, by close of play. In the first two days' play, 835 runs had been scored, 20 wickets had fallen and 231 overs had been bowled, a rate of progress hard to imagine in county cricket today.

On the third day, Sussex followed on, and just managed to save the innings defeat. Dwyer was bowled by Douglas for 2, making that quite probably the most initial-laden dismissal in cricket history, and Essex were left needing five runs to win. The Sussex captain, Charles Smith, who took only nine wickets in his 14 seasons of first-class cricket, bowled the four balls required for Essex to win. Bill Reeves and Walter Mead, numbers eight and 11 in the first innings, were the pair who hit off the runs, for a ten-wicket victory.

Kent's main challengers for the title, the reigning champions Yorkshire, were playing at Aylestone Road in Leicester, where once more the runs flowed. The home team won the toss and decided to bat, and finished the first day on 388 for 7, against a Yorkshire attack that included Wilfred Rhodes, George Hirst and Schofield Haigh, three of that county's best of all time. Against this attack, Leicestershire's opening batsman, the comparatively unknown Cecil Wood, hit 148 out of 262 runs scored while he was batting, and the brothers Vivian and Reggie Crawford both made useful contributions to the score. The Crawford fraternity, like the Hutchings, had a third first-class member, Jack of Surrey, who the next day would hit a ball very nearly over the Lord's pavilion. All three were playing for the county of their birth: Vivian and Reggie were born in Leicester, but Jack, the youngest by four years, was born in Coulsdon, Surrey.

On 10 August, a day when Yorkshire's chances of retaining the title took a hard knock at Canterbury, the Leicestershire innings was ended at 425, and Yorkshire set about beating that total. Thanks largely to a century from Rhodes, and big contributions from 'Long John' Tunnicliffe and David Denton, Yorkshire reached 314 for 3 by close of play on the second day, but the pitch was looking more and more the likely winner of this game. *Wisden* was not very complimentary about Rhodes's innings, describing him as being lucky not to be caught when he had made 26, and playing 'several bad strokes'. Denton on the other hand 'played best for Yorkshire, his 80 being practically faultless'. Yorkshire batted on into the third day, bringing their total up to 483, including a vigorous 60 from Haigh batting at number nine, but a first innings lead of just 58 was never going to be enough to force a win on such an easy batting wicket. George Hirst, the man who would finish the season with over 2,000 runs and 200 wickets, had a quiet game, scoring only 23 and taking two wickets for 95 runs. Leicestershire batted out the day, and the match, on 169 for 5, and Yorkshire had to be content with a draw.

Meanwhile at Edgbaston, Warwickshire were playing Derbyshire, the team that would end the season bottom of the table by some distance, winning only two of their 20 games, losing 17 and drawing just once. This match, their 16th of the summer, turned out to be the draw. Derbyshire won the toss and, as was almost always the case until more recent times, chose to bat. The Warwickshire attack was by no means the most feared on the county circuit, but their opening bowler Sam Hargreave, bowling left arm at the same sort of pace as Charlie Blythe, took four wickets as Derbyshire lurched to 162 all out. Tom Hallam, an opening bat who played only ten games for Derbyshire in his career, six of them in 1906, hit the highest score of that short career in making 68 before being run out, and one of Derbyshire's all-time worst batsmen, Billy Bestwick, made 20 not out with some cheerful hitting at the end. Bestwick, who played for Derbyshire as a very effective right-arm fast-medium bowler for so long that he even played first-class cricket alongside his son Robert in the 1920s, played 323 first-class matches without ever scoring more than 39. His career batting average of 4.71 is among the very worst on record for somebody who has played so many games.

By close of play on the first day, Warwickshire had reached 152 for 4, just ten runs shy of Derby's total, with their batting linchpin, Willie Quaife, well set. Quaife also played until he was in his fifties and alongside his son Bernard in the Warwickshire side. When Derbyshire played Warwickshire at Derby in June 1922, the Bestwicks, father and son, were playing for Derbyshire and the Quaifes, father and son, were playing for Warwickshire. This remains a unique combination in English first-class cricket, although it is common enough on the village green.

On 10 August, Warwickshire took their total up to 303, and Derbyshire had to bat again, 141 in arrears. Warwickshire must have been expecting to have the game wrapped up by lunch on the third day at the latest. However, contrary to expectations, Derbyshire batted with far more backbone the second time around. Derbyshire's captain, the 44-year-old Levi Wright, and Tom Hallam put on 101 for the first wicket, and by close of play, with Derbyshire on 167 for 3, the arrears had been wiped out and a close game of cricket could be expected on the third day. Sam Cadman, Derbyshire's long-serving all-rounder, hit 94 and the West Indian Charles Ollivierre, described in *Wisden* as 'generally a sort of brilliant disappointment', made 74. By the time that Derbyshire were all out for 357, leaving Warwickshire 217 to win, there was only about an hour and 40 minutes left to play. Warwickshire, deciding they could not lose the game, had a go at chasing the target, but finished the match on 115 for the loss of four wickets, with Willie Quaife on 55 not out. Derbyshire had secured their only draw of the summer against the odds.

By the end of this round of matches, it appeared that Surrey were poised to take the title. The scoring system, which gave counties one point for a win, minus one point for every loss and nothing at all for a drawn game, encouraged positive cricket, and also required a sophisticated mathematical mind as well as plenty of pencils and paper in those pre-calculator days to work out which team needed to do what to take the title. Surrey had played 23 matches, of which they had won 16 and lost only two, giving them 14 points and 88.89 per cent of the available points per completed game. Yorkshire, with 11 points from their 15 completed matches out of 23 played, were second, on 73.33 per cent. Kent were lying third, with nine points from 13 completed games, having won 11 matches, lost two and drawn four, to give them a score of 69.23 per cent. No other county was really in the race now. All three teams had five matches still to play, meaning that if they won all their games, Surrey could finish with 91.30 per cent, Yorkshire with 90 per cent and Kent with just 77.77 per cent. In 1905, Yorkshire had secured the title with a 71.42 per cent score, so all three teams were still definitely in the running, with Kent the long odds outsiders. Yorkshire and Surrey both had a fixture list comprising 28 games, while Kent only played 22. Playing fewer games was not necessarily an advantage, as each loss would count for a bigger percentage drop than for those counties who played more. That summer, Northamptonshire only played 16 championship games, and Middlesex and Somerset only 18, but they all finished well down the table.

What happened next was enough to keep the excitement bubbling for the rest of the summer as first one county and then another claimed an advantage. Surrey had already beaten Yorkshire at the Oval at the end of July, which gave them a big boost towards the title, but the day after they returned from Lord's with victory against Middlesex under their belt, they took on Lancashire, smarting from defeat at Canterbury at home. For much of the game Surrey were in control, securing a first innings lead of 82 in a low scoring game, thanks largely to excellent bowling by the Yorkshire-born Walter Lees (6 for 53) and the dangerously quick Neville Knox (4 for 39).

But Lancashire fought back, and dismissed Surrey for 143 in their second innings, leaving the visitors needing 226 runs to win. Lancashire knocked off the runs for the loss of just four wickets, although Spooner, who went on to make 92, was dropped off the first ball of the innings. Had that catch been held, Lancashire might have wobbled and the outcome of the championship could have been very different. In Surrey's second innings, Lancashire's wicketkeeper Billy Findlay took four catches and let through no byes, begging the question of why he was not preferred to Worsley in the Canterbury game, a selection that would have solved all

Chevallier Tayler's problems of getting Lancashire's players to pose for him.

Kent had already beaten Surrey twice during the summer, but had fared much less well against Yorkshire. Given that Yorkshire were the reigning champions and had several England players in their superbly gifted side, it was not surprising that Kent had not done well against them. What was surprising was how well Kent played against all the other teams, once the season got properly under way. Their very first county game of the summer was against the champions, at Catford, which resulted in an easy win, by 119 runs, for Yorkshire. Kent managed to draw the game against Yorkshire in the return match at Sheffield in June, but neither match was their finest hour, in cricketing terms, at least. One small incident in the Sheffield match shows the way that both Kent and Yorkshire, under the benevolent dictatorship of Lords Harris and Hawke respectively, played their cricket. Arthur Fielder clean bowled Lord Hawke in the first innings for 4, but although the stumps were a mess and Fielder had not overstepped the line, Slug Marsham recalled his Lordship because there was some thought that the bails had been blown off by a gust of wind a split second before the ball demolished the stumps. Lord Hawke refused to return to the crease, believing he had been fairly dismissed, and was later known to repeat his view that Kent were 'one of the most sporting sides in England', a compliment that Lord Harris would have appreciated and happily returned to his friend. These days the umpires would be conferring, the television replays would be shown from a variety of angles on an endless loop, and no doubt Lord Hawke, on walking, would have been recorded as 'retired, out' rather than bowled, thus denying Arthur Fielder his sixth wicket of the innings.

Yorkshire had failed against Surrey earlier in the season, but now had the chance of revenge, at Sheffield in late August. Since their drawn game against Leicestershire, they had drawn against Middlesex in a very rain-affected match at Leeds, and then brushed Warwickshire aside at Harrogate, dismissing their opponents for under 100 in each innings and winning by an innings and 91 runs. Their match against Surrey at Sheffield, beginning on 20 August, was seen by many as the game that would decide the identity of the eventual champions. As it turned out, the many were wrong. Yorkshire won the toss and batted, but apart from Denton and Hirst, nobody got to 20, and the side were all out for 144 within three hours. This looked to give Surrey the advantage, but Hirst and Rhodes got among them and Surrey could only manage 154, a lead of ten runs. Now the advantage of batting first looked to give Yorkshire the edge. By close of play on the second day, Yorkshire had reached 188 for 7, a lead of 178, with Rhodes on 92 not out. If Yorkshire could make another 50 runs the next morning, Surrey would have a very difficult task ahead.

In the event, Rhodes was out for 94 very early in the morning session, and Yorkshire could only manage 225 all out, leaving a target for Surrey, with openers Hayward and Hobbs in fine form, which should have been gettable. But Surrey dropped Hobbs down the order to bat at number six, and promoted Crawford to open in his place. Surrey then got off to a terrible start, being 19 for 3 at one stage, and 44 for 4 when Hobbs made his belated appearance. By now Hirst and Haigh were doing the damage, and Surrey could do nothing to limit it. Hobbs ended on 38 not out, and Haigh with five wickets for 31 runs, as Surrey crumbled to 113 all out, to give Yorkshire an unexpectedly comfortable victory by 102 runs. Now the white rose county was the favourite to win the title.

But then Yorkshire were on the wrong end of the closest game of this or any season, when they lost to Gloucestershire by a single run. Kent, who had won every single match since beating the touring West Indians in mid-July, were now the favourites. Since the Lancashire match, they had beaten Somerset and Worcestershire and in the aftermath of Yorkshire's disaster at Bristol, had to face Middlesex at Lord's to consolidate their place at the top of the table. Middlesex batted first and thanks to Fielder and Blythe, were all out for 143, but Kent did not press home the advantage well, and by the close of play on the first day had made only 129 for the loss of seven wickets. The large crowd that had come to Lord's to see the champions elect in action went home wondering if they had merely been watching the runners-up elect. The next day's play, however, reinforced the idea that Kent were the champions in waiting. Dick Blaker, who had been on 7 not out at the close of play on the first day, took his score to 86, an innings that was either 'magnificent' (Cloudesley Marsham) or 'very lucky' (*Wisden*), according to your point of view, and together with the tail-enders Marsham, Huish and Fielder, took Kent's first innings total to 266, a lead of 123. This proved decisive, and with Blythe bowling at his best (7 for 66 in 40.3 overs) in Middlesex's second innings, they struggled to reach 181 early on the third morning, leaving Kent just 59 to win. Hutchings, Kent's batsman of the summer, did it almost single-handed, coming in with the score on 27 for 2, and hitting 33 not out while his partner Jack Mason scored just 1. Now all Kent had to do was to avoid defeat by Hampshire in their final game, at Bournemouth. If they did that, then whatever Yorkshire or Surrey did in their final match would be of no account.

The match turned out to be a one-sided slaughter. The weather was remarkably hot all over the country during those last few days of August and the first days of September: on 2 September, the highest September temperature ever known in Britain was recorded in Yorkshire, but even on the south coast the players and the crowds basked in temperatures over 90°F (32°C) throughout the match. Hampshire won the toss and batted, on what Kent's captain Marsham described as a perfect wicket, but somehow got themselves all out for 163, early in the afternoon session. They had taken only 41 overs to reach that total, scoring at almost four runs an over, but Blythe (6 for 67) and Fielder (3 for 65) proved too much for them. At one stage the score stood at 75 for 8, but then Langford at number nine and Badcock at ten hit out and brought some slight respectability to the score. Badcock's 48 came in only 30 minutes of hefty blows. Kent then had time to build a solid total, and this they did. Cuthbert Burnup hit 179 and Kenneth Hutchings 124, their partnership of 189 coming in only 90 minutes. Hutchings brought up his hundred in a mere 65 minutes and by close of play on the first day Kent had made 302 for 3, a lead of 139 after a day in which 465 runs were scored. On the second day the massacre of the Hampshire bowlers continued. Mason, Humphreys and Blaker all scored fifties, and the only man not to reach double figures was the last man, Fielder, who was 3 not out when the Kent innings finally closed at 610, scored in almost exactly six hours, off 131.2 overs, a rate of 4.6 runs an over. Hampshire faced the enormous task of scoring 447 just to avoid the innings defeat. At this stage in the game, it was clear that Kent would avoid defeat and be crowned champions for the first time.

Hampshire made a much better fist of things the second time around. Thanks mainly to a magnificent innings of 158 not out by Hampshire's South African Test cricketer Charlie Llewellyn, Hampshire made 410 all out, but this was not enough to avoid an innings defeat.

Kent had done it! County champions for the first time!

Kent's title was greeted with great acclaim around the country, with even Lord Hawke at Yorkshire sending congratulations to his great friend Lord Harris. Typical of the reaction around the country was an article in the *Athletic News* of 31 August that year. 'We are delighted to see Kent at the head of the table for the County Championship, and trust that, having climbed to the top of an inclined plane, they will remain in that altitude. Everybody admires Kent for the sporting character of her cricket, for the spirit of her amateurs and for the calibre and character of her professionals.' Even so, the writer had to put in a small dig against Kent, when he went on to say that they 'prefer Men of Kent and Kentish Men to all others – although they are not quite so rigid about the birth qualifications as Yorkshire and Notts'. Yorkshire's captain at the time, Lord Hawke, had actually been born in Lincolnshire, although nobody really liked to mention it.

There was still one more game for the county to play before the season finished – Champion County v The Rest of England. The match was scheduled as a four-day game, at the Oval from 10 September. The Rest fielded a very powerful side, including Spooner and Tyldesley from Lancashire, Hirst, Rhodes and Haigh from Yorkshire, Surrey's Tom Hayward and their captain Pelham Warner from Middlesex. Kent had not lost a game since mid-June but this was a very big challenge.

The Rest won the toss and batted – no surprise there. Kent fielded the same 11 men who had beaten Lancashire, apart from Jack Mason who was unavailable for business reasons. He was replaced by the promising colt, Frank Woolley. As ever, Fielder and Blythe did most of the bowling, sending down 90 of the 118.2 overs required to dismiss The Rest for 392. Hayward, Tyldesley, Hirst and the Essex batsman Frederick Fane all hit fifties, and Claude Buckenham, the Essex bowler who was not supposed to be much of a batsman, hit 49 not out. Kent responded well, and by close of play on the second day had made 312 for the loss of five wickets, putting them perhaps marginally ahead at that stage. Hutchings and Woolley had both made fifties, and Blaker and Humphries were well set, so Kent should have been hoping for a total of 450 or more. But from the third morning onwards, the game was all for The Rest. Kent slipped to 365 all out, a small deficit but a significant one, and The Rest turned the screw. Tyldesley hit another century, bringing his total of runs off Kent bowling during the year past 500, and Warner and Fane both hit fifties. Fielder and Blythe bowled another 67 overs between them, and on the fourth morning, with the score on 344 for 7, Marsham brought himself on to bowl. His first ball dismissed Buckenham, caught by Seymour in the gully, and The Rest promptly declared, leaving Kent an improbable 372 to win in less than a day. They never got anywhere near it, being skittled for 120 within 40 overs. James Seymour made 48, but only Woolley, Blaker and Dillon of the rest even reached double figures. Claude Buckenham took 6 for 45 and Hirst 4 for 73. It was a disappointing end to an otherwise triumphant season for Kent.

Kent had played 22 games in the championship, winning 16 and losing just two. From 9 June, when they lost to Lancashire at Old Trafford, until the end of the season they were unbeaten. They played three other first-class games: against MCC at Lord's in May, a game they lost by 69 runs; against the touring West Indians at Catford in July, a match they won by an innings and 14 runs; and their final match as Champion County against The Rest. If we are to analyse the team's averages, we see that despite the Herculean efforts of Arthur Fielder and Charlie Blythe, it was the batting that was the real foundation of Kent's success. Cuthbert Burnup finished the season top of the national batting averages, ahead even of the hyper-prolific Tom Hayward of Surrey, and Kenneth Hutchings was third in the list. Ted Dillon and Jack Mason were not much further down, all with averages over 40, and Dick Blaker averaged 39.52. With a line-up like that, and with solid support from James Seymour, Punter Humphreys and the new boy, Frank Woolley, it was no wonder that Kent scored quite so heavily and so fast.

The fielding was exceptional, too. James Seymour was acknowledged as a superb close fielder in the slips or gully, and Hutchings, Mason and Woolley all earned the highest praise for their efforts in the field. The close catching in particular, built around the wicketkeeping of Huish and the slip cordon including Mason, Woolley and Seymour, was of the very highest order, a fact that W.G. Grace himself acknowledged when he stated a few years later that 'there is not a bad fieldsman among them, and it is to this fact very nearly as much as anything else that they owe their run of success'. Cloudesley Marsham was interviewed by a reporter from the *Kent Messenger*, and said that only once, at Manchester against Lancashire, did the fielding go to pieces. As the reporter added, 'in praising others who had shone in the field he did not mention what we all know – that he himself is alone equalled by Jessop at cover point'. Catches win matches, and Kent were undoubtedly the best fielding side in England.

He was also asked which opponents he considered the strongest of the summer. Without hesitation, Marsham replied, 'Lancashire. Surrey too greatly depends on Hayward and Yorkshire too much upon Hirst to be a consistently good eleven.' All three counties had been beaten during the course of the summer, but Lancashire had caused Kent the most problems.

The bowling was, in 1906 at least, hugely dependent on two men, Fielder and Blythe. Blythe had not been fit for all of the summer, a badly damaged hand keeping him out of the side in June and July, causing him to miss seven county games, almost one third of the season. Nevertheless, he and Fielder bowled almost 1,700 overs between them, while all the other bowlers used during the season bowled only 1,420. The pair took 248 wickets between them, as opposed to 156 taken by all the rest of the team. What's more, Fielder was a fast bowler, opening the bowling off a long run all through the summer without missing a game. We may argue that he was not expected to do much with the bat, nor throw himself about too much in the field, but he averaged almost 12 with the bat and was never a passenger in the field. His bowling partnership with Blythe was crucial to Kent's triumph, but if he had broken down at any stage in the summer, it is hard to imagine that Kent would have won the title. As far as *Wisden* were concerned, Fielder was the man 'to whose fast bowling Kent more than anything else owed the championship'. To build on their success in 1906, Kent would have to build up their bowling attack. Luckily, they had part of the answer already in the team: Frank Woolley, who modelled his bowling on that of his hero Blythe, would go on to become one of the most prolific of all Kent bowlers, overtaking Fielder on the all-time list, but never quite catching up with Blythe, who took 2,210 wickets for his county in only 16 seasons. Woolley finished with 1,680 in a career that stretched to 1938, and Fielder with 1,150, taken between 1900 and the outbreak of war in 1914. It is a remarkable fact, as an aside, that all of the five most prolific wicket-takers in Kent's history have been bowlers whose stock ball turned away from the right-hander. Three, Blythe, Underwood and Woolley, were left-handers, and the other two, Freeman and Wright, bowled leg breaks. Quite what this says about Kentish wickets, I am not certain.

And so the 1906 season was over, on the pitch at least. The players could now relax until the spring. There were no overseas tours, no Test matches, no months playing grade cricket in Australia. The amateurs went back to their day jobs and the professionals found ways to earn money in the winter, often by coaching or by more manual labour, on farms or factories around the county. There were a few celebratory dinners to attend, of course, to relive the glories of the summer of 1906, but the focus in Cloudesley Marsham's mind, and no doubt for Lord Harris too, was how to keep on winning in the seasons to come.

The Match

IMAGINE the scene. The sun is shining. As one correspondent to the *Kent and Sussex Courier* writes of his trip to Canterbury, 'The city is en fete. The narrow streets are crowded. Chinese lanterns hang across in strings from nearly every house and flags by the hundred. We creep along with crowds of other motors and in this old-world place with reminiscences of the far off past on every side, our motor seems almost an outrage, but it was a very comfortable and delightful one.' On that bright summer's day in 1906, just as much as in the first quarter of the 21st century, the past, the present and the future mix, sometimes a little uneasily, during Canterbury Week. The fourth day of the 65th Canterbury Cricket Week is about to begin. The Canterbury City Council and the local Chamber of Commerce have between them stumped up £100 to put bunting around the streets of the city, and within the St Lawrence Ground, some 18 tents have been erected to house the great and the good of Kentish society, as they drink, eat, gossip and, occasionally, watch the cricket. Over the previous three days, and before a huge crowd, Kent had demolished Sussex, their oldest county rivals, by an innings and 131 runs, and today, Thursday, 9 August 1906, had been designated 'Ladies' Day'. As the local papers reported, 'the whole ground resembled a picnic party of monster proportions … Ladies smiled and gentlemen joked and all was merry as a marriage ball'. A crowd of 13,435, a record for the ground, are eager for the start of the game against Lancashire, the side that had lowered Kent's colours in the game at Manchester earlier in the summer.

At this point there is a slight hiatus. The appointed hour for the game to start, 12 noon, passes without any players emerging from the pavilion. Nobody seems too worried by the delay – the picnic party of monster proportions carries on even without the promised entertainment by men in white flannels. It turns out that the public transport systems of 1906 are no more reliable than those of the 21st century, and the Lancashire team have been delayed on their trip from Manchester. As the *Morning Post* put it, 'Lancashire, following their unlucky reverse at the hands of Yorkshire, had to come up from Manchester by special train on Wednesday night, then journey down to Canterbury in the morning; consequently, they arrived late.' In those days, matches began when all the players were ready, not when the clock struck a certain hour, regardless of whether there was a full complement of players on the ground. When the Lancashire team finally arrive, the toss is quickly won by Kent, whose captain, Cloudesley 'Slug' Marsham, decides to bat. At 12.25pm, the Lancashire team, led by their captain Archie MacLaren, stride out into the Canterbury sunshine.

There was a general expectation in the morning papers and among the crowd at the ground that there would be one change from the team that beat Sussex the previous day. This would give the highly promising colt Woolley a game, but at the last moment, it was decided to stay with a winning team, and the same 11 men who had trounced Sussex took on Lancashire.

The pitch was made for batting. Kent opened with Ted Dillon and Cuthbert 'Pinky' Burnup, two of the six amateurs in the Kent eleven. It was said that Kent under the chairmanship of Lord Harris always insisted on having at least three amateurs in every county eleven, but on this occasion they were running well above their minimum requirement. Burnup, who had barely played in 1905 because of his business commitments, came into the Kent side at the end of July 1906, and then opened the batting in every game until the end of the season. Dillon was his most regular opening partner, but during the summer, Kent tried no fewer than 11 different opening partnerships, featuring nine different players.

The combination of Alec Hearne and Ted 'Punter' Humphreys began the batting in seven of the 25 matches that Kent played that summer, but the long-serving Hearne had been dropped after the match against Gloucestershire a few weeks earlier, and Humphreys was now batting at number six. Dillon performed his usual tricks of adjusting his pads, fiddling with his gloves and fidgeting at the crease, but did not last long. He was caught by Poidevin for 8, with the score on 9. A disappointing start, maybe, but this brought Kent's most reliable professional batsman, James Seymour, to the crease. In perfect weather, he and Burnup took the score to 107 for 1 at lunch, with few alarms apart from one chance from Seymour to MacLaren in the slips when the total was 81, but it slipped through the Lancastrian's fingers. It proved not to be too expensive a miss. Shortly after the lunch break, a sumptuous occasion for spectators and players alike, MacLaren

redeemed himself by catching Seymour for 50, leaving the score
at 109 for 2.

This was the cue for Kent's batting hero of the summer,
Kenneth Hutchings, to take guard. Batting with a fluency and
grace which he never really recaptured after this one outstanding
summer, Hutchings put on a further 99 runs in an hour and ten
minutes with Burnup, before the opener was run out. Hutchings
was not only a mercurial batsman, he was also a mercurial runner,
and sensing a two where Burnup only saw one, they found
themselves both at the same end. Burnup, on 94, sacrificed his
wicket in favour of Hutchings, a noble gesture. 208 for 3. Burnup's
departure brought no respite for the Lancashire bowlers, as the
next man in, J.R. Mason, was in equally fine form. Not long after
tea, the crowd broke into cheers, long and loud, as Hutchings
hit the runs that not only brought up his century but also raised
the team's 300. It was a superb exhibition of attacking batting.
As *Wisden Cricketers' Almanack* put it, 'in the course of an hour
and 50 minutes ... Hutchings and Mason hit up 201 runs, and
were still together at the drawing of stumps, Hutchings being
167 and Mason 71'. By the end of the day's play, Kent were on
409 for 3, and MacLaren and his men must have wondered what
they could possibly have done to prevent, or at least slow down,
the onslaught.

This was Hutchings's golden hour, the highest score of his
career. His strokes peppered the boundaries, with at least one
big hit disappearing into one of the 18 tents around the ground.
The crowd loved it and basked in the splendour of this carefree
batting display, an amateur batsman of the golden age of cricket
at his beautiful and ruthless best. But Kent wanted to win the
game, so personal glory was not considered. 409 was a good score,

probably a winning one, so as the crowds drifted away after a thoroughly satisfactory first day's play, Slug Marsham and his men considered what strategy they should follow over the next two days. The decision was straightforward – attack and pile on a few more runs before exposing the Lancashire batsmen to the Kent bowling attack, led by Arthur Fielder and Charlie Blythe.

The next morning, Friday, 10 August 1906, dawned bright and clear, a few summer clouds drifting indolently across the sky as if they too wanted to stay and watch the action down below. Hutchings and Mason resumed their attack, but after only 12 more runs had been added to the overnight total, the partnership was broken. The Lancashire captain Archie MacLaren was proving rather butter-fingered, having dropped Hutchings much earlier in his innings, to compound his lesser error against Seymour, but he made partial amends for his mistake and this time held on to a chance off the bowling of William Gregson, a Scottish-born fast bowler who only played five first-class matches in his entire career, all for Lancashire in 1906. Hutchings departed for 176 to prolonged cheering from the crowd, which was not quite as large as on the first day but still very considerable, and who were also no doubt a little disappointed not to have seen a repeat of the previous day's batting brilliance. Nevertheless, during his spectacular innings Hutchings had reached the milestone of 1,000 runs for the season, and had also broken at least two bats. Mason followed Hutchings into the hutch a few runs later, having made 88. He had also been dismissed by Gregson, whereupon Frank Harry, the Lancashire opening bowler who up to this point had had a dreadful time at the hands of the Kent batsmen – no wickets for 147 runs – suddenly came into his own. He hit exactly the right length and made batting very difficult for the remaining

Kent batsmen, who admittedly were having a go at everything in the pursuit of quick runs. Harry took five wickets for nine runs within three overs, and Kent found themselves all out for 479, 70 runs on from their overnight score, having lost seven wickets in 55 minutes that morning.

This was not, from Kent's point of view, a very bad thing; 479 was a very good score, and Frank Harry had shown that good bowling could also reap its own rewards on a wicket that nevertheless should still have a few runs left in it. There was plenty of time to get among the Lancashire batsmen, although past experience had taught them that there were plenty of fine batsmen in the Lancashire team, notably their number three bat Johnny Tyldesley, who had made a double century against Kent earlier in the summer. But they need not have worried. Off the final ball of Arthur Fielder's first over, he dismissed Reggie Spooner, a man who had made his England Test debut against the Australians the previous summer, for a duck. At the other end, Charlie Blythe, bowling as ever in his cap, made short work of both Harry Makepeace (caught behind for 6) and Johnny Tyldesley (caught by James Seymour for 19), and by the time that Jack Sharp was run out by a smart piece of fielding by Hutchings, Lancashire were deep in trouble at 67 for 4. In today's world we would be a little surprised that the opening bowlers were not both fast bowlers, but it was not really until Ted McDonald and Jack Gregory of Australia opened the bowling for their country in England in 1921, and swept all before them, that captains began to understand the advantages of giving the new ball, hard and shiny, to the two fastest bowlers in the team. And anyway, if you have Charlie Blythe on your side, why would you not give him the ball at the first opportunity?

This was the session of play that Lord Harris wanted Albert Chevallier Tayler to immortalise, with the sun at its height and Blythe bowling to Tyldesley as the Kent fielders bent keenly to their task, and the huge crowds – over 7,000 people came to watch the second day's play – added colour and life to the boundary's edge. As far as Harris was concerned, this proved that God was in his heaven and all was right in the world.

As the day wore on, Lancashire's position became more and more dire. *Wisden* summed up their entire innings with the single damning sentence, 'Lancashire batted in very disappointing fashion.' In barely two and a half hours' play, the visitors were all out for 169 in 46.3 overs. Blythe took five wickets for 80 and Fielder four for 81. They bowled virtually unchanged through the innings: Punter Humphreys bowled one over, a maiden, but otherwise it was all Fielder and Blythe.

These days a county captain may take a look at his two leading bowlers after they have each bowled over 20 overs and decide that they need a bit of a rest, and that therefore he would not enforce the follow-on. But that was now and this is then. Marsham had no hesitation in asking Lancashire to follow on, 310 runs in arrears, so Arthur Fielder and Charlie Blythe began again. They clearly did not need any rest, as the Lancashire batsmen did no better the second time around. Within a few balls, Reggie Spooner, one of the best and most elegant amateur batsmen of his generation, got himself out, bowled by Blythe, for his second duck of the day. By the close of play, Lancashire had stumbled to 78 for 4, with Sharp and MacLaren having engineered some sort of a revival from the depths of 20 for 4. MacLaren's innings, while important for Lancashire, did not please all the members of the crowd. As the official history of the club records, 'In the second innings of Lancashire, Mr A.C. MacLaren made a big off drive, and the ball, clearing the ring, struck the forehead of an elderly gentleman with so much force as to necessitate his removal to the hospital.' The unfortunate victim of MacLaren's off drive, who was identified as Walter Archer of Chartham, was tended to by the St John Ambulance men who were in the ground, and then taken to the Kent and Canterbury Hospital, which as luck would have it was, and still is, right next door to the ground. There he was treated for concussion and kept in overnight, but on the Saturday he was well enough to go home. A not very serious but almost inevitable injury at a cricket match where a hard ball was being hit fairly regularly into a crowd of several thousand people nevertheless attracted enough attention to live on in public memory down the years, and give Mr Archer his own tiny niche in Kent's cricketing history.

On the first day, 409 runs had been scored for the loss of three wickets, but on the second day 317 runs had been scored for the loss of 21 wickets. For the mathematicians among us, this shows that roughly nine times as many runs per wicket were scored on day one compared with day two. This was not because of a sudden deterioration in the wicket – it was a sudden deterioration in the quality of the batsmen, and an improvement in the quality of the bowlers playing on it. Kent now had the match by the throat and were not going to let go.

The next morning, another bright summer's day, Kent set about finishing off the match. Sharp went early on, after only two runs had been added to the overnight total, caught behind off Fielder. Arthur Fielder then ran through the Lancashire card, dismissing numbers two to eight in 16 overs of controlled accuracy and hostility. As his captain said, Arthur Fielder 'has never bowled better than this season, keeping, as he does, an excellent length, and he varies his pace more than formerly. He makes the ball go away with the arm as well as nip back from the off.' Fielder finished with second innings figures of 7 for 49 in 16 overs, and match figures of 11 for 130 in 38.3 overs, his best of the season. Lancashire were all out for 115, the last six wickets falling for 35 runs in scarcely half an hour. Kent's victory, achieved before lunch on the third day, by an innings and 195 runs, was their biggest win of the season.

At the conclusion of the match, the Lancashire captain Archie MacLaren, a patrician but somewhat argumentative cricketer with truly Victorian ideals of fair play and sportsmanship, could only comment that 'in every department of the game, the display of the home side was faultless'. MacLaren was one of the great batsmen of his day, holder of the then record highest first-class score of 424, made against Somerset at Taunton 11 years earlier, but he was not a great captain. Too stiff and unbending in his attitudes, he did little to inspire his teammates. He was captain of his county for a dozen years, but 1904 was the only season when Lancashire, always a strong side on paper, won the championship under his leadership. He also captained England 22 times in his 35 Test appearances, but with little success. He won only four of his games in charge, losing 11 and drawing seven.

In this match, though, the fault was hardly with his captaincy, although comments were made about the attitude of the Lancashire batsmen on the third morning. The batting of Hutchings, and to a lesser extent of Burnup, Mason and Seymour, and the bowling of Fielder and Blythe (who finished with match figures of 8 for 107 in 33.4 overs) were, if not entirely faultless, of a different class to anything that Lancashire had to offer.

MacLaren was not the only one with a few words to say at the end of the match. According to the local cricket reporter, writing in the *Whitstable Times*, 'a large company assembled in front of the pavilion to see the presentation of the money collected on the ground on the previous Tuesday and Thursday for the Kent professionals'. Lord Harris took up his favourite theme of the way in which Kent played, their 'fine spirit' as well as their actual skills on the field. Harris then went on to explain how the money collected would be divided up, in a public manner which would not go down too well with the county professionals of today, whether we are talking about the professionals on the cricket pitch or in the HR department. Fielder got £30, Huish, Woolley and Blythe £15 each, and Humphreys, Seymour, Hearne and Fairservice £12 each, with Hardinge and Hubble being allotted £10 each. Several of these men had not played in the Lancashire game, but were clearly seen as intrinsic to the success of the eleven. Huish, who was the unofficial but generally acknowledged senior professional, responded in a manner that would seem obsequious to us today, but which was the norm in those class-stratified days. Lord Harris spoke again, to congratulate the entire team, and Slug Marsham thanked his Lordship for the compliment. Even then, the impromptu speeches were not over. The Yorkshire-born Albert Craig, known as the Surrey Poet because he used to sell his rhymes at the Oval, followed up all this mutual Kentish backscratching with what was described as a 'lengthy, interesting and witty speech', which no doubt included several lines of his doggerel, which he had been selling at Canterbury Week since the 1890s. When finally he wound up his oration, he called for three cheers for Lord Harris and Kent's two chief administrators, A.J. Lancaster and Tom Pawley. The crowd heartily responded.

Gradually, Kent's season was moving from the playing of cricket to cricket speeches, cricket presentations and cricket dinners.

While Kent were beating Lancashire so well at Canterbury, their second XI was in Felixstowe, playing a two-day game against Suffolk, which began on 10 August. Several of Kent's regular first XI were playing in this side, professionals who made way for the amateurs in August. Jack Hubble, Frank Woolley, Wally Hardinge and Bill Fairservice were all in Suffolk, a quartet who appeared 41 times between them in the senior side in 1906. The captain was William McCanlis, the man who ran the Tonbridge Nursery which had been so successful in supplying cricketers of great quality to the county XI. Also in the team was Frank Woolley's older brother Claud, who never graduated to the first team at Kent but who went on to have a long and reasonably successful career with Northamptonshire. Kent easily beat Suffolk, by six wickets, thanks mainly to runs from Hubble, Fairservice and Hardinge, who between them scored all but 30 of the runs off the bat in Kent's first innings, and Henry Preston, who had to wait until the next season for his first-class debut, who took seven wickets for 63 runs in Suffolk's second innings. It must have been very exciting to learn of the first team's victory when they returned from Felixstowe, but it must also have been a little galling for the four first team semi-regulars to learn later that there would be a painting of the victorious team which did not include them. But even if Lord Harris could have foreseen that Woolley would go on to become probably Kent's greatest cricketer of all time, it is unthinkable that he might have chosen a different game to immortalise.

The Lancashire match was Kent's 11th win of the championship summer, and they went on to win five more matches and claim the championship for the first time by a slender margin from Yorkshire. The way the champions were calculated in those days was fairly straightforward – a county gained one point for each win, and lost one point for each loss. Unfinished games were ignored, and the title was decided by the greatest percentage of points taken from finished games. Kent played a total of 22 championship games in 1906, of which they won 16 and lost two, while four games were drawn. This gave them 14 points from 18 finished games, a score of 77.78 per cent. Yorkshire, the runners-up, played 28 matches, of which eight were unfinished. Of the other 20, 17 were won and three lost, giving them 14 points from 20 finished games, or 70 per cent. Kent won all of their last three games, but Yorkshire, who were the reigning county champions, lost their last but one fixture, against Gloucestershire at Bristol. Gloucestershire, no longer much of a force after the glorious Grace years, were given no chance of success against the mighty White Rose, but they won by the very narrowest of margins – one run, with Gilbert Jessop getting Yorkshire's last man lbw just as Yorkshire looked to have the game won. If Yorkshire had won that game, they would have finished with 16 points from their 20 finished games, a score of 80 per cent, and thus would have retained the title. And Chevallier Tayler would never have painted his masterpiece.

KENT v LANCASHIRE

Played at the St Lawrence Ground, Canterbury, 9, 10, 11 August 1906
Kent won the toss and chose to bat

KENT

Mr E W Dillon	c Poidevin b Dean	8
Mr C J Burnup	run out	94
Jas Seymour	c MacLaren b Gregson	50
Mr K L Hutchings	c MacLaren b Gregson	176
Mr J R Mason	c Dean b Gregson	88
E Humphreys	b Harry	18
Mr R N R Blaker	c Worsley b Harry	7
Mr C H B Marsham	c Worsley b Harry	0
F H Huish	c Poidevin b Harry	7
C Blythe	not out	8
A Fielder	c Tyldesley b Harry	4
Extras	(b 8, lb 6, nb 5)	19
Total		479

Fall of wickets 1/9, 2/109, 3/208, 4/421, 5/440, 6/459, 7/459, 8/466, 9/475, 10/479

Lancashire Bowling

	O	M	R	W
Dean	21	6	86	1
Harry	39	7	156	5
Poidevin	10	1	53	0
Gregson	38	3	125	3
Sharp	10	0	40	0

The Match

LANCASHIRE

Batsman	Dismissal 1st	Runs	Dismissal 2nd	Runs
Mr R.H. Spooner	lbw b Fielder	0	b Blythe	0
J.W.H. Makepeace	c Huish b Blythe	6	b Fielder	9
J.T. Tyldesley	c Seymour b Blythe	19	c Seymour b Fielder	4
Mr L.O.S. Poidevin	c Seymour b Fielder	45	c Seymour b Fielder	0
J. Sharp	run out	25	c Huish b Fielder	32
Mr A.C. MacLaren	st Huish b Blythe	22	c Mason b Fielder	39
F. Harry	not out	26	c Mason b Fielder	3
Mr A.H. Hornby	b Fielder	6	c Humphreys b Fielder	7
H. Dean	b Blythe	0	b Blythe	1
W.R. Gregson	c Dillon b Blythe	10	c Seymour b Blythe	13
W. Worsley	b Fielder	2	not out	0
Extras	(b 4, nb 4)	8	(b 4, lb 1, nb 2)	7
Total		169		115

Fall of wickets: *1st Inns:* 1/0, 2/25, 3/28, 4/67, 5/113, 6/121, 7/143, 8/144, 9/160, 10/169

2nd Inns: 1/1, 2/10, 3/11, 4/20, 5/80, 6/84, 7/92, 8/93, 9/111, 10/115

Kent Bowling

1st Inns:	O	M	R	W	2nd Inns	O	M	R	W
Fielder	22.3	4	81	4		16	4	49	7
Blythe	23	1	80	5		10.4	5	27	3
Humphreys	1	1	0	0		2	0	15	0
Mason						7	3	17	0

Umpires: A.J. Atfield and V.A. Titchmarsh

Kent won by an innings and 195 runs

The Players

LORD Harris was insistent that the match that Albert Chevallier Tayler should portray should be the match against Lancashire, and that it should show the entire Kent team so that they were clearly identifiable, while also being seen to be playing a proper game of cricket. There is no question that Harris decided on the Lancashire game almost at the same time that he decided on the concept of a painting as a memorial to his county's success, but it is also clear that Harris had not won the agreement of Lancashire to be painted in a losing light before Tayler began planning his painting.

Harris would have given Tayler the list of all those players who represented Kent in that game, as well as the names of the umpires and opposition batsmen, but until Lancashire gave their agreement, neither Harris nor Tayler could be sure that it would be Kent v Lancashire, rather than Kent v Sussex or Kent v Worcestershire, which were the only other matches the county played at Canterbury that year. There was, I suppose, the dreadful prospect that no county would give permission for their

team to be portrayed as losers, and that therefore the painting
would have to be a fictitious game, but still featuring the Kent
XI in the field. For that reason, Tayler asked most of the players
who had played for Kent that summer, whether or not they were
in the side that beat Lancashire, to sit for him, so that he could,
if need be, include their likeness in the finished painting.

In the end, Tayler needed to portray 11 Kent players, two
Lancashire men and one umpire. He did not attempt to portray
any of the Kent grandees who would have been watching from
the tents around the ground; this painting was to be a very early
example of the artist focussing on the game itself rather than the
social milieu. The Kent players were, in batting order:

The Rugby-Playing Shipbroker

Edward Wentworth Dillon is portrayed in the distance, in front
of the pavilion at long-on. His face is barely distinguishable,
and while this could simply have been because that was where
he fielded, he may also have been given the least favourable
position in the painting because he played only eight of Kent's
22 championship games in 1906, the fewest games for the county
that summer of all the Kent players on the field that day.

Ted Dillon was born on 15 February 1881 at Penge, making
him 25 years old in 1906. Penge was a comparatively small hamlet
on the south-eastern edge of London, near Bromley. It may now be
part of Greater London, but in Victorian times was still definitely
in Kent. Dillon's father was a well-to-do shipbroker, and Ted was
the fourth child. He was educated at the Abbey School in nearby
Beckenham, and then he went on to Rugby, where he excelled at
all sports, but most notably cricket and rugby football. He was
an elegant and prolific left-handed batsman at schoolboy level,

and already somebody whose talent had been noticed by the Kent County Club. He made his first appearance for the second XI in August 1898, but his first-class debut two years later, while still a boy at Rugby, was for W.G. Grace's London County against Worcestershire at the Crystal Palace. Dillon marked his debut with a century, scoring 108 in the first innings and 29 not out in the second, and taking two wickets for 54 runs. The day after that game finished, he was selected for the Kent first team for the first time, and hurried off down to Taunton to play against Somerset. Kent won that game by an innings, but Dillon did little. Still, it was enough for Kent to keep him in the county side for the final four games of the summer, and by the end of the summer he had scored 292 runs for the county, at an average of 36.50, as well as taking three wickets with his leg breaks, for 77 runs. Clearly Kent had a valuable young talent on their hands, a man *Wisden* described as 'the best school batsman of the year'.

On leaving Rugby, he progressed to Oxford University, where he won his blue for cricket in 1901 and 1902, and played no fewer than 15 matches for Kent in between playing for the university and attempting to catch up with his studies. He first opened the batting in a first-class game when Oxford University played Somerset at the Parks in Oxford. The university had been dismissed for 81 in their first innings, with Dillon batting at number six and scoring just 4, but in their second innings, chasing a target of over 500 to win, Dillon was promoted to open the batting with his future county captain Slug Marsham, and he scored 143. This was not enough to save the game, but it established Dillon as an opening bat and from then on this seemed to be where he preferred to be in the batting order. His first experience of opening for Kent came at Worcester in late

July, when he opened the batting once again with Marsham, and together they put on 210 for the first wicket. Marsham made 102, but poor Dillon just missed his first century for Kent, being dismissed on 99, caught off the bowling of the last of the underarm lob bowlers, George Simpson-Hayward. In the event, he did not have to wait long for the magic three figures. During Canterbury Week a week later, Dillon compiled his first century for Kent, 103 not out, as Kent secured a draw in a difficult game against Essex. By the end of the season, he had scored over 1,000 runs for the first time, and was already being seen as an England batsman of the future.

His opening partnership with Cuthbert Burnup had begun in 1901, and in 1902, the pair put on 243 together against Hampshire at Tunbridge Wells, Burnup making 102 and Dillon 137, as Hampshire suffered a massive loss by an innings and 195 runs. A little earlier that season, in June against Nottinghamshire at Gravesend, Dillon achieved the comparatively rare feat of carrying his bat through the Kent innings, when he made 38 not out, out of a total of just 86. The next highest scorer was extras, with 16. Luckily for Kent, the match was ruined by rain, and no result was possible. From January to April 1902, Dillon ignored, it seems, the demands of his tutors and examiners at Oxford and toured West Indies with R.A. Bennett's privately raised team, led by B.J.T. Bosanquet, the inventor of the googly. Later that summer, he played for the second time for Oxford against Cambridge at Lord's, and having opened the batting the previous year with his great friend Marsham, this time, under Marsham's captaincy, he opened the batting with Billy Findlay, the wicketkeeper who would feature rather more prominently in *Kent v Lancashire 1906* than Dillon himself. The world of the cricketing amateur in Edwardian times was a small one. He also played twice against the touring Australians, first for Oxford University and then for the South of England. He did not score particularly heavily in either match, but had the pleasure of fielding while the immortal Victor Trumper hit a century at the Parks, and also had his first opportunity of batting with W.G. Grace in the match for the South at Hastings.

After leaving Oxford, Dillon moved into his father's world of shipbroking, but this did not at first seem to limit his appearances for Kent. In 1903, he played in 20 championship matches for Kent, as well as two other non-championship games, two for other teams, and at the end of the year, three more games touring with Kent to Philadelphia. Philadelphia, a bastion of cricket in America long after baseball had taken over as the national summer game, had one very good player – possibly even a great player – in the fast bowling all-rounder John Barton King, but otherwise their players were scarcely of county second eleven standard. Kent took out a fairly strong side and duly dominated the matches.

Dillon was back in time to change his sports clothes and play rugby for Blackheath, as a centre three-quarter. His reputation in that sport was also rising rapidly. In 1904, business commitments took over much of the time he was usually able to allot to cricket, meaning that he was only able to play in eight games for the county. It was not a particularly successful season for him, his best score of 76 coming in his first appearance of the summer, against Middlesex at Catford in June. However, he was clearly less preoccupied with business matters over the winter as he was able to accept the invitation of the England rugby selectors to play for his country in the home internationals against Ireland, Scotland and Wales. He was to play rugby once more for his country, against Wales the next winter, but despite all the early promise, Dillon was never chosen to play for England at cricket.

In 1905, he played 15 championship games for Kent, as well as one against the touring Australians. When his business commitments allowed, he was one of the first names on the team sheet, and it proved to be perhaps the best summer of his career. He finished the season with 1,310 runs for the county, top of the batting averages with an average of 48.51, and a highest score of 141. In the official history of Kent, Cloudesley Marsham notes that Dillon 'headed the field, hardly failing in a single match'. However, Dillon's greatest triumphs would come a few years later, when he was appointed captain of the county side in 1909, a position he held until the end of the 1913 season. In those five seasons, Kent were placed first, first, second, third and first, making Dillon still the only captain in the county's history to have won more than one championship. Kent, in the years immediately before the First World War, were undoubtedly the strongest team in the country, but they still required a very fine leader, and in Dillon they found one.

Dillon's tenure as captain was hugely successful, but it did not prompt Lord Harris to commission any more paintings as the championships piled up. The usual dinners followed the triumphs, of course, including a 1909 civic reception in Canterbury, at which the mayor read out a message of congratulations from, among many others, the Archbishop of Canterbury, Randall Davidson. It was rather more formal than even that occasion required, and perhaps not the words that a true fan of Kent cricket would have used: 'Please convey to your eminent guests an expression of my proud recognition of the county's prowess.' After that message was read out, there was a blast on the Burghmote Horn, an ancient piece of civic regalia dating back to the middle of the 12th century, which was originally used to summon the city bailiffs to the court known as the Burghmote. Nowadays it is blown only on special occasions such as the installation of a new mayor, or the death of a monarch. Or Kent winning the championship, I suppose.

Dillon's captaincy of Kent may have been statistically the most successful of all, but many good judges would say that Marsham was a better leader, and that Dillon had a stronger team at his command, notably the ever-improving Frank Woolley and, from 1909, the remarkable leg-break bowler Douglas Carr. What is more, Dillon's business commitments meant that he could not be a full-time captain, and in 1909 Jack Mason, who had led the side at the turn of the century, stepped in to lead the side on the six occasions that Dillon was unavailable. In 1911, too, Dillon missed several matches firstly because of an eye injury picked up playing squash and then because business commitments got in the way. After the third title triumph under his leadership in 1913, Dillon stepped down from the leadership, handing over to Lionel Troughton, and did not play at all in 1914.

On 3 September 1913, the magazine *Vanity Fair* paid Dillon the compliment of featuring him in their series of *Men Of The Day,* with a caricature showing him wearing his Band of Brothers blazer and white flannels, with his left hand in his pocket and his right hand holding a cricket bat. The title of the portrait was *The Champion County,* and the brief paragraphs about Dillon were both flattering and denigratory at the same time. 'Kent's yearly bid for the County Championship', they wrote, 'dates from Mr Dillon's acceptance of the captaincy in 1909 … This year they are champions once again.' They note that his career at Oxford, 'like that of many other great men, was abbreviated'. Pointing out that Dillon had twice recorded a pair that summer might be seen as somewhat tactless in an article that is meant to be in praise of its subject, but to point out that 'his bowling average this year is remarkable' seems to be going too far. 'If he were not too good a sportsman to care about averages, the topic might be irksome. It will suffice to say that he does not head the list.' In fact, he had taken two wickets for 109 runs in 21 overs, which may not be much good, but there have been many worse analyses, both before and since. But the tribute ends with what seems to have been a very widely held view at the time: 'Mr Dillon is captain of the most popular sporting county.' Nobody begrudged Kent their success.

When war broke out in 1914, Dillon enlisted almost immediately, along with many of the Kent cricketers of serving age. He was 33 years old and was commissioned into the Royal West Kent Regiment, eventually reaching the rank of captain and company commander of a battalion. He spent much of the war in North Africa and the Middle East, having fought at Gallipoli in August and September 1915, and then in Egypt and Palestine, where he was wounded. He also took part in the Battle of Jerusalem, the British Army's successful attempt to capture Jerusalem from the Ottoman Empire in late 1917, and was subsequently transferred to the Economic Section of the Intelligence Corps in Cairo, where he served for the remainder of the war.

The war did not quite mark the end of his first-class career, however. In 1919 he was tempted to make a comeback, but after one game for a scratch eleven against Oxford University and two games for Kent, he realised that at the age of 38 he was not still the free-scoring batsman he had been a decade earlier. Once again he turned his attention fully to his business, but in 1923 he was recalled to Kent's colours when due to a set of unforeseen circumstances, several players were unavailable. He was asked to lead the side at Trent Bridge against Nottinghamshire, in Lionel Troughton's absence, but his final game for the county proved to be an unmitigated disaster. Nottinghamshire batted first, and after Charlie Wright and George Collins had reduced the hosts to 24 for 3, their captain Arthur Carr (165) and Wilfred Payton (154) put on 323 for the fourth wicket, which is still, almost 100 years on, the largest fourth wicket stand ever compiled against Kent. Nottinghamshire declared early on the second morning on 421 for 9, and Kent then lost all 20 wickets over the course of the rest of the day. In their first innings they were all out for 179, having lost their ninth wicket on 93, and during the course of the innings their best batsman, James Seymour, suffered a badly bruised wrist. In their second innings they were all out for 97, and the game was lost by an innings and 145 runs. Dillon, who had once previously been dismissed first ball in both innings of a game, made 0 and 0, and clearly realised that at 42 his first-class playing career was finally over. Kent's official captain that summer, Lionel Troughton, who was two years older than Dillon, also retired at the end of the 1923 season, and Kent were destined to spend most of the interwar years in a position to challenge for the title, but never quite reaching the heights that they had attained from 1906 to 1913.

Wisden described the left-handed Ted Dillon's batting style as 'very free' and said that he 'used his long reach to the best advantage. Going in to meet the ball, he drove straight and to the off with great power and placed his forcing strokes skilfully.' In his career for Kent he played 223 matches and scored 9,415 runs at an average of 28.88. He scored 12 centuries, with a highest score of 141, and also took 27 wickets with his occasional leg spin. In all cricket, he scored 11,006 runs and took 74 wickets, which seems to show that his bowling was very undervalued by Kent. For his county over 14 full seasons, he took just 27 wickets at an average of 48.92, but for all other teams, he took 47 wickets at an average of just 23.51. Kent, of course, did have some great bowlers at that time, so perhaps Dillon's subtle leggies were not needed, except in emergencies.

Ted Dillon died aged 60, on 20 April 1941, at his home in Totteridge, Hertfordshire.

The True Corinthian

Cuthbert James 'Pinky' Burnup was born on 21 November 1875, and thus was 30 years old during Kent's first championship-winning season. Like his opening partner Ted Dillon, he hailed from the fringes of south London, having been born in Blackheath.

He was educated at Malvern College, far away from his home town, and soon demonstrated his outstanding sporting prowess. He was in the Malvern XI for cricket for three years from 1892, and was also an outstanding racquets player. Going up to Clare College, Cambridge, he won his blue for cricket for three years from 1896, and also won three blues for football. In some ways football was to become his first sport, as he played once for England at that sport, but never for England at cricket. His one cap for football was in 1896, when he was still an undergraduate at Cambridge. He played on the left wing, but although his career as an amateur for Corinthian FC was long and successful, his one match for England ended in defeat at the hands of the Scots for the first time in two decades.

Burnup's first-class cricket career began in 1895 when he was invited by W.G. Grace to play for the Gentlemen of England against I Zingari, which in those days was a first-class fixture. Batting at number nine, the 19-year-old Burnup scored an unbeaten 66 in the Gentlemen of England's first innings, playing against the likes of F.S. Jackson, A.G. Steel and A.E. Stoddart, England captains all, and alongside England Test cricketers C.B. Fry and Gregor MacGregor, not to mention W.G. Grace and his son W.G. Grace junior, who was also a Cambridge undergraduate and who chose this game to make 79, the highest score of his not too successful career. Burnup also opened the bowling in both innings, and took the last three wickets in I Zingari's first innings. It was a heady start to his career, but it was not until the next summer, as an undergraduate at Cambridge, that his career really got under way. He played regularly for Cambridge until the university match (which Cambridge lost) and then played for Kent for the rest of the summer. He scored 54 on his championship debut against Gloucestershire at Gravesend (but Kent still lost by nine wickets), but by the end of the season had scored 629 runs for the club, at a shade under 30 runs per innings. He also hit his first century for Kent, 101 out of Kent's total of 196 against the touring Australians.

He then missed almost all the 1897 season, as he was playing football in South Africa with Corinthians. He played only once for Kent, against Nottinghamshire at the Bat and Ball Ground, Gravesend, but his contribution was significant – 108, his highest first-class score and his second century for Kent in consecutive games. His return in 1898 was eagerly awaited.

Pinky – he got the nickname either because he was not a tall man, and was thought of as the little finger at the end of the forward line, or because of his bright red hair – Burnup left England for Cape Town immediately after the university match, and spent two months as part of the 14-man squad that played 23 matches in South Africa. This was only a couple of years before the outbreak of the Second Boer War, at a time when travel in South Africa was not without danger and hardship. It was the first tour by any European football club outside Europe, but despite the alien conditions and often rock-hard pitches, the Corinthian team won 21 of its matches and drew the other two, scoring in total 113 goals and conceding just 15. The Corinthian spirit was summed up by their refusal to have anything to do with penalty kicks. If one was awarded against them, the goalkeeper would merely stand by the goalpost until after the kick was taken, and if one was awarded to them, they deliberately kicked it high or wide. As another Corinthian, C.B. Fry, remarked, the penalty kick rule was 'a standing insult to sportsmen to have to play under a rule which assumes that players intend to toe tip, hack and push opponents and to behave like cads of the first kidney'. This Corinthian spirit of fair play was also followed by the Kent cricket teams which Burnup and several other Oxbridge amateurs represented.

Pinky Burnup's first match for Kent in 1898 did not happen until after the university season was finished, but from the moment he came into the side against Yorkshire at Maidstone in the middle of July, he was a first-choice batsman for the county. In his second game for Kent that summer, he improved his top score to 131, giving him three centuries in four outings over three years and from there, although the centuries did not come in quite such profusion, there is no doubt that Burnup was now a vital cog in Kent's batting line-up. By the end of the summer of 1898, Burnup had scored over 1,000 runs in a season for the second time, and he then toured Philadelphia with the Kent XI. In 1899, his first full season down from university, he really came into his own. After a slightly slow start, he began scoring fifties on an almost weekly basis, culminating in 150 against Gloucestershire at Bristol. His efforts in two games against the touring Australians were not quite as telling as they might have been, which probably left him out of the England selectors' plans, but in Kent's game against the tourists, Burnup twice improved his career-best bowling figures, with 3 for 7 in the first innings, and 5 for 44 in their second. Kent won the match by two wickets.

In 1900, Burnup achieved what may well be a unique bowling feat. Playing for MCC against Derbyshire at Lord's at the end of May, Burnup was hit for ten runs off one ball by the Derbyshire captain, Samuel Hill Wood. This was only possible because of an experimental rule being tried by MCC that year. In order, as they hoped, to restrict the dominance of bat over ball that the cricket authorities had perceived, MCC experimented with running a net all around the playing area, between two and three feet high, in an attempt to reduce the number of boundaries that were scored. It soon became clear that not only did players and umpires find it very hard to understand the rule, but that also it did not limit the scores at all. The rule stated that any ball getting lodged in the net would count for two runs plus any actually run, and any hit over the net would score three in total. Confusion abounded because nobody was quite sure whether the two runs were added as soon as the ball hit the netting, and whether the ball then became dead, or whether the batsmen could continue running until the fielder had disentangled the ball from the net and thrown it back to the middle. Any hit to the net could easily get five or six runs, but there was a strong disincentive to hitting the ball out of the ground, and scoring only three. How would T20 have worked if this rule had stayed in place? Hill Wood's ten runs off Burnup was achieved by him hitting the ball to the netting, the batsmen continuing to run, and eventually two more runs being added to the already large total when a wild throw back to the middle resulted in overthrows.

The game between MCC and Derbyshire was the fifth game in which the net system had been tried, and it was to prove the last. After that, the idea was abandoned, but Burnup's unfortunate record remains. No doubt he bore the ignominy with true Corinthian spirit, and he had the consolation of hitting the highest score of his career, 200 against Lancashire at Old Trafford, just ten days later. In that innings, he took 150 minutes to make his first 50 runs, but only 40 minutes to score the final 50. This was typical of his style, able to adapt his batting to the situation, sometimes slow and dependable, sometimes flashy and brilliant.

Kent had come third in the County Championship in 1900, under the leadership of Jack Mason, and high hopes were held for the coming year. In 1901, however, they slipped down to seventh place, although Burnup had another good season, scoring 1,780 runs with five centuries. In 1902, however, he reached his personal peak. He scored over 2,000 runs at an average just below 40, with six centuries, and he was chosen as one of *Wisden Cricketers' Almanack's* Five Cricketers Of The Year. As *Wisden* noted, 'Burnup is a versatile batsman with many ways of scoring, and he can get runs on all sorts of wickets.' They also praised his fielding – 'a cricketer whose work in the outfield is every bit as fine as his batting'. In what was a wet season, Burnup 'played so finely on all sorts of wickets that a place in the English team in one or two of the Test matches would have been by no means beyond his deserts'. Cuthbert Burnup, however, never played for England in a Test match.

The nearest he got was in the winter of 1902/03, when he toured Australia and New Zealand with Lord Hawke's side, and played in many of the big games, including those against New South Wales, Victoria and South Australia. In 1903, however, he was appointed captain of Kent in succession to Jack Mason, who stepped down because of his business commitments.

Burnup's one season in charge was neither a success nor a failure. Once again, he scored over 1,000 runs in the season, but at a lower average, 31.36, than in any season since he began playing for Kent. The team finished eighth in the table, one place lower than in 1902, but with a very similar playing record. It was another wet summer, and Burnup found run-scoring very difficult at the start of the summer. As the weather warmed up, and as he got used to the stresses of captaincy, his cricket blossomed, and as the official county history notes, 'the fielding of the side was probably better than any other county. Blaker, Burnup and Hutchings especially distinguished themselves in this department.'

At the end of the 1903 season, Burnup's business interests took him abroad, and he did not play any cricket at all in 1904. The captaincy was taken over by Cloudesley Marsham, and although at the time the change was forced by Burnup's business commitments, in retrospect the change can be seen as the beginning of the years of Kent's greatest success.

In 1905, too, Burnup was unavailable for much of the year. He played just two matches for Kent, the first against MCC at Lord's in May that year, but he only made 1 and 6 as MCC won easily. He played again a day later, against Nottinghamshire at Gravesend, but only scored 6 and 0, as Notts won by an innings and plenty. He was clearly very out of practice and neither he nor Kent seemed to want to prolong the comeback that season. But then came 1906, his astonishing comeback year. As *Wisden* remarked with pleasing understatement, 'As he had only taken part in one county match in 1905, his return to the eleven in better form than ever was an immense help. Of all Kent's batsmen … he was the soundest.' He had by this time established a reputation as a dour batsman, leaving the dashing strokes to Kenneth Hutchings, but there was great value in knowing the limits of his skills and playing within them, as his average in the championship that summer, 69.75, showed.

The championship summer proved to be Burnup's last hurrah with Kent. He played just three games for the county in 1907, against Hampshire, Gloucestershire and Worcestershire in June and July, but did little of note, and after that he devoted himself full-time to his business interests as a stockbroker. In the Hampshire game, he did little except watch James Seymour overtake his record score by a Kent batsman, as Seymour compiled 204, to beat Burnup's mark set seven years earlier. In November that year, Burnup married Miss Beatrice Hope Bowen, and retired from top-class cricket.

Cuthbert Burnup served on the Kent committee from 1908 to 1911, but was never appointed president, as so many of his amateur contemporaries were. His connections with Kent cricket faded and when he died, in 1960 at the age of 84, he was living in north London. In his first-class cricket career, which lasted from 1895 to 1907, he scored a total of 13,614 runs at an average of 36.79, including 26 hundreds and 81 fifties. He also took 106 catches, not to mention 98 wickets with his gentle off spin.

The Man Who Fought the Taxman – and Won

James Seymour was born on 25 October 1879, at Brightling, a small village north of Bexhill-on-Sea in Sussex. Before his tenth birthday, the family moved to Pembury, near Tunbridge Wells in Kent. He quickly became a Kent man through and through. His brother John, two years younger, played for Sussex for three seasons before moving to play for Northamptonshire but James Seymour's allegiance to Kent never wavered. In 1900, aged 20, he began his cricketing career as a professional with London County, W.G. Grace's vanity project, and he played a couple of first-class games for them that summer. In his first match, against Derbyshire at the Racecourse Ground, he batted well down the order and scored 1 and 25 not out. He also took two wickets for 54 runs in 20 overs of off spin, and was in his early days clearly thought of as a bowler who bats a bit, rather than what he became, a solid and reliable number three whose bowling was only needed in the most hopeless of circumstances. His only other first-class game that summer was against MCC at Lord's a couple of weeks later, and whatever Seymour had done in the nets in that fortnight obviously made a difference, because he was asked to open the batting with the great man himself. It was not a success, Seymour being bowled for a duck. In the second innings, he and W.G. were both relieved of the responsibility of opening, but it made little difference. At number three, Seymour made just 7. His bowling was hardly used – 0 for 26 in five overs – and London County went down to an innings defeat. However, the season did not end there: Seymour played a few games for Kent Club and Ground, and an innings of 66 not out impressed Captain William McCanlis so much that he offered the young man a place on the ground staff at Tonbridge, the home of his famous nursery.

He had one more game for London County in 1901, against Derbyshire again, but this time at London County's home ground of Crystal Palace. Whether W.G. was upset that Seymour had switched his allegiance to Kent by joining the Tonbridge staff, or whether his form warranted it, is impossible to say, but in this game Seymour batted at number 11 (1 not out) and did not bowl as his team beat Derbyshire by an innings. He did not play for London County again, although one of his teammates in his final game for them was George Beldam, whose photography so inspired Albert Chevallier Tayler.

At Tonbridge, on the other hand, things were going very well and Seymour, a man of diminutive stature but iron determination and a very sound defence, improved so much under the guidance of McCanlis that he made his debut for the county in 1902, and played 20 games for them that year. From the start he was established as an important member of the side, and, indeed, the only professional batsman to hold down a regular place in the top order throughout all their glory years (apart from Frank Woolley who was, of course, much more than just a batsman). His return in 1902 was not prolific – just 595 runs at under 20 per innings, but he was seen as exceptionally promising, and also as a wonderful slip fielder.

In Chevallier Tayler's portrait he is seen to the far right of the painting, fielding at gully, and if the picture is docked for space purposes in books and magazines, his is the image that disappears, but his importance to the team as a close fielder cannot be overestimated. One of the reasons that Kent were so dominant in the decade before the First World War was the brilliance of their fielding, and of their close catching in particular. In their long careers, Frank Woolley held 773 catches for the county, and Seymour held 659. Nobody else is within 200 catches of them. Seymour held 40 or more catches in a season six times, easily a record. Fred Huish, the wicketkeeper, held 902 catches in his career and stumped a further 352 slow-moving batsmen, so the combined tally of these three – 2,686 dismissals – shows how much Kent owed to the alertness of their close fielders.

Seymour enjoyed a very long and fruitful career with Kent. He scored 1,000 runs in a season 16 times between 1904 and 1926, and hit 53 centuries in the process. His total runs for Kent over his 25-year career, 26,818, puts him fourth on the all-time list behind Woolley, Hardinge and Ames, but he never tasted Test cricket. It is an interesting fact that of the 12 top run scorers of all time for Kent, four of them never played for England and another two each won only one Test cap. Do the consistent but unflashy run accumulators in Kent just not feature on the England selectors' radar? (Not that radar had been invented when Seymour was playing, of course.)

Seymour, of whom *Wisden* wrote, 'as a county player he was in the highest class', achieved several significant personal successes during his career. He was the first Kent player to score two hundreds in a match, a feat he achieved against Worcestershire at Maidstone in 1904. He scored 108 in the first innings and 136 not out in the second, a score that was not only the highest of his career to date but which also involved a last-wicket partnership of 103 in 35 minutes with Arthur Fielder, who made 37, also the highest score of his career thus far. In that match, Seymour scored 244 runs out of 512 off the bat, most of them with patience and dogged determination, but the last few with gay abandon, and Kent won by 204 runs.

In 1907, Seymour scored the first of three double hundreds for the county, 204 against Hampshire at Tonbridge. It was the record score by a Kent batsman at the time, but in 1911 he beat his own record, scoring 218 not out against Essex at Leyton. This innings included a last-wicket partnership of 102 with Arthur Fielder, one fewer than against Worcestershire seven years earlier. Fielder this time made 61. He was becoming a useful number eleven.

Seymour's record did not last long, however. Two years later, Frank Woolley scored 224 not out against Oxford University, and although Seymour's record for championship matches lasted through the war, in 1923 Woolley scored 270 against Middlesex at Canterbury, and Seymour's record was gone forever. Seymour's third double hundred, however, 214 and also against Essex, at Tunbridge Wells in 1914, is still the record by a Kent batsman at that ground.

Seymour 'was not a classic batsman' according to *Wisden*, 'but he possessed many strokes both skilful and attractive. His flash past cover point was a thing of special delight'. However, his true legacy to cricket, and to all professional sportsmen, was not in his batting or his slip fielding ('he ranked with the greatest' said *Wisden*), but hard won in the law courts. In 1920, his 19th season as a Kent professional, he was awarded a benefit and having been on a professional cricketer's notoriously poor wages for all that time, certainly needed any help that his benefit could give him. In case it appears that the Kent committee were very begrudging in granting benefits, it should be noted that he had originally been granted a benefit in 1915, but the Great War intervened, so he had to wait a further five years. He chose the match against Hampshire during Canterbury Week as his benefit match, and despite being run out for a duck in the first innings, he made 74 in the second innings and helped Kent to win by 165 runs. Frank Woolley took 11 wickets in the match, and made the highest score on either side, 80, which must have pleased the large Canterbury crowds. All in all, Seymour had a very good benefit.

According to the official records, Seymour's benefit match raised £939/16/11d, although the Kent CCC committee minutes show a figure of £1,492/8s/6d. Either way, it was a very useful sum, and it attracted the attention of the Inland Revenue who wanted their share. Seymour, a doughty fighter for the rights of professional sportsmen, felt instinctively that this was unfair, and in this he had a strong supporter in the shape of Lord Harris, who took up Seymour's cause with gusto. It has to be remembered that professional sportsmen in those days were not considered capable of handling their own affairs, and the rules of Kent CCC stated that 'the Committee reserve to themselves an absolute and unfettered discretion as regards Benefit Matches, the collection of subscriptions in connection with such matches, and dealing with the net proceeds of such matches in any way they may think desirable in the interests of the beneficaire [sic]'.

The case was fought through several layers of court action, with the first court finding in favour of Seymour, but then having the verdict overturned on appeal by the Inland Revenue. The final appeal to the House of Lords was concluded on 24 May 1927, almost seven years after the match which had raised the money. One of the judges deciding the case was Lord Harris's brother-in-law, a remarkable conflict of interest, but the judgement held that 'the award of the benefit match to the cricketer was not a profit accruing to him in respect of his office or employment, but was in the nature of a personal gift and not assessable to Income Tax'. The judgement concluded by stating that 'a benefit is not usually given early in a cricketer's career, but rather towards its close. Its purpose is to express the gratitude of his employers and the cricket-loving public for what he had already done, and in appreciation of his personal qualities.'

As *The Cricketer* commented later, 'Practically all his brother professionals owe to him their undying gratitude for the forethought and courage required by any individual who is capable of standing up against the demands of the Inland Revenue.' As the Kent historian Derek Carlaw wrote, 'Present day recipients of tax-free six figure benefits may like to stop counting their money long enough to speculate on what might have happened (a) if Lord Harris had not been prepared to pull every available string on behalf of professional cricketers and (b) if the Commissioners of Inland Revenue had displayed a little more nous and chosen a county in whose professionals Lord Harris had no paternal interest.' All benefits for all sportsmen remained tax-free for 90 years, until 2017 when the then chancellor, George Osborne, decided to limit the tax-free amount to £100,000, a sum beyond the dreams of James Seymour, but all too easily surpassed by the overpaid professionals in many sports today.

Seymour retired at the end of the 1926 season and became a cricket coach at Epsom College. He used his benefit money to buy a small fruit farm near Marden in Kent, but he did not enjoy it for long. He died suddenly in September 1930, aged only 50, leaving a widow and three children.

The *Beau Idéal* of Kent Cricket

Somewhat surprisingly, given the pivotal influence he had on Kent's championship year, Chevallier Tayler has painted Ken Hutchings far in the distance on the deep extra cover boundary, just to the right of two flagpoles. Kenneth Lotherington Hutchings was born in Southborough, near Tunbridge Wells, on 7 December 1882. He was the youngest of four brothers, three of whom played first-class cricket. His elder brothers William and Frederick were both good cricketers who represented Kent a few times, but were never in the class of Kenneth. The fourth brother, John, like his three siblings, played for Tonbridge School, alma mater of many Kent cricketers including four Cowdreys who have played for Kent, as well as the former England Test player and from 2018 the national selector, Ed Smith, right down to Zak Crawley who scored his first first-class hundred in 2018. Hutchings's father Edward was a surgeon who 'made many a hundred in local matches in the Southborough neighbourhood' and was apparently 'a slashing hitter'. His mother Catherine had a brother, Edward Colebrooke, who had played for Oxford University in 1880, and for the Gentlemen of Kent.

Kenneth, or 'Hutch' as he was known to his teammates and the Kent cricketing public alike, was captain of the Tonbridge eleven in his last two years at the school, 1901 and 1902, when *Wisden* first noticed him and described him as a 'very fine player'. He was a superb racquets player, a game that requires among other things lightning reactions and very strong wrists. These qualities also helped him become a superb fielder in the covers, with a throw that is remembered as one of the fastest and best that the game has seen. Hutchings played for Kent for the first time in that summer of 1902, in late August against Worcestershire at Tonbridge. He made 10 and 1 as Kent won by nine wickets. Unlike many gifted sportsmen of his era and class, he did not go to Oxford or Cambridge, which gave him time to play for Kent in 1903. He turned out for them 11 times, without giving much indication of what a brilliant player he would become. His batting average at the end of the season was a little under 30, but he did have the satisfaction of scoring his first century, 106 against Somerset at Taunton.

After going with the Kent team on their tour of Philadelphia in the autumn of 1903, he then stepped back from the county scene for a couple of years, playing for Kent just once in 1904 and twice in 1905. In 1904, he scored 30 and 66 in a drawn match against Sussex at Tunbridge Wells, but such was the perceived strength of Kent's batting that summer that he was not selected for the Canterbury Week games, even though he made himself available. In 1905 he played against Sussex and Middlesex, consecutive games at the Angel Ground, Tonbridge, but Hutchings scored only 87 runs in total as Kent lost both matches fairly easily. So there was no indication that 1906 would be his *annus mirabilis*.

He came into the Kent side on 18 June, against Hampshire at Tonbridge, and scored 39. He shared a partnership of 98 in fifty minutes with Frank Woolley, who was in the process of compiling his first first-class century, which helped Kent win by an innings. 'Hutchings and Woolley in partnership' wrote one nostalgic writer, 'while Edward VII was king – the tang of hops, the beauty of roses, the sad poignancy of lilies'.

Thereafter, Hutchings was a permanent member of the side. In the next match, once more against Middlesex and his fourth consecutive county game at Tonbridge, he saved the day with 125 in the first innings and 97 not out in the second. Kent, chasing 292 to win in a little under four hours, finished the game on 253 with nine wickets down, still 38 runs behind Middlesex. Hutchings did not get his second century of the game, eschewing the chance of hitting a boundary off the final ball in case he got out, but his 97 was probably the most important innings he played all summer. If he had been out, and Kent had lost, they would not have been champions. The legend of Hutchings's summer of '06 was born.

For the record, Hutchings did score two centuries in a match the next year, against Worcestershire at Worcester. He made 109 and 109 not out and the match was drawn. But in 1906 the next game was up in Yorkshire, at Bramall Lane against the reigning champions. To Hutchings they were all alike: he scored 131 and 50 not out as the match ended in a draw, thanks largely to Hutchings's second innings, which staved off defeat. By now, after three matches for Kent, he had scored 442 runs at an average of 147.33. Press reports were full of the power and purity of his batting, notably his straight driving. Several fielders noted that the ball was coming at them much harder than was the case with other batsmen, and even the great George Hirst was said to have stood a further yard or two towards the boundary when Hutchings was facing. Frank Woolley, much later on, said that in all his cricket career (which lasted until 1938) he had never seen anybody hit the ball as hard as Hutchings did in 1906.

Games against Leicestershire and Worcestershire followed. Hutchings did little against Leicestershire, a game that Kent won by eight wickets, but at Worcester he was back to his best. Picked for Worcester was his elder brother William, who had moved from Kent to try his luck elsewhere, but his luck was out. One person whose luck was not out was the Kent captain Cloudesley Marsham, who won the toss for the first time in 18 matches.

Whether this marked the end of the longest run of losing tosses ever experienced by one captain is not known, but it cannot be far off the record. On winning the toss, Kent made 576, thanks mainly to 154 from Alec Hearne, in his final season with Kent after 23 seasons of loyal and very brilliant service to the club. Hutchings made 94, adding 140 in 90 minutes with Hearne, and breaking two bats in the process. Worcestershire responded with 361 and were invited to follow on. They saved the innings defeat quite comfortably, finishing on 277 for 5, but one of those wickets was W.E.C. Hutchings, caught Hubble bowled K.L. Hutchings, 30. Hutchings and Burnup bowled the most overs in the home side's second innings, almost as though Kent were hoping they would declare and set a target. They did not.

Hutchings was then picked for the Gentlemen against the Players at Lord's, and became one of his Kent teammate Fielder's ten wickets in the first innings of the game. He also fell to Fielder in the second innings, which presumably gave the bowler bragging rights in the bar afterwards. Despite that, the Gentlemen won the game. Against the West Indians in his next game, at Catford, Hutchings did little with the bat but took four wickets for 73 runs in the tourists' second innings, his best analysis to that date. He never did take five wickets in an innings, but he took 16 of his 24 first-class wickets in 1906, including 4 for 15 in his last but one match of the summer, for the Gentlemen against the Players in a festival game at Scarborough in September. He finished the summer third in the national batting averages, behind his Kent colleague Pinky Burnup and the prolific Tom Hayward of Surrey, with 1,597 runs at an average of 53.23. *Wisden* chose him as one of their Five Cricketers Of The Year, but this was his apogee; he never quite attained that peak of brilliance again.

Wisden was fulsome in its praise. 'Batting so remarkable and individual as his has not been seen since Ranjitsinhji and Trumper first delighted the cricket world. Not in the slightest degree resembling either of these famous players, Hutchings has a style that is entirely his own.' It added that 'whatever the future may have in store for him, he was very great indeed in 1906'. The modern writer David Frith described Hutchings as 'bare-headed, suntanned, [who] built his elegant game on daring driving'.

1906 was the first of six consecutive seasons in which Hutchings scored 1,000 runs, but only in 1910 did he really challenge the heights he reached in 1906. He remains a slightly unfulfilled talent, but still a man who was briefly one of the great batsmen of his era. The word 'remarkable' is used time and again in descriptions of his cricket, implying a simplicity of style and a unique way of going about his cricket. In 1907/08 he toured Australia with MCC, playing in all five Tests. In his second Test, at Melbourne, he scored 126 – the first Kent player to score a Test century – as England scraped home by one wicket, but otherwise did not stand out. He played two more times for England, in the fourth and fifth Tests against Australia at home in 1909, but although he made a fifty in the fifth Test, which was incidentally the debut Test for two of his Kent colleagues, Frank Woolley and Douglas Carr, he was never selected again.

On 14 August 1907, just a fortnight after he had come back after six weeks out with a badly injured hand, caused by a fast ball from the South African opening bowler Kotze, he was the subject of a *Vanity Fair* caricature, by Spy (Sir Leslie Ward), entitled *A Century Maker*. The artist had chosen to portray him crouching in the field, in a very similar manner to the way Chevallier Tayler posed Humphreys or Fielder in his painting, which had only just been shown in public for the first time. The brief article accompanying the portrait confirmed that his batting was what excited the crowds. 'He drives with extraordinary vigour' and is a 'favourite with the crowd wherever he plays, because he evidently goes in to hit, and scarcely lets a loose ball pass without punishment'. The *Daily Telegraph*, in a tribute to him after he died, described him as 'a typical man of Kent, in that his cricket was splendidly characteristic of his county – bright, free, sparkling – Hutchings at his best was the most engaging batsman of his day'. The newspaper went on to say that 'on any wicket, against any bowling – circumstances did not matter – he was magnificent'. This somewhat hyperbolic panegyric ended with the thought that 'not in this generation have we seen his equal'. Hutchings was a player who excited that kind of passion, on his day as great as any player of his era.

Ken Hutchings retired from cricket at the end of the 1912 season, having by then been a member of three championship-winning sides. He scored a total of 10,054 runs at an average of 33.62, barely half the average he achieved in his great year of 1906. His 176 against Lancashire at Canterbury that summer remained his highest score. In his final four matches, he scored just 15 runs in seven innings, and although he was given the honour of captaining the side in his final county match, against Sussex at his hometown ground in Tonbridge, a game that Kent won by seven wickets, he no doubt realised that his time at the top was up, and he switched his focus to earning a living. His business career was based in Liverpool and he moved to Formby, just north of the city. He played cricket for the local club when business commitments allowed, and when war broke out in 1914, he was quick to volunteer, being just short of his 32nd birthday.

He was commissioned into the 4th Battalion of the King's Liverpool Regiment, and arrived in France in April 1915, where the battalion was attached to the Royal Welsh Fusiliers. He spent the summer in the trenches, but was invalided home in October. After an operation, he took some time to regain fitness, and it was not until July 1916 that he was declared fit enough to return to his comrades in Belgium, still in the trenches near Ypres. Soon the whole division headed south, towards the Somme where the battle had been raging without any real progress on either side for some time. It was to be Ken Hutchings's last journey. In the first week of September 1916, Lt Kenneth Hutchings was killed in action. He was hit by a shell as his platoon defended a position in woodland near the village of Ginchy against strong German attacks, and he died immediately.

In the *Daily Telegraph* of 10 September 1916, next to the headline, 'The Capture of Ginchy', is a tribute to Ken Hutchings, which begins to show what Hutchings meant to cricket lovers. 'A great cricketer has fallen, in the person of Kenneth Hutchings, killed in action in France. Lovers of our great national pastime will deplore his death, though as patriots they would not have been content for his life to have been spared by the ignoble shirking of paramount duty …. All the same, we shall all be forgiven for lamenting the untimely death of this brilliant athlete – a man who had it in his power to delight great masses of his fellow countrymen by the mere witchery of his batsmanship. There was scarcely a county in England that at one time or another had not felt the force of his brilliant powers of punishment – powers which like Victor Trumper he could bring to bear equally on good as on indifferent or bad bowling. He was an outstanding ornament of the game and until he dropped out of first-class cricket no name stood higher on that roll of brilliant batsmen which Kent in her marvellous renaissance has given to the cricket world. That he fell playing the game to the last will not be doubted for an instant by those who knew him best.'

The Solid All-Rounder

At first slip in Chevallier Tayler's painting is Jack Mason. John Richard Mason, always known as Jack, was born at Blackheath on 26 March 1874, one of seven brothers, two of whom, Charles and James, also played first-class cricket. He was described in the 1907 *Kent History* as 'perhaps the finest all-round gentleman player Kent has ever had', and his statistics lend support to that claim. He was educated at Winchester College in Hampshire, and played for four years in their first XI, captaining the side in his final year, 1893. Writing in the 1894 *Wisden*, C.B. Fry stated that 'there can be no doubt that J.R. Mason was the best public school bat of the year …. His success for Kent stamps him as a performer of phenomenal merit.' Fry predicted a fine future for the young man. To many men who had seen both players in their prime, Mason reminded them of Walter Hammond, the great Gloucestershire player of the interwar years, straight of back, leaning into a supremely elegant and powerful cover drive or cut, bowling energetic fast-medium and quite brilliant in any close catching position.

Despite being a pupil at the intensely academic Winchester College, Mason, like Hutchings a few years later, did not go on to Oxford or Cambridge, or indeed any university, but instead became articled to a firm of solicitors as he studied for his qualifications as a lawyer, and this allowed him to play cricket for Kent, to the exclusion of almost everything else. It would be wrong to suggest that his period of studying for the law was as long as W.G. Grace's years of studying to be a doctor, but there is little doubt that Mason's heart was on the cricket field rather than among his law books for the first years of his adult cricketing life.

Mason made his first-class debut on 27 July 1893, at the age of 19, opening the batting for Kent against Sussex at Beckenham, only a few days after leaving Winchester for the last time. He made 31 and 14 not out as Kent won by nine wickets, a promising debut indeed. Kent kept him in their side for the rest of the summer. At Blackheath, they lost by an innings to Yorkshire, but Mason had the satisfaction of his first bowl for Kent, and his first two wickets. His first match for Kent at Canterbury was particularly memorable, as it was against the visiting Australians, and Kent won by 36 runs, after following on. Mason did not do much, scoring only 14 and 18 as opener, and took just one wicket, but the experience of being in a side that bowled out the Australians for 60 when they needed only 97 to win would remain with him for a long time. The Australian bowling attack of Giffen, Trumble, Harry Trott and Turner should have been enough to ensure an Australian victory, but Alec Hearne, Mason's opening partner, took 5 for 35 and Walter Wright 4 for 24 in the tourists' second innings, and gained a great victory. The Australian tourists of 1893 were not the strongest, and this was their eighth defeat of the tour, but it was all the same a notable triumph for Kent.

In the next game, against Nottinghamshire at Canterbury, Mason scored 49 and 50, his two best scores of the summer to date, and a few days later took six wickets for 70 at Lord's, his first five-wicket haul, to help Kent to a win by just 12 runs. Mason was quickly becoming an important part of the Kent eleven. In the final match of the season, against Sussex at Hove, he scored

48 and 52, beating his highest score by 2 and his best match aggregate by 1. In Kent's first innings, all 11 batsmen reached double figures, but none reached three figures, a comparatively rare achievement in any form of cricket.

By the end of his first season, Jack Mason had scored 336 runs at an average of 25.84, and had taken 14 wickets at 24.14. These were very impressive figures for a 19-year-old. After a winter no doubt spent poring over his law books, Mason was ready for a full season of county cricket, but although he played 20 matches, his summer was not as successful as the experts had predicted. He did score his first century, 102 against Lancashire at Tonbridge at the end of June, but a season's batting average of 17.40, and just five wickets at 46 runs each were poor returns for a young man of his promise and talent.

In 1895 things began to get better. He scored over 1,000 runs for the first time (a feat he would achieve in each of the following seven seasons) with a top score of 142 not out, and he took 24 wickets, although at over 40 runs apiece. The upward curve continued and in 1897, the year in which Lord Harris played his final championship match for Kent, he had a particularly good summer. He hit the highest score of his career, 183 against Somerset at Blackheath, a game in which he also took 5 for 20 in Somerset's second innings to bring Kent victory. *Wisden* thought so highly of his efforts that year that they chose him as one of their Five Cricketers Of The Year. His selection as one of the five seems to have been partly through lack of many outstanding candidates (the other four were Gilbert Jessop, a fair choice, Frank Druce of Surrey, Willis Cuttell of Lancashire and Fred Bull of Essex), and also because of one innings for the Gentlemen against the Players at Lord's, when Mason top-scored with 62 in the first innings. Despite this, the Players won the game. *Wisden* described Mason as doing 'splendid work for his county', but it was a bad year for Kent, who won just two and lost ten of their championship games. Despite their view that 'there is no need to dwell at length on the doings of the Kent eleven in 1897', *Wisden* did acknowledge that 'in Mr J.R. Mason, the county possessed one of the finest all-round cricketers in England, for not only was his batting as good as ever, but he often bowled with conspicuous success, and his fielding in the slips was uniformly brilliant'.

That winter, Mason was chosen to tour Australia with the MCC team led by A.E. Stoddart, and he played in all five Test matches, but he was not a success. He scored a mere 129 runs in ten innings, and took just two wickets for 149 runs. He was never selected for England again. In a way, this was a pity, because his best season was yet to come, and Stoddart's side lost the series 4-1, so the fault was not solely Mason's. *Wisden* gave him the benefit of the doubt, suggesting that he 'did a lot of good work for the eleven'. He began the tour in excellent form, against state sides in Adelaide and Melbourne, but then had what *Wisden* called 'a long spell of bad luck', before beginning to find his form again as the tour ended. 'However, he fielded superbly at slip, and was one of the best change bowlers on the side.' Although it might not have been true of Stoddart's team in Australia, the idea that catches win matches begins to come through as a major reason why the Kent team were so successful in those years before the First World War. With magnificent fielders like Mason, Hutchings, Seymour and Huish, among others, in the side, it must have been exceptionally difficult for opposition batsmen to find the gaps often enough to set challenging totals.

In 1898, Mason was appointed captain of Kent, a position he held for five seasons. In 1900, he led them to third place, but otherwise could not bring them to a position from which they could make a realistic challenge for the title. In 1899 he scored 1,220 runs, including 181 not out against Nottinghamshire, in what was at the time the highest partnership ever for Kent. He and Alec Hearne (162 not out) put on an unbroken stand of 321 for the third wicket, a record that stood for 35 years until it was beaten by Bill Ashdown and Frank Woolley in 1934. W.G. Grace, in his ghosted newspaper column of the day, wrote that 'I am glad to be able to chronicle the fact that Jack Mason has at last shown his proper form, and gave, with Hearne, a grand display of batting.' Two weeks later, Grace might have regretted Mason's return to form, as they batted together for the Gentlemen against the Players at Lord's. Grace, then a few days short of his 51st birthday, was on 78 and looking good for his century when Mason, 'overlooking his partner's 51 years and inhibiting bulk', as David Frith delicately put it, called for a short run and Grace was run out by several feet.

1900 was, from a personal point of view, Mason's best season for Kent. He scored 1,828 runs that summer, at an average of 53.76, and took 86 wickets at 19.51. In every season that he captained the side he took at least 70 wickets, with 118 at 20.44 in 1901, his best year's work. Those figures included his career best analysis of 8 for 29 against Somerset at Taunton. When he was not captain, he never took more than 55 wickets in a season, although in several of those years he did play fewer matches. All the same, it seems to show that Mason had more faith in his own bowling than other men did. In 1902 he played for the only time in his life for MCC, against Cambridge University. It turned out to be a one-sided slaughter, and by the time MCC had reached 442 for 3, all the top three batsmen, Plum Warner, Pinky Burnup and Jack Mason, had scored centuries. This was Mason's only innings for MCC, so he must be one of the very few who finished with a first-class average for MCC of over 100. MCC finished on 607 all out and won by an innings and 146 runs.

By 1903, Mason's law career began to impinge too much on his cricket, and clearly there was a need to earn a living and not merely collect the expenses that came the way of the amateur cricketer in those days. Having played over 20 matches in each season of his captaincy, in 1903 he played only nine games for Kent, including both of the games in Canterbury Week. *Wisden* was sure that his absence for much of the season had a big impact on the side's success, describing him as a captain who 'fulfilled his duties with conspicuous ability, managing his bowling with great judgement, setting his side an excellent example in fielding, and making himself extremely popular with all those who worked under him'. There had originally been some doubt as to whether he would be available at all, but he found time to play for almost half the season, either because there were few lawsuits in need of settling in Kent, or else because his partners were able to cope without him.

Between 1904 and 1907, Mason played at least ten matches for Kent each season, and twice, in 1904 and 1906, averaged over 40 with the bat. In those same four years he took 160 wickets at around 24 runs each, and took 82 catches. Even though he could not give his full time to cricket, it is no wonder that the Kent committee welcomed him into the side whenever he was available. In 1909 he topped the national batting averages with 783 runs at 65.25, an average over 20 runs better than the next man. In that summer, when Kent again finished as champions,

Albert Chevallier Tayler's painting Kent v Lancashire 1906, *shows Colin Blythe, the Kent left-arm spin bowler bowling to J.T. Tyldesley of Lancashire, at the St Lawrence Ground in Canterbury. The painting shows all the Kent players who took part in the match*

Kent, county champions, 1906. Back row, left to right: Woolley, Huish, Hearne (scorer), Fielder, Blythe. Middle row: Burnup, Blaker, Marsham, Hutchings, Mason. Bottom row: Fairservice, Humphreys, Hearne, Seymour

(Left) Richard Blaker, whose grandfather and twin daughters also represented Kent

(Right) Colin 'Charlie' Blythe, the tragic hero of the painting

Ted Dillon, who went on to become Kent's most successful captain

Arthur Fielder, who took 11 wickets for
130 runs in the match

Kenneth Hutchings: the highest score of his career
changed the game

Pinky Burnup,
the Corinthian
footballer and
cricketer, one
of the Empire's
Cricketers, as
portrayed by
Chevallier Tayler

Jack Mason, in 1906 Kent's greatest ever all-round cricketer

Fred Huish, the senior pro and first in the line of great Kent wicketkeepers

Punter Humphreys, the young batsman who became a great coach

James Seymour, whose successful case against the Inland Revenue changed the lives of professional sportsmen

Johnny Tyldesley, seen from the front by Chevallier Tayler, a year before he immortalised his backside

J. T. Tyldesley.

A. Chevallier Tayler.
1905.

Cloudesley Marsham, captain of the side, picked for his leadership and connections as much as his cricket

Billy Findlay, the Lancastrian who wasn't playing, but who went on to be a pillar of Kent cricket

Albert Chevallier Tayler (left) with his friend and fellow cricket-loving artist, Henry Scott Tuke (right)

George Beldam, the cricketing photographer who was the inspiration for Chevallier Tayler's 48 portraits of The Empire's Cricketers

*Lord Harris – the
portrait that introduced
him to Chevallier Tayler*

Lord Harris.

A Chevallier Tayler

Tayler gave his Eton v Harrow at Lord's 1886 *to MCC, where it is still on display in the pavilion*

Girl Shelling Peas, *a typical example of Chevallier Tayler's romantic realist work at Newlyn*

he scored hundreds in three consecutive games. But by 1912, his career was finishing. After five games for Kent in 1911, he did not play at all in 1912. During the season, he got married and on the occasion of his wedding, the club opened a testimonial fund for him, despite the fact that he was an amateur and a member of the county committee. The fund raised a little over £750, and at the end of Kent's match against Worcestershire at Catford that July, he was presented with a silver salver and a candelabra by Lord Harris. He came back to play one championship match in each season of 1913 and 1914, and his final first-class match was a post-war festival game against the Australian Imperial Forces XI at Attleborough in Norfolk. He was 45 years old, and scored 18. He did not bowl nor take a catch.

Jack Mason did not end his association with Kent County Cricket Club with his retirement as a player. He first joined the committee in 1898 and remained a member until 1938, when he was elected president of the club. The second oldest member of the team in Chevallier Tayler's painting, Mason was the last but one to die, aged 84 on 15 October 1958, peacefully at his home in Sussex.

The Young Professional

The man at silly mid-on, at the extreme left of the painting, is Ted 'Punter' Humphreys. Edward Humphreys was born at Ditton, not far from Maidstone, on 24 August 1881. He was the ninth son of Henry and Kate Humphreys – like many of his Kent teammates, he had plenty of brothers and sisters to play with as he grew up. He acquired the nickname Punter, by which he was universally known as an adult, but nobody seems to know how he came by it. Derek Ufton, the former Kent wicketkeeper-batsman who was coached by Humphreys after the war, remarked that he did not gamble as he had too little money to waste any of it.

According to the 1891 census, his father was by then landlord of the Walnut Tree Inn, a pub at Ditton, just to the south-west of Maidstone. In 1897, aged only 15, he gained a trial for Kent, as a slow left-arm bowler, and the following season became one of the first players to be taken on the ground staff at Tonbridge by Captain William McCanlis, to be part of the nursery which was set up that year. He became a professional player for Kent in 1898, just before his 17th birthday, and spent his days in a highly organised and disciplined coaching regime, designed to get the best out of the young men who were considered to have the necessary spark of talent. The Tonbridge Nursery was of its time a very advanced cricket school, with training programmes designed to suit each individual cricketer, and extensive notes taken to record every player's progress. It did not yield results overnight, but by 1906, it could be seen that the backbone of Kent's championship-winning side were graduates of McCanlis and the Tonbridge Nursery.

Humphreys was one of the first, and one of the best. He played his first game for Kent, against Surrey at the Oval, at the end of July 1899, shortly before he turned 18. He was picked as a bowler, batted at number eight, scored 0 and 5, and took his first two first-class wickets for 49 runs. Surrey won the game. He played two more games that summer, against the Australians at Canterbury – a real honour for such a young man – and against Warwickshire in the last but one game of the season. The game against the Australians was a real triumph for Kent, who won the match by two wickets, inflicting only the third defeat in 35 matches on the tourists. Humphreys did little in the game – he was the one man who did not bat as Kent chased down 138 to win – but the experience of playing at Canterbury in front of a crowd described on the first day as 'by far and away the biggest ever seen on the St Lawrence Ground' would have been invaluable.

However, from then his progress was slow. In 1900, he played nine games in the championship, but finished the season bottom of the county batting averages, with only 67 runs in 12 innings, 40 of which were scored in the second innings of the first game of the season, and also bottom of the bowling averages, with one wicket for 180 runs. Many a player has disappeared forever after seasons like that. But clearly Kent saw something in Humphreys, and they were right to persevere.

Humphreys's career as a slow left-arm bowler was largely peripheral by this time, because that slot in the side had been filled by Charlie Blythe, an altogether greater spinner than Humphreys – or indeed practically everybody else who has ever played for Kent – could hope to be. His progress as a batsman continued to be steady, but hardly very quick. In 1901, he played 17 of the county's 23 championship games, and yet when *Wisden* made the comment that 'fully represented, Kent had a capital eleven' in 1901, the 11 names that were then listed did not include Humphreys. He scored only 373 runs at 13.32, and took 18 wickets for 553 runs, an average of a little over 30 per wicket. Indeed, *Wisden* commented that 'two batsmen of whom something is likely to be heard in future are K.S. Singh and the young professional Murrell'. Kanwar Shumshere Singh, who has some claim to the title of Kent's first overseas player, was educated at Rugby and Cambridge, but played just twice for Kent, once in 1901 and once in 1902. In the first of those games, against Surrey at the Oval, he shared a stand of 115 in under an hour for the seventh wicket with Joe Murrell, who hit 68 not out while Humphreys, batting at number four, hit 14 and 21 in a generally low-scoring game which Kent won by 110 runs. Murrell's 68 was originally recorded as 70, but after the innings was over, the captains were consulted and one of his drives, which was originally given as a six, was deemed to have pitched within the boundary and two runs were deducted from his score and the total. That was the highest score that Joe Murrell (christened Harry Robert, but universally known as Joe, no doubt for the same reason that Colin Blythe was known as Charlie) ever made in 27 games for Kent, and despite moving to Middlesex in 1906 and playing for them for a further two decades, he never scored a first-class century. Kent made the right decision in sticking with Humphreys rather than Murrell.

In 1902, Humphreys played a further 15 games for the county, but his batting average did not improve: he ended up with 217 runs at 10.85, a very meagre return, and a further 18 wickets at the improved average of 24.94. In 1903 he continued to struggle, averaging just 15.23 with the bat, but in 1904 there came a transformation. Promoted up the order, often opening the batting with Alec Hearne or Pinky Burnup, he totalled 1,545 runs in the season at an average of 35.11, twice as many as in any previous season. He also, for good measure, topped the bowling averages with 26 wickets at 17.61 each. 'Humphreys was nothing less than a revelation,' said *Wisden*. Having been dropped from the side at the end of the 1903 season, his resurgence in 1904 was completely unexpected, but highly appreciated.

He hit his first three centuries for Kent, but one of his more remarkable innings was against Lancashire at Old Trafford that year when Kent were very easily beaten, by an innings and

128 runs. Kent's first innings of 122 was bad enough, but in the second innings, they could only manage 42 all out. However, Humphreys made 24 of these runs, while nobody else could muster more than 6.

His first century for Kent came against Nottinghamshire at Trent Bridge in June. It was obviously a very good batting track as Notts piled up 602, and in reply Kent could only manage 356, thanks mainly to a remarkable 82 not out from Colin Blythe, the highest score of his career, and 97 by Punter Humphreys. He was back out again a few minutes later, as Kent followed on and Blythe, who had obviously not removed his pads in the meantime, opened the batting with Humphreys. This time Blythe made only 3, but Humphreys went on to make 131, as Kent totalled 263 for 4 and saved the game. Joe Murrell, incidentally, was playing in that match and made 8 and 2 not out. His star was waning just as Punter's was on the rise.

Although Humphreys had a slight dip in form in 1905, he was a regular member of the side in 1906, only he and James Seymour as professionals in the batting line-up. His bowling was useful that summer, too, especially when Charlie Blythe was injured. His 7 for 33 against Middlesex in the draw at Tonbridge proved to be the best analysis of his career. However, his real purple patch would come a few years later. In the winter of 1908/09, he went out to New Zealand to coach, and played three games for Canterbury during his time there. In his one Plunket Shield game, he took 10 wickets for 120, and he ended up with 25 wickets in those three matches, at an average of 12.52. His coaching must have worked on himself as much as on any of his pupils, because when he came back for the 1909 season in England, he was in better form than ever before. He hit the highest score of his career, and the highest score of Kent's season, when he made 208 against Gloucestershire at Catford. This form continued until the war, 1914 being the seventh consecutive season in which he scored more than 1,000 runs. Punter Humphreys spent several winters coaching in New Zealand and in the West Indies, and from January to March 1913 toured West Indies with an MCC team led by Arthur Somerset, the former Sussex player who was by now in his late fifties. Humphreys had a very successful tour: in nine first-class games he averaged over 40 with the bat and took 40 wickets at 16.75 runs apiece.

The war came at the height of Humphreys's career. He was just 34 when war was declared, and despite having family responsibilities which could have kept him out of active service, he joined the Royal Navy in 1917 and served until early 1919. He was then offered the post of cricket coach at Uppingham School in Rutland, which he took. This meant he was not available to play for Kent until the summer holidays, but from August he was welcomed back as a regular member of the side, even though the team were doing very well in the championship race, considering the blows that the war had dealt to the eleven. His cricket in the eight championship matches he played in 1919 was not spectacular, 59 being his highest score of the year. The next summer, 1920, he played just twice for Kent, but he made only 18 runs in four innings and took no wickets. His final game for the county was against Middlesex in Canterbury Week, a game that Middlesex won by five runs. Keeping wicket for Middlesex that day was Joe Murrell, the man *Wisden* had tipped as a future star, while ignoring Humphreys completely all those seasons ago. Humphreys finished his career with 16,603 runs at an average of 27.95 and 379 wickets at 24.57, figures that are the hallmark of a true all-rounder, even if as a bowler he spent most of his career in the shadow of Charlie Blythe. 15,308 of those runs were scored, and 306 of those wickets were taken, for Kent. His seventh-wicket partnership of 248 with Arthur Day against Somerset at Taunton in 1908 remains the Kent record over a century later. He also took 229 catches in his career, mostly at short leg or mid-on.

Humphreys became an excellent coach. He was helped by the fact that in his first season at Uppingham he had A.P.F. Chapman in his team, the outstanding schoolboy batsman of the year and a future captain of Kent and England. He also visited West Indies a number of times in the winter, and coached very successfully there. Such was his reputation as a coach that in 1929 Lord Harris, now in his late seventies but still the power at Canterbury, persuaded Punter to come to Kent, to take over from Gerry Weigall, who was retiring. Humphreys stayed until 1948, playing a big part in the development of such players as Chapman, Gerry Chalk, Doug Wright, Arthur Fagg and Godfrey Evans, among many more. He was a taciturn man, not given to long speeches, but whatever he did say was very much to the point. He was a popular sight at all Kent's grounds, usually to be seen smoking a small cheroot as he cast a benign eye over his charges. His final contact with the first-class game was as umpire in a match between Kent and the Combined Services, a team that included future Test cricketers Peter May and Alan Oakman, in May 1949, just six months before he died.

The Hard-Hitting War Hero

Dick Blaker is standing at mid-off, to the right of the pavilion as Blythe turns his arm over to bowl. Richard Norman Rowsell

Blaker was born in Bayswater, in London, on 24 October 1879. He was the fourth child of Harry Campbell Blaker, a solicitor, and Edith (nee Rowsell). His father had played a few games for the Gentlemen of Sussex in the 1860s, and his grandfather, also Richard, had won his blue at Cambridge in 1842 and 1843. Richard senior, who became vicar of Ifield in Sussex, is one of those whose portrait is included in the famous depiction of the cricket match between Sussex and Kent at Brighton, which was first published in 1849. This gives the Blaker family a unique double of two different generations being portrayed as part of the most famous cricket artworks of their times. Cricket was certainly in his blood.

Young Dick was educated at Westminster, where he had a stellar sporting career, captaining the cricket team for four years, and also playing at centre-forward in the football XI. He went on to Cambridge, where he gained three blues for cricket from 1900 to 1902, as well as four for football from 1899. He first played for Kent, where his family now lived, in 1898, when he was 18 years old and still at school. His first match was against Middlesex at Lord's, and Kent were beaten by an innings. Blaker made only 4 and 17 not out, but the not out innings was after coming in with four wickets down and holding up one end while the remaining wickets tumbled from 138 for 4 to 165 all out. He was retained for the next match, the return against Middlesex, at Catford. Middlesex still won, and Blaker made 0 and 7. Then he went up to Cambridge.

He played a few games for the university in 1899, but did not win his blue. He played ten games in all that summer, five for the university and five for Kent, but his highest score was only 39 not out. His first game of the summer for Kent was once again

168

versus Middlesex, this time at Maidstone, meaning his first three championship games had all been against Middlesex, and on three different grounds. In his next match, against Gloucestershire at Bristol, he took his first first-class wicket with his somewhat erratic fast right-arm bowling. He was very rarely used as a bowler, taking only nine wickets in his entire career, but in this match, ten of the Kent team, including the wicketkeeper Huish, had a bowl, so it was more by luck than good bowling that the wicket fell to Blaker. The opening bowler Walter Wright, whose last game for Kent this proved to be, was the only man who did not bowl in Gloucestershire's second innings. The match was drawn.

In four years at Cambridge, Blaker scored 1,030 runs at an average of 22.39, adequate but not exceptional figures. His career at Kent was not, if judged statistically, that much better, but he was the sort of man and the sort of cricketer that the Kent hierarchy liked. He was a Corinthian, for a start, playing football with Pinky Burnup and sharing the same values of selfless fair play. At this time, Kent were fortunate to have several very fine amateur batsmen, and some not quite so very fine, but because of the careful stratification of the social aspects of top-class cricket, perhaps especially of cricket in Kent, selection of the top six in the batting order seemed to depend on who you knew as much as what you knew. Dick Blaker fitted in extremely well. One could argue that Ted Humphreys disproves this theory, in that he, as a professional, was given plenty of opportunities to prove his worth, but there is no doubt that the top order of Kent's batting was very inconsistent; when it worked it really worked, but when it didn't, it needed the steadiness of the likes of Seymour and Woolley to help them out of trouble. Fortunately for Kent, in 1906 all the amateur batsmen had good summers.

Blaker never scored 1,000 runs in a season, but after he came down from Cambridge, he was never able to play a full season. In early 1902, while still at university and presumably not too worried about the prospect of examinations, he toured the West Indies with an all-amateur side run by R.A. Bennett, a man who had played a few games for Hampshire. They played matches in Barbados, Jamaica, Trinidad and British Guiana (now Guyana), and had three matches against a representative West Indies XI. Blaker enjoyed the trip and took two wickets for one run in the only over he bowled in the game in Trinidad, but he did little else to prove he had unusual talent. Batting on matting did present difficulties for all the batsmen, but Blaker's Kent colleague Ted Dillon managed to do rather better.

After graduating, Blaker followed his father's profession and went into the law. He soon realised, like Jack Mason, that it was not possible to combine cricket and law in such a way that he could enjoy a full summer of cricket without it affecting his legal studies, and so after 1903, when he played 18 championship matches, he found that his opportunities were limited. His batting style was, in the manner of many of his fellow amateur batsmen of the day, aggressive and somewhat leg side in direction. He was also an exceptionally good fieldsman in almost any position, a fine slip but was just as likely to be found in the outfield away from the bat. *Wisden* particularly picked out Burnup, Hutchings and Blaker as three who helped make Kent the best fielding side in the country.

Blaker's two best seasons were 1905 and 1906. He finally hit his first first-class century playing for Kent against Gloucestershire at Catford in 1905, hitting 120 out of 194 added while he was at the wicket in just 75 minutes, before being stumped off the bowling of another mighty hitter, Gilbert Jessop. Blaker finished the season with 786 runs, his highest season's total, at 39.30, and took that form into 1906.

In 12 championship appearances in Kent's great year, Blaker scored 605 runs at an average of 40.33. He also made the highest score of his career, 122 against Sussex at Canterbury in the match before the Lancashire game. He and Pinky Burnup put on 191 for the seventh wicket in just under two hours, before Blaker was bowled. The partnership changed the course of the game and allowed Marsham, the next man in, to play with equal freedom until he, too, reached his century. Burnup, who had been playing carefully and rather slowly until Blaker came to the crease, took his score to 141, and with Marsham's 119 to add to Blaker's quickfire 122, Kent reached 568 all out. Even Charlie Blythe hit 53. Sussex were then bundled out twice to give Kent an innings victory.

This, as it turned out, was almost Blaker's swansong. He played only five games for the county in 1907; in his final championship innings, against Surrey at the Oval, he made 41, batting at number nine but top scoring for Kent as they went down to an innings defeat. After one last game against the Gentlemen of Philadelphia in 1908, he was lost to the first-class game at the age of 28. He made a duck in the first innings of his final match, but made 1 not out in the second, as Kent won by four wickets, so he walked off the square at Canterbury for the last time undefeated. In his first-class career he had played 162 games and scored 5,359 runs at 22.61, not a good enough return for a man of his explosive talent.

Ten days after finishing his cricket career, he married Miss Mary Godby at Eltham parish church. It was a sumptuous affair with 250 guests including several of his Kent amateur colleagues. The dashing Kent batsman then settled down to a very conventional life as a civil servant within the judiciary. In 1913, his wife gave birth to twin daughters, Joan and Barbara. At the very end of 1915, despite being 36 years old, Blaker enlisted in the Army Reserve as a private, but by the middle of 1916 had been accepted as an officer cadet and underwent several months of training in Scotland. He was commissioned into the Rifle Brigade at the end of the year, but almost immediately went down with pneumonia and was unable to take up his commission straight away. It was not until September 1918 that Lieutenant Blaker was able to join his battalion in France. On 4 November 1918, just a week before the Armistice was signed, Blaker's company were ordered to attack, and in fierce hand to hand fighting, they advanced along a railway cutting near Louvignies in northern France. For his gallantry on that day he was awarded the Military Cross. The official citation spoke of his 'most conspicuous courage' as he 'came single-handed on two enemy machine guns in action. He dashed between the guns, capturing them both and their teams. Seeing his men a short distance ahead, and held up by machine gun fire from a house on their flank, he again took them single-handed, clearing the house and capturing two officers and 28 other ranks.' This was, unquestionably, the greatest piece of soldiering performed by any Kent player during the Great War, a complete contrast to the routine civil service life that he had left and would now go back to.

Neither the war nor his retirement from playing cricket marked the end of Blaker's association with cricket, or with Kent. From 1920 until the end of his life, he was on the Kent committee for 20 of those years, and was president of the club in 1950. In his acceptance speech at the 1950 Annual General Meeting, Blaker said that 'I want to instil into young players that they still have feet to use. Some people seem to forget where their left foot is.' He also regretted that 'one does not see fieldsmen on the boundary nowadays. This was most disappointing as it is most exhilarating to a fieldsman to hear the crowd telling him what to do when a catch is coming his way.' As the local paper said in its report, '(Laughter)'. Sadly Dick Blaker became only the third President to die in office. His *Wisden* obituary noted that 'during the last Canterbury Week, his tent was the centre of pleasant entertainment, but he showed signs of ill health and in little more than a month passed away'. His death came after an operation for peritonitis in September 1950. He was a few days short of his 71st birthday.

One of his most important legacies to both the club and the game of cricket in its widest sense came through his twin daughters. Both Joan and Barbara became fine cricketers in their own right, the Blaker Twins being the backbone of many top women's teams from the mid-1930s until the 1950s. Both women were fine batsmen, although they never quite earned selection for England. Barbara, a forcing right-hand batsman like her father, was chosen to tour Australia and New Zealand in 1939/40, but the war caused the tour to be cancelled. Kent has always been a stronghold of women's cricket, and the part played by the Blaker Twins in building up that reputation in the years either side of the Second World War is at least as significant as the part played by their father in 1906.

They were a true Kent family. If you take a walk along the promenade at Hythe, one of the ancient Cinque Ports, you will pass a bench with the inscription, 'Dedicated to the cricketing

Blaker Twins, Barbara A. Hamilton April 1913–April 2005, and Joan R. Smith April 1913–August 2001. Loving and happy memories of walks in Hythe'. To the end of their long and active lives, they were part of the cricket heritage of the county, as much as their father and great-grandfather.

The Captain

Standing at cover, in front of the tower of Canterbury Cathedral and looking every bit the man in charge of operations, the Kent captain Cloudesley Marsham is shown as a vigorous and confident figure taking a central place in Chevallier Tayler's painting. Cloudesley Henry Bullock Marsham, named for his five-times great-grandfather Admiral of the Fleet Sir Cloudesley Shovel, was born at Stoke Lyne, near Bicester in Oxfordshire, on 10 February 1879. He was born into Kent aristocracy, both cricketing and social, as not only the nephew of George Marsham, who had been a committee member since 1875 and who would be president in 1886, but the second cousin of the fourth Earl of Romney, who was president in 1880, when his young cousin was just learning to walk. His father, also Cloudesley, was described as 'the best Gentleman bowler of his day', his day being the 1850s and 1860s. Several other members of his family were also involved in Kent cricket – the fourth Earl's brother, Rev. John Marsham, played twice for Kent in 1873, two uncles both played for Oxford University and MCC sporadically in the 1850s and 1860s, and his brother Francis played one game for MCC and one for Kent, both against Oxford University in 1905. Somewhat bizarrely, he captained Kent on the one occasion that he played for them. Cloudesley Marsham's son Algernon also played half a dozen games for Kent in 1946, but did nothing to eclipse his father's fame.

Young Cloudesley lived at Harrietsham, near Maidstone, where his father was rector, and in due course was sent to Eton, where he first acquired the nickname 'Slug'. This name was bestowed upon him by his fellow Etonians for no other reason than that it had been applied to several generations of Marshams who had preceded him there, but it stuck with him for life. Both he and his younger brother Francis answered to this name. Cloudesley played in the Eton first XI in 1897 and 1898. He then went up to Oxford, as was the family tradition, and won his blue for cricket in the three years from 1901. In the Oxford team of 1901, Marsham opened with Ted Dillon, and Billy Findlay kept wicket. Dick Blaker and another Kent stalwart, Sammy Day, were playing for Cambridge. Despite Marsham's 100 not out in the second innings, the match was left drawn. Young Cloudesley had made his debut for Kent in 1900, at Trent Bridge against Nottinghamshire. He scored 4 and 23 in a match Kent lost by 12 runs, but he did enough to retain his place for three more matches that summer, against Somerset at Blackheath, against Surrey at the Oval and against Essex at Leyton. 1901 was a better season for Marsham but he only played three games for Kent, against Sussex and Lancashire at home and against Worcestershire away, and then was not picked again. In 1902, his last season as an undergraduate, he made something of a breakthrough, playing ten championship games and finally scoring his first 50 for the club in his fifth game of the season, against Somerset at Mote Park, Maidstone.

In the next game, at Trent Bridge, he scored his first century for Kent, 120 against Nottinghamshire. For good measure, he scored 54 in the second innings, but the match was drawn. He played his first Canterbury Week that year, too, and helped his team beat Surrey by an innings by scoring 92 as his excellent form continued.

In 1903, Marsham played very little. The reason was simple. 'C.H.B. Marsham, who had made considerable strides as a batsman in the previous season, went off so completely that he dropped out of the eleven,' according to *Wisden*. All the same, with Pinky Burnup going overseas and thus giving up the captaincy, the Kent committee asked Marsham to take over the reins for 1904. It was not a decision that was greeted with unanimous acclamation, but his leadership soon proved to be the strongest part of his game. *Wisden* was altogether kinder than it had been a year earlier. 'C.H.B. Marsham, who could not have hoped, when he succeeded Burnup as captain, that his first year of leadership would be crowned with such success (Kent came third, their highest placing to date) played at least two fine innings.' They were no doubt referring to his 95 at Tonbridge against Lancashire, in a losing cause, and his 92 not out against Yorkshire at Tunbridge Wells. There were no hundreds for Kent for Marsham in 1904, although when playing for MCC against Oxford University at Lord's that June, he hit 161 not out, the highest score of his career. In that game he batted with Ranjitsinhji, who made 142, and together they put on 107 in under an hour. Once Ranji was out, Marsham put on 175 in a little under 90 minutes with his Kent teammate Alec Hearne, who made only 39 of those runs. Those who thought of Marsham as a sound but painstaking batsman, dour in the Burnup mould, would have to eat their words.

1905 was not such a good year for either Marsham or Kent, although he was deemed to have captained the team 'zealously', a further example of *Wisden* damning with faint praise. He was widely criticised at the time for putting Lancashire in to bat in their game in Canterbury Week, and losing the game by eight wickets. It would have been an innings defeat if Blythe and Fairservice had not added 120 for the ninth wicket in the Kent second innings. The match was Fred Huish's benefit game, but he made just four runs and Blythe, his partner in luring so many batsmen to their doom, bowled poorly. Marsham was vilified for not following W.G. Grace's dictum of 'If you win the toss, bat. If you are not sure, think about it, and then bat.' Today cricket has changed to the extent that fielding first is seen as an advantage in county cricket, especially in early season games, but in Edwardian times, it was always a case of win the toss and bat. *Wisden* generously suggested that in the same situation, many other captains would have done the same thing, but clearly there were question marks over Marsham's skill as a captain as Kent prepared for 1906.

The disastrous Lancashire game of 1905 made victory in the same fixture a year later all the sweeter, and for Marsham the whole season was a triumph, even if his personal form was not spectacular. His one century, against Sussex in the first game of Canterbury Week, was an excellent innings, but he still only averaged 25 for the season, and was one of eight different batsmen to make a century for Kent that summer, all but one of whom finished with a better average than him. But was he a Brearley, worth his place in the 11 purely for his captaincy skills? Could he be carried by the other ten simply for his strategic and tactical skills? The simple answer to this is no. Marsham was a fine captain, but he was not a genius. He did not have Brearley's degree in people. But he was a lucky captain: in 1906 there were no serious injuries to key members of the side, and several of the team blossomed that summer in a way that nobody could have dared hope for at the start of the season. He also had one other priceless gift as a captain, the ability to listen. He was often quoted as saying that he regularly spoke to his more experienced teammates, by which he mainly meant Fred Huish and Alec Hearne, and was not too proud to put their thoughts into action. In those days when it was almost unthinkable that a professional cricketer should be captain, the amateurs who turned out to be the best leaders often deferred to their senior professionals. From Jack Hobbs to Alec Bedser at Surrey, from Phil Mead to Derek Shackleton at Hampshire and from Fred Huish to Les Ames at Kent, among many others, the senior pro had wielded an influence on and off the field that an amateur captain ignored at his peril.

1907 was the season after the Lord Mayor's Show. Many players failed for one reason or another to deliver the performances they had done in 1906, and in Marsham's case, the fall was precipitous, even if not from a very high peak. In 18 championship matches, his highest score was 31, and his average only a whisker above 10. His captaincy, too, did not have the magic of the previous summer. Canterbury Week, once again pitting Kent against Sussex and Lancashire, resulted in one draw and one defeat, a stark contrast to the triumphant Week of 12 months earlier. Yet despite slipping from first to eighth place in the table, Kent drew large crowds wherever they went. The policy of playing county matches in several different towns was seen as what we would now describe as a piece of brilliant marketing, with one contemporary writer noting that 'having county matches at a number of grounds makes for prosperity. In various directions there is a large local public to draw upon, and just now the same spirit of enthusiasm prevails everywhere'. Kent's cricket under Marsham was no doubt played in a style that drew the crowds, but whereas in 1906 the whirling blades of Hutchings and his colleagues had brought victory after victory, there was criticism of Kent a year later that they were suffering from 'too much brilliancy'. The writer added that 'one thing must be said for Kent cricket in 1907, whatever its shortcomings, it was so full of life and energy as always to be exhilarating to look at'. Marsham probably considered that a reasonable epitaph for the year.

In 1908, Kent and Marsham bounced back. The change from two years earlier in the batting was almost total, with the top three run scorers all being professionals – Seymour, Hardinge and Woolley – who all passed 1,000 runs for the county, but fourth on the list was Marsham, with 960 runs in championship matches, and 1,004 in all matches, the second and last time he passed 1,000 runs in a season. His successes included two centuries in successive games at Tonbridge, opening the batting against Gloucestershire and Essex, and creating two victories for his side in the process. It was a remarkable turnaround but it was also his last fling. At the end of the year he found that his business commitments meant that he could not continue the captaincy, and although he said that he hoped to play whenever he could get away from the office, in fact he played only twice for the county, against Sussex and Somerset, both away from home in August. He did little in either game, apart from being hit for 43 runs in 27 balls by the Somerset batsmen as the match faded into a high-scoring draw. His commitment to cricket, however, was not in doubt as he accepted an invitation that year at the age of just 29 to join the Test selection committee, the first Kent man to be appointed a Test selector. This meant he spent much of his cricketing hours watching other players rather than getting into his flannels himself. In 1910, Marsham played one early season game for Kent against Cambridge University, and that was the end of his first-class cricket until the war. He married in 1911, and no doubt home life as well as business life began to get in the way.

In 1919, at the age of 40, he captained the Gentlemen of England against Oxford University, without achieving much except another appalling bowling analysis (0.5-0-8-0, plus one wide). Even that game was not quite the end of his career. In July 1922, when his old friend Lionel Troughton was not available to captain the side against Notts, Marsham came out of retirement and led the side. He won the toss, and no doubt remembering the drubbing he had been given when he put Lancashire in in 1905, he chose to bat. However, the weather proved to be the winner, washing out almost all of the game after tea on the first day. There was time for Marsham's final innings of his career, cleaned bowled for 1 as Kent were dismissed for 185, but although Nottinghamshire got to 112 for 4 on the third day, no result was possible. Thus, at the age of 43 and five months, Slug Marsham put down his bat for the final time.

In his first-class career, Cloudesley Marsham played 174 matches and scored 5,878 runs at an average of 22.78. He scored seven hundreds and took 89 catches, as well as two wickets with his very rarely used right-arm slows. He died young, aged just 49, in 1928. His sudden and unexpected death was felt by many. At a meeting of the Kent County Council shortly after Marsham died, the chairman, Lord Cornwallis, recalled Marsham's influence 'in the field of public business', while Lord Harris, as involved with county political matters as much as cricketing ones, added that Marsham had 'the superb quality of leading men and enthusing his own spirit into them, and extracting from them the highest excellence'. His funeral, at St Mary's Platt on 23 July 1928 was attended by a congregation swelling well into the hundreds, including Lord Harris, Jack Mason, Dick Blaker, Fred Huish and Ted Dillon, and there were over 80 wreaths around the grave. *Wisden* summed him up by writing that he was 'a hard worker and a keen trier in the field. He inspired his men by fine example. As a captain he secured unfailing support and unswerving loyalty from those under him, while a charming and courteous disposition endeared him to all opponents'. And he secured his immortality by leading Kent to their first ever championship, and thus being portrayed in a central position in Chevallier Tayler's epic work.

The First Great Kent Keeper

Frederick Henry Huish was born in Clapham, south London, on 15 November 1869, making him the oldest member of the Kent team depicted in Chevallier Tayler's painting. He is the wicketkeeper, viewed largely from behind, but with just a few bristles of his fine moustache visible as he crouches down to wait for Tyldesley to make a mistake against the wiles of Charlie Blythe. It would probably be wrong to describe Huish as the first in the line of great Kent keepers which stretches down through the likes of Ames, Levett, Evans, Knott and Jones to Billings of the present day, but he is certainly the first of the great Kent keepers of the overarm era. His statistics remain to this day the yardstick for all Kent wicketkeepers.

Huish first played for Kent in 1895, but he had made one appearance for the Gentlemen of Kent against the Players of Kent three years earlier, in a game at Beckenham. This match did not have first-class status, and Huish, later to be one of the longest-serving professionals on Kent's staff, played as an amateur, but he still did enough in the game for the county to keep an eye out for him. His brother Francis, also, was a good enough cricketer to be tried out by Kent, and in 1895, both brothers made their debuts for the first team, although somewhat surprisingly, they never played together in the Kent eleven. Fred was the first to make his debut, against Warwickshire at the beginning of June. The match was drawn but Fred got the first of over 350 stumpings, off Fred 'Nutty' Martin, Kent's fast-medium opening bowler. He played the next game, against Lancashire at Old Trafford, but got injured during the match and thus missed two months' cricket. In June and July while Fred was recovering from injury, Francis, a bowler, came into the team, and played five games for the county, four of them in the championship, in each of which Kent used a different wicketkeeper. Francis took 11 wickets at an average of just under 40, including 5 for 52 in the first innings of his first county match, against Sussex, but then was dropped and never played in the first team again. Three weeks later, Fred, recovered from injury, regained his place in the team and became a fixture in the side for the next 15 years at least. As *Wisden* noted in its summary of Kent's season, 'A cause for regret was that F.H. Huish, a young professional wicketkeeper, who looked like supplying the want so badly felt by Kent, should have broken his collarbone almost at the commencement of the season, in the match against Lancashire at Manchester.' From the outset, Huish was identified as something special.

Fred Huish is one of the great unsung heroes of Kent cricket. Although he was the first-choice wicketkeeper for two decades, he never played Test cricket and only once represented the Players in the big domestic match of each season, the Gentlemen v Players at Lord's. He is thus often overlooked when the list of great Kent keepers is compiled – Ames, Evans and Knott are the great triumvirate, Levett, Jones and Tylecote all won Test caps as wicketkeepers, and Sam Billings has ODI and T20 international caps, but Huish, who played more games for Kent than any of them, was never called on to play for his country. Of course, there were far fewer Test matches in those days, but the door was barred to all other wicketkeepers by the brilliance of Dick Lilley, of Warwickshire, who was certainly a better batsman than Huish and who missed only one Test match in England between 1896 and 1909. Lilley did not travel with MCC to South Africa in 1905/06, nor to Australia in 1907/08, when the wicketkeeping places went to Jack Board of Gloucestershire in South Africa, and to Joe Humphries of Derbyshire, six years younger than Huish but no better as a batsman. Both men performed adequately in Lilley's place, but it is in retrospect a major surprise that Huish was not picked for either tour. Once Lilley retired, and he was only three years older than Huish, his place in the England side was taken by Tiger Smith of Warwickshire and then by Herbert Strudwick of Surrey. These were all very fine wicketkeepers, but Huish lost nothing in comparison with them.

Huish, the oldest member of the 1906 side, was four and a half years older than the next oldest, Jack Mason, who in turn was 20 months older than Cuthbert Burnup. It is a curious fact that these three oldest members of the team were the last three to die, all living into their eighties. At the start of the 1906 season, Huish was 36 years old, had been a capped player for ten years and had received a benefit the year before. After his handful of games in 1895, the year in which Kent finished bottom of the table for the first and only time in their history, he became a regular in 1896, and won his county cap that year. *Wisden* again enthused over him, concluding that 'Huish has youth on his side, and as he is an extremely keen cricketer, there is every prospect of his making still further development and remaining for several seasons to come the regular wicketkeeper of the Kent eleven.'

There is no doubt that Huish was no batsman. In his first four summers, he failed to average even 10, and his highest score in those years was a mere 26 not out. He took plenty of catches and made some excellent stumpings, but the runs did not come. In those years he helped in the dismissal of over 150 batsmen, a high total in those days, especially as these were the seasons before Blythe came into the Kent side. He had no serious competition for his place, but we know that he realised the need to score runs in the lower order, and over the years his batting certainly improved. However, a final first-class batting average of just under 13, and a highest score of 93 in 497 matches is not very impressive, even given the state of wickets when he began his career, and the generally lower scores made. His wicketkeeping, however, was without parallel.

Fred Huish made 1,311 dismissals in his career, at a rate of 2.64 dismissals per game. That may not look particularly impressive, but when compared to other wicketkeepers, it is remarkable. Herbert Strudwick, who dismissed 1,495 batsmen in 674 matches, averaged just 2.22 wickets per match, and Dick Lilley, who got rid of 911 men in 416 matches, was marginally worse at 2.19 per game. Tiger Smith averaged only 1.77 dismissals a game, and later long-serving Kent keepers could not match Huish's rate. Les Ames, even with the astonishing Tich Freeman to keep to, only averaged 1.88 dismissals per game (although in many games he did not keep wicket), and Alan Knott, with Derek Underwood as his fellow destroyer and modern fast bowling to encourage nicks through to the keeper, was Huish's nearest rival, averaging 2.63 dismissals per game. But of these other wicketkeepers, only Strudwick, with a career batting average of only 10.88, was at Huish's level as a batsman. All the others averaged twice as much as Huish, and Ames, who also scored over 100 hundreds, averaged 43.51 over his career. In county games in the early years of the last century, the wicketkeeper was not necessarily meant to know which end of the bat to hold, but at Test level it has always been an issue, and that is why Lilley, averaging pretty much exactly twice that of Huish with the bat, played 35 Tests and Huish played none.

Fred Huish was very much appreciated by the hierarchy and the crowds at Kent. His keeping was unostentatious but ruthless, quick but fair in the Corinthian sense of the word. It was said that if he took a catch or made a stumping, no other Kent player dared appeal unless and until Huish had appealed. 1906 was a particularly good season for him, as it was for almost all the Kent eleven, as not only did he eliminate 64 batsmen, but also averaged nearly 18 with the bat, half as much again as his career average. He also scored four fifties, having scored only five in his previous 11 seasons of cricket. Among those fifties was his highest ever score, made against Somerset at Gravesend. At one stage Kent were 119 for 6, chasing Somerset's first innings total of 178, and when Huish went in to bat, the score was 157 for 7. Batting first with his captain, Slug Marsham, and then with Bill Fairservice, Huish hit 93 in an hour and a half spread over two days, full of crashing cuts and drives, to bring Kent's total up to 322 all out, which set Kent up for a ten-wicket win later on the second day. It was most un-Huish-like but very effective.

In 1908, for the first time he dismissed more than 80 men in the season, a fact that went almost completely unnoticed at the time. Although Huish was known to be a very fine wicketkeeper, the role was not one that seemed to be appreciated very much. *Wisden's* records section of the time, which included records for a big hit and throwing the cricket ball, made no mention of any wicketkeeping records at all, and it was not until 1911 that Huish made people sit up and take note of what he was up to behind the stumps. In that year he had a most remarkable season. He took 62 catches and made 39 stumpings, a total of 101 dismissals in the year, the first time in cricket history that a wicketkeeper had reached this target. In the game against Surrey at the Oval, he stumped nine batsmen and caught one, still a record total for a Kent wicketkeeper. He took four stumpings off Douglas Carr, the leg break bowler, one off Blythe and four stumpings and a catch off Woolley, whose analysis in the second innings was 7 for 9. It was a very exciting match, which Surrey eventually won by nine runs, and appropriately for a game which featured such astonishing wicketkeeping, it was played for Herbert Strudwick's benefit.

Huish's statistics are still remarkable, over a century on. He and Les Ames are the only Kent keepers ever to have dismissed 100 men in a season, and he and Jack Hubble are the only two Kent keepers to get rid of as many as ten in a match. Nobody else has ever stumped nine men in a match. Since his era, only six other keepers have dismissed 100 or more victims in a season, and Huish still ranks sixth on the all-time list of most dismissals by a wicketkeeper, behind only Bob Taylor, John Murray, the aforementioned Strudwick, Alan Knott and Jack Russell.

Not content with his achievements in 1911, in 1913 he did it again. He caught 69 batsmen and stumped 33, giving him a total of 102 victims. In 1914, at the age of 44, his performance slipped a little from his previous very high standards, but he still ensnared 73 victims. His final game, the last of the season against Hampshire at Bournemouth on 31 August, resulted in an innings defeat for Kent and a pair and just one catch for Huish. His ready replacement, Jack Hubble, was already in the team as a batsman and occasional keeper, so whether he would have played another season in 1915 is open to doubt, but by the time the war ended in 1919 he was almost 50 and his playing days were over.

He lived on for another 42 years after his retirement, and died on 15 March 1957, at Northiam, just over the Kentish border into Sussex, where he had lived for a number of years. In his later years, he used to come to watch Kent occasionally, and the memory of the old man that remains is of a smartly dressed gentleman who, despite being a professional wicketkeeper for two decades, had almost completely unmarked hands. His contemporaries, and most wicketkeepers before and since his time, bear the scars of years of active service behind the stumps, but Huish emerged unscathed.

The image we have of Huish a century on is of a man who, to quote Ronnie Corbett in the famous upper-, middle- and lower-class sketch with Ronnie Barker and John Cleese, knows his place. The details we have of the speeches he gave at dinners celebrating the several triumphs of Kent during his long career are full of humble appreciation for the leadership given by the amateurs, and of the friendship they bestowed upon him. The idea of equality in a cricket eleven, as in society as a whole, was not something he could have imagined, let alone practised or even tolerated. In those socially highly stratified days, Huish knew his place. And his place was behind the stumps.

The Best-Loved Man in Cricket

The left-arm bowler about to deliver the ball, the man that Lord Harris felt deserved much of the credit for bringing the championship title to Kent for the first time, is Colin Blythe, wearing his cap at a jaunty angle as he always did. Blythe, known to all his teammates and admirers as 'Charlie', for reasons that have never been clear, was born at Deptford on 30 May 1879. His parents, Walter and Elizabeth, were not rich – his father worked as a manufacturing hand at Woolwich Arsenal – and young Colin was sent to Alverton Street School in Deptford. He left school as soon as he could, and joined his father as an engineer at Woolwich Arsenal. Blythe was never a strong man, suffering from a form of epilepsy throughout his life, but he had two great loves in his life, cricket and music. He was a fine violinist, who played semi-professionally in orchestras when cricket permitted, but his tendency to fits meant that he often had to miss a number of matches. His cricket career, wonderful though it was, might have been even more successful had it not been for his debilitating medical condition.

He was discovered by Captain McCanlis in 1897, at the Rectory Field in Blackheath, where Blythe had gone to watch Kent play Somerset. While there, he asked if he could bowl in the nets at Walter Wright, the fast-medium opening bowler for Kent, which he did, in his ordinary shoes and working clothes. Both McCanlis and Wright liked what they saw and as a result of this little spell, he was invited to come to Tonbridge to join the newly established nursery. It was a major decision for Blythe to give up his job at Woolwich Arsenal, but he loved cricket more than munitions, and he took the risk. In 1898 he played his first game for the second XI, against Sussex second XI at Hove. He took 1 for 28 in 14 overs, and batted at number 11, and then did not play for the seconds again until the equivalent game in 1899. This time he took 1 for 60 in 18 overs, nothing to get too excited about, but just a couple of weeks later, he made his first-class debut for Kent against Yorkshire at Tonbridge. He was an instant success, clean-bowling the Yorkshire batsman Frank Mitchell with the first ball he bowled, but that was almost the extent of his success in the game. He also clean-bowled the Yorkshire wicketkeeper David Hunter with the last ball he bowled in the game, but 2 for 66, and a duck when he batted, was not particularly good. Blythe is one of only three Kent bowlers to have taken a wicket with the first ball they bowled in first-class cricket, the others being the far less renowned George McCanlis, younger brother of Captain William who discovered Blythe, and Gerald Hough, who never took another wicket after that first-ball success against Essex in 1919.

Kent won Blythe's first game by eight wickets, and Blythe was persevered with, playing in each of the final four county games of the season. In each of these games, he was one of only three professionals, Huish and Alec Hearne being the other two, alongside eight amateurs. Against Surrey at Blackheath, where two years earlier he had been a mere spectator, he took six wickets in the match for 39 runs, and although the game was badly rain-affected and thus drawn, Blythe was beginning to show how deadly he could be when the wicket suited him. He ended the season with 14 wickets for 310 runs, and *Wisden* commented that 'the pressing need of Kent is new professional bowling', especially slow bowling. 'Blythe may, of course, develop into the man required, but he has not yet done enough to justify one in predicting a great future for him.'

In 1900, Blythe took exactly 100 more wickets than in 1899. *Wisden* was now able to be more effusive about Kent's young left-arm spinner. 'His brilliant form came as quite a surprise to the general body of cricketers. Probably those who knew his skill were prepared for what he did, but to outsiders he was a revelation.' His easy action, which is so well caught by Chevallier Tayler in his painting, meant that he could bowl for hours without tiring, and although his natural finger-spinning action tended to take the ball away from the right-handed batsman, it was the ball that went straight on with the arm that caused the most difficulty and captured many of his wickets. He was already being compared with James Wootton, the slow left-armer of the 1880s, who took over 500 wickets for the county and set the standard for Kent's professional spinners.

Over the winter of 1900/01, Blythe was seriously ill, and as a result was not as strong in 1901 as he had been the year before. As the season wore on, he regained his strength, but although he bowled more overs, over 800, than any other Kent bowler, his tally of wickets dropped to 93, the only English season in his career in which he did not take at least 100 wickets. He was, however, chosen to tour Australia that winter with Archie MacLaren's MCC team, and he played for England for the first time. In the first Test, at Sydney, which England won by an innings, Blythe not only took seven wickets for 56, but also equalled his highest first-class score to date, 20. The next four Tests, however, were lost, and Blythe, who had been hampered by a finger injury for much of the tour, returned to England with a reputation that was neither diminished nor enhanced. Among those with him on the tour was J.T. Tyldesley, his eternal opponent in Chevallier Tayler's painting.

Back in England in 1902, Blythe was back to his best form, although he was not picked for any of the Tests against the touring Australians, Rhodes of Yorkshire being preferred. He took his first eight-wicket haul, 8 for 42 against Somerset at Maidstone, and finished the season with 127 wickets. In 1903, he improved yet further, taking 142 wickets during the summer and achieving his first nine-wicket analysis, 9 for 67 against Essex in the first game of Canterbury Week. As a result of his bowling that summer, *Wisden* chose him as one of their Five Cricketers Of The Year, noting that as far as Kent were concerned, 'for the large majority of their victories, the team were indebted to this young cricketer'. Slightly grudgingly, *Wisden* pointed out that like all spinners, he was at his best when the wicket was affected by rain, but they also paid him the great compliment of quoting Ranjitsinhji's opinion that he was more difficult to play than Wilfred Rhodes. They finished off his tribute with the view that 'he is a bowler pure and simple, his batting counting for little or nothing'.

Blythe had a successful tour of South Africa in the winter of 1905/06, but back in England, 1906 was his least prolific season of all, with only 111 wickets to his name. This was largely because he was forced to miss four county games from mid-June to mid-July when he opened a cut on his hand while fielding against Hampshire at Tonbridge, and the injury proved slow to heal. But he was back in harness well in time for Canterbury Week. His first game after his hand had healed was against the West Indian touring side at Catford, a match considered first-class but against such poor opposition that Lord Harris, then in his mid-fifties, ventured a comeback and scored 33. Blythe, who was born nine years after Lord Harris had first played for Kent, took seven wickets for 86 in the West Indians' first innings, and finished with ten wickets in the match, which Kent won by an innings. The rest of the summer was an enjoyable march to glory for Blythe and all his teammates.

In 1907, Blythe achieved his best analysis, 10 for 30 against Northamptonshire at Northampton. It was an astonishing game, as rain took out half of the first day and all of the second, but still Kent forced a win. After Kent had made 254 all out in their first innings, thanks to fifties by Wally Hardinge and Ken Hutchings, Blythe came into his own. Bowling unchanged throughout the two innings, he finished the game with 17 wickets for 48 runs, all taken in one day. At one stage in their first innings, Northamptonshire had lost seven wickets with just four runs on the board, and two of them were leg byes. Thanks to some lusty hitting from Northamptonshire's number nine, George Vials, who made 33 not out, the home side limped to 60 all out. Following on, Vials opened the batting (having presumably not taken off his pads) but was dismissed by Bill Fairservice for a single. Blythe then scythed through the rest of the side, taking 7 for 18 in 15.1 overs. Northamptonshire were all out for 39 and Kent won by an innings and 155 runs. In all cricket, only Jim Laker, with 19 wickets for 90 runs in the Old Trafford Test against Australia in 1956, has achieved better match figures than Blythe's, and only Hedley Verity and Tom Goddard have equalled his feat of taking 17 wickets in a day.

1907 was the first of four hugely prolific seasons for Blythe. Before the season began, he married Miss Gertie Brown at the registry office in Tonbridge on 11 March, and perhaps spurred on by the contentment of a settled home life, took 183 wickets that year, 197 in 1908, 215 in 1909 and 175 in 1910. He took a further 91 wickets on overseas tours in the winters of 1907/08 and 1909/10, a total of 861 wickets in four years. Kent, needless to say, benefited hugely from his success, and took the title in 1909 and 1910. Not that he really slowed down in the years up to the war – he took 653 wickets in the final four years of his career. But more than the number of wickets he took was the style in which he took them, in which he played cricket and conducted every aspect of his life. He was every boy's hero. As *Vanity Fair* wrote of him in 1910, 'Every schoolboy knows something of Blythe, and treasures it up with the diligent care all too soon to be transferred to politics or petticoats. Every youngster worth his salt can tell you that Blythe was an engineer at Woolwich Arsenal, can tell of his South African and Australian trips, of his slow left-hand teasers, of his spasmodic unreliability as a batsman, and his present position as third in the list of bowling averages.'

Blythe's career ran in parallel with that of Wilfred Rhodes of Yorkshire, who was generally considered to be at least Blythe's equal as a left-arm spinner, and was certainly a much better batsman, and this unfortunate coincidence, alongside Blythe's continuing health issues, limited his Test appearances. Rhodes, who made his first appearance for Yorkshire one year before Blythe, in 1898, and continued playing into his fifties in 1930, took more wickets than anybody else in the history of the game, but at an average very similar to Blythe's, both men averaging under 17 runs per wicket. Not that Rhodes had it all his own way. The newspaper report of Blythe's marriage in 1907 pointed out that 'since the arm of Rhodes lost its cunning, Blythe has had no equal as a left-handed bowler'. *Wisden* noted that the Yorkshireman's 'continued advance as a batsman did not compensate for his marked decline as a bowler'. Indeed, the

England selectors (of whom Cloudesley Marsham was now one) picked Blythe over Rhodes for the matches against South Africa in 1907, and were rewarded by Blythe's 26 wickets at ten runs each in just three games. In the second Test that summer, he took 8 for 59 and 7 for 40, the first time anybody had ever taken 15 wickets in a Test in England.

Jack Hobbs, writing in *The Cricketer* in 1925, said that 'what I think many people did not realise was that Blythe could not only spin and swing the ball, but was remarkably clever in flighting it, and to this I ascribe the fact that the Kent slow bowler was almost equally effective, compared with other bowlers, on a good hard wicket. On soft wickets he was sometimes unplayable.' The article was entitled *Bowlers I Dreaded Facing*. Jack Hobbs, the most prolific batsman in cricket history, put Charlie Blythe at the top of his list.

It will always be one of cricket's what ifs?, wondering how Blythe would have bowled had he survived the war. He would have been 40 in 1919, and had already stated that he would not play on after the war, but instead take a coaching post at Eton College. However, he could easily have changed his mind and the prospect of him bowling in tandem with the only man to have taken more wickets for Kent than him, Percy 'Tich' Freeman, would have been mouth-watering. They did play together a handful of times in 1914: in Freeman's first ever championship match, against Surrey, Blythe took 9 for 97 in Surrey's first innings, while Freeman remained wicketless. In Freeman's next match, at Edgbaston, he claimed the first of his 348 five-wicket hauls, while Blythe had to make do with 2 for 4 in 8.1 overs! In their seven games together, Blythe took a total of 38 wickets at precisely 15 apiece, while Freeman took 28 at 24.57 each. With

Woolley in the attack as well, Kent's record in the 1920s might have been very different if that shell had not exploded next to Charlie Blythe in November 1917.

Blythe, aged 35 and an epileptic, did not have to volunteer for service in the Great War, but although it took him several attempts to persuade the army he was fit for service, he joined the Kent Fortress Engineers, along with his great friend Claud Woolley, Frank's brother, before the end of 1914. In late 1917, they were posted to France, shortly after Blythe had played his last game of organised cricket, aptly at Lord's, for the Army and Navy against an Australian and South African side on 18 August. Remarkably, although *Wisden* noted that Blythe 'was not really well enough to play', he was still deemed well enough to go to fight at Passchendaele. On 8 November 1917, while working one evening on the front line, a shell landed behind the British lines and Sergeant Blythe and two others were killed instantly. Claud Woolley was injured, but survived.

The death of Charlie Blythe caused an outpouring of sadness and regret, and not just among the cricket fraternity. 'His personal qualities were such that he was universally popular,' noted the *Kent & Sussex Courier*, an understatement about a sweet-natured cricketer, loved by his fellow cricketers, whether teammates or opponents, and by all who came to see him play. His success, both on the cricket field and as a man, according to one of his obituarists, lay 'to a large degree in what schoolboys would call "cheek". Such sangfroid as his has rarely been equalled.' He went on to write that 'we shall all miss that perky, thin figure, with the cap cocked on one side of its head, and all with a soul for cricket will miss even more the sight of him having a duel with some great batsmen'. He was generally considered the most exciting bowler of his age to watch, imaginative, full of variations and never afraid to take on the big hitters. And now he was gone.

At a meeting of the General Committee of Kent CCC on 12 December 1917, a resolution was passed to create a permanent memorial to Blythe, and in August 1919 a Memorial Fountain was unveiled at the St Lawrence Ground, erected to the memory of Blythe and other Kent cricketers who died in the Great War. Lord George Hamilton, the 1919 president of Kent, said of Blythe at the dedication ceremony that 'although fragile in physique, he had the heart and head of a lion'. A quarter of a century later the names of those who fell in the Second World War were added, and it still stands at the ground today, having been restored and repositioned in time for the centenary of Blythe's death. Each year, on 8 November, a ceremony is held at the memorial, where wreaths are laid by the president and captain of the county club, as well as by representatives of the local regiment. The inscription is simple:

> To the memory of Colin Blythe of the Kent Eleven, who volunteered for active service upon the outbreak of hostilities in the Great War of 1914–18, and was killed at Ypres on the 8th Nov 1917, aged 38. He was unsurpassed among the famous bowlers of the period and beloved by his fellow cricketers.

The Fast Bowler

When people first see Chevallier Tayler's painting, they look at the little brass nameplates on the bottom of the frame, to see which cricketer is which. It comes as a surprise to some to discover that although somebody took the trouble to name ten of the Kent players, the final one is just listed as 'a fielder'. Surely the artist knew who he was painting? Yes, he did. 'A fielder' was really a bowler. Arthur Fielder, crouching at the edge of the shadow at silly point, was the man who bore the brunt of Kent's bowling, alongside Charlie Blythe. Two more different characters, and bowlers, it would be hard to find. Arthur Fielder was born at Plaxtol, a little village not far from Sevenoaks where there is still a thriving cricket club, on 19 July 1877. His father was a bailiff on a nearby hop farm, and as soon as he was able, young Arthur was taken on as a farmhand, which is possibly how he acquired his nickname (they all had rather more imaginative nicknames than the cricketers of today) 'Pip'. Always a keen sportsman, with a special talent for cricket, he was spotted by Captain McCanlis and taken on as a young professional at the Tonbridge Nursery from 1897. He did not play for Kent's first team until 1900, and then only in one match, against Essex at Leyton. As debuts go, it was spectacularly undistinguished: in a drawn match, Fielder took no wickets for 40 runs in the one innings he bowled, and was clean bowled for a duck when he batted.

His next chance did not come for a further two years, when he played for Kent against MCC at Lord's. If his first match had been unimpressive, his second was even more so. In Kent's first innings, he was listed as 'absent hurt', and although he made a gallant 0 not out in the second innings, he was unable to bowl throughout the game, and Kent lost by one wicket. Things could quite clearly only improve from here, and in 1903 they did. Having waited three seasons for his first wicket, he took 70 in 1903 and bowled with such fire that he was chosen to go with Pelham Warner's team to Australia in the winter. He replaced Walter Bradley in the Kent 11, Bradley being one of that rare breed, an amateur fast bowler, but Kent hardly noticed the absence of a man who had taken 536 wickets for Kent in nine seasons. Fielder was a genuinely fast bowler in his prime, coming in tirelessly off a long run, and able to deceive even the best batsmen with his away swing.

In 1903, he played 18 matches, of which 14 were in the championship. For Kent he bowled over 400 overs, the second most used bowler of the summer, although the busiest, Blythe, bowled over twice as many. It was not until 1904, when he played 22 matches and took 98 wickets, that it became clear that he and Blythe, with help from Mason, Fairservice and the ageing Alec Hearne, would have to be the backbone of Kent's bowling attack. Fielder was by far the quickest of all these bowlers, but his workload was second only to Blythe's. All things considered, he remained remarkably fit throughout his career, which was brought to an end by the war, and although his final tally of 1,150 wickets for Kent was dwarfed by those of Blythe (2,210) and Woolley (1,680), Fielder still holds the record as the fast bowler with most wickets for the county, and would still get into many people's all-time Kent XI as one of the opening bowlers.

Fielder's tour of Australia in 1903/04 was not a success. He played in two Test matches, but took only one wicket, that of Clem Hill in the third Test at Adelaide. Bizarrely, he was picked for the second Test, having been left out of the first, and batted at number 11, but did not bowl at all in the game. He was not picked for the fourth or fifth Tests. In 1904, back in England, he put his disappointing winter behind him and bowled his heart out for Kent. *Wisden* was complimentary in its usual backhanded way. 'Fielder … did a lot of good work on the hard wickets, and without being in any sense a great fast bowler, was often effective.' It would take the little yellow book another couple of years to revise its opinion. In 1905, *Wisden* looked to have made a correct judgement: Fielder was left out of almost half the county games and took only 44 wickets for the county, at a cost of over 32 runs apiece. Furthermore, he retained his position at the bottom of the batting averages, an even less effective batsman than Huish or Blythe. According to his captain, he was handicapped by a weak leg that summer. He had his moments – eight wickets in an easy victory against Hampshire, and 7 for 89 against Gloucestershire at Catford – but there were too few of these, and ever more frequently Blythe would open the bowling with Bill Fairservice, although even *Wisden* admitted that there was nobody who could bowl in partnership with Blythe as well as Arthur Fielder.

It was, therefore, something of a shock when Fielder played as well as he did in 1906. This was not just a return to his old form, it was a major advance on anything he had achieved up to that date. Although Blythe was the leading wicket-taker for the county in their championship season, and although the arrival of Woolley as a regular member of the eleven took a great deal of pressure off the two leading bowlers, it was probably the huge step change in Fielder's penetrative bowling that made the significant difference. His weak leg was obviously weak no more. Most of the Kent eleven portrayed by Chevallier Tayler had a wonderful season in 1906, and for many it was their best ever year, and the coincidence of 11 players at their peak meant that Kent were nigh on unbeatable, but Fielder's year was brilliant by any standards. He took 186 wickets in all matches, including 18 five-wicket hauls, and on six occasions he took ten wickets or more in a match. For the players against the Gentlemen he took all ten wickets in an innings, the only time this feat was ever achieved in these games, which were 100 years old in the year he did it. Given that more often than not, it was Charlie Blythe bowling at the other end, a man who himself had ten five-wicket hauls that summer, and four times took ten in a match, Fielder's statistics look all the more impressive. Finally, *Wisden* agreed, picking him as one of their Five Cricketers in the 1907 edition.

In 1907, Fielder's superb form continued as he approached his thirties. He took 172 wickets in all games, at an average of 16.12, the best season's average he ever achieved. In the course of the summer, he bowled 977.2 overs, a huge workload for a fast bowler, but it earned him a second trip to Australia. This time, he was far more successful, playing in four of the Tests and taking 25 wickets. Blythe, who was also on this tour, was left out of four of the Tests, but the irascible S.F. Barnes, Crawford of Surrey and Fielder bore the brunt of the bowling in a losing cause. England lost four of the five Tests that winter, but the one that ended in victory, the second Test at Melbourne, was a personal triumph for two Kent players, Hutchings and Fielder. Largely because of Hutchings's first innings century, England were left needing 282 to win, but wickets tumbled so that when Arthur Fielder came in at number 11, to join Sydney Barnes, England still needed 39 to win. It was a foregone conclusion that Australia would wrap up victory in a matter of balls, but the two bowlers kept their batting heads, and managed to hold on for a one-wicket victory. With the scores level, the pair went for a very risky run, but Hazlitt's throw from cover missed the stumps and England, and Barnes and Fielder were home. It could be argued (and was) that this was by no means the strongest team England could have sent to Australia, but all Fielder and all the rest of the touring party could do was to try to grab the opportunities presented. For Fielder, it was not quite enough. When the Test teams for the series against South Africa in 1907 were picked, Neville Knox of Surrey and Ted Arnold of Worcestershire were preferred.

If Fielder was a poor batsman, which he was, he nevertheless enjoyed one more moment of batting glory in 1909. Against Worcestershire at Stourbridge in July, it was with one hour left to play on the second day that Fielder strode to the wicket, last man in. Kent were on 320 for 9, facing a Worcestershire first innings total of 360. Fortunately for Fielder, the man at the other end was Frank Woolley, who was enjoying a great season which would culminate in his first Test appearance for England. Kent, who had begun the season rather badly, needed every victory they could muster if they were to regain the championship after three years, and Fielder, who had not been fully fit for much of the season, needed to show his worth to the side. By the close of play on that second day, Kent had moved to 439 for 9, with Fielder on 67 not out, the highest score of his career. He had scored these runs out of 119 added by the last-wicket pair in that last hour of the day, while Woolley at the other end closed the day on 136 not out. The next morning, the pair continued with equal vigour, adding a further 116 runs in the first 80 minutes of the day. When Woolley was finally out for 185, the highest score of his career to that time, Fielder was left not out on 112, the only time in his life that he ever scored a hundred. The pair had put on 235 for the last wicket, still a last wicket partnership record for the County Championship over a century later. This gave Kent a lead of 195 runs, and although Fielder was given no time for a breather after his batting efforts, he (3 for 67 in 25 overs) and the rather more rested Blythe (7 for 44 in 24.5 overs) bowled Kent to an innings victory. Six weeks later, they were crowned county champions again.

In 1911, Fielder was granted a benefit, choosing the Canterbury Week match against Lancashire, no doubt hoping for a repeat of the 1906 game. Unfortunately, the result was very different, with the visitors winning by nine wickets, but at least Fielder made a few runs and took four wickets, and more to the point, collected a total of £1,174/10/3d from the Canterbury Week crowds. 1912 was a very poor season for Fielder. Kent had an excess of injuries and unavailability to contend with, and very few of the amateur batsmen on whom Kent had relied for so many seasons were able to play regularly. Fielder, although available all summer, was in such poor form that he was dropped from the side. In 14 matches for Kent, he took only 28 wickets at an average of 35.75. He must have feared that at the age of 35, his cricket career was finished, but in 1913 he came back strongly, taking 116 wickets at an average below 20, playing his part in Kent winning their fourth title in eight years. The editor of *Wisden*, who had never been numbered among Fielder's strongest supporters, conceded that for a man who 'seemed in 1912 to have come to the end of his career as a fast bowler', he came back in 1913 'in such a surprising way that in county matches alone he took 105 wickets. He was not quite so fast as in his early days, but he bowled very finely in many matches, keeping the ball on or outside the off stump with remarkable accuracy.' He went on to say that 'without a good fast bowler, Kent would have had no chance of winning the championship'.

In 1914, Fielder bowled well, if not as incisively as in 1913, and at the age of 37, he was no doubt thinking of retirement. But the war came along and made up his mind for him. When cricket began again in 1919, he had retired. He lived on for 30 more years, dying in 1949 shortly after his 72nd birthday. There is a story of him in hospital, seriously ill and not long before the end of his life, nevertheless being thrilled to learn that the man in the next bed recognised him and had seen him bowl in his prime. Fielder's last few days on Earth were spent having long chats about cricket. He was a man of immense charm, and fairly immense girth, and if not the very fastest of bowlers, his speed was enough, as one of his obituaries noted, to make every wicketkeeper stand well back to him. As *The Times* wrote of him in 1909, 'On his day – generally a hot day, when the muscles are most elastic and the bowler, like the sprinter, gets more pace out of himself – [Fielder] is little, if at all inferior to Richardson in his prime. His fault is that he takes too long a run, which is a waste of energy.' To be compared to the great Tom Richardson was a compliment indeed, even if he did take too long a run.

Kent, in winning four championship titles in eight years, were lucky enough to have a strong group of players who did not change very much over the years. This core of talent, created to a great extent by Captain McCanlis and his Tonbridge Nursery, but topped off with a pool of remarkable amateur batting talent, created a sense of unity and team spirit over the period which gave the county a head start over many of their rivals. Six of the players who feature in Chevallier Tayler's painting played for the county in every championship year – Blythe, Dillon, Fielder, Huish, Humphreys and Seymour – and six more who are not in the painting also played at least one game for Kent each championship year. They are the amateur brothers Arthur and Sammy Day, and the professionals Bill Fairservice, Wally Hardinge, Jack Hubble and Frank Woolley. All six of these men feature on the supplementary banner created by Chevallier Tayler, along with Dillon and Hutchings, who are in the main painting too, and Alec Hearne, perhaps the best of Kent's all-rounders before the arrival of Frank Woolley, the man who effectively took his place in the team in 1906.

* * * *

The painting does not feature only the 11 Kent players: there are two Lancashire batsmen and an umpire whose portraits are just as much an integral part of the picture.

The Record Breaker

The batsman facing up to Blythe in Tayler's painting, showing none of his face but much of his backside, is J.T. Tyldesley. John Thomas Tyldesley was born at Worsley in Lancashire on 22 November 1873. He made his debut for Lancashire in 1895, and in his second game for the county, against Warwickshire at Edgbaston, scored 152 not out. The cricket cognoscenti picked him out straight away as somebody to watch, and although he did little else of note that summer, nor in 1896, he made his breakthrough in 1897 and confirmed his place in the Lancashire side with over 1,000 runs in a season for the first time, and three centuries, which were scored in successive innings. He then scored over 1,000 runs in every season up to the First World War, and, for good measure, in 1919 too, when he was 45 years old. Four times he scored over 2,000 runs in a season and in 1901 his total was 3,041, with nine centuries at an average of over 55. He played 31 times for England between 1898/99 and 1909, scoring four hundreds for his country, but his Test career was not as successful as his county figures would have suggested. In Tests he averaged 30.75, and in all cricket he scored 37,897 runs at an average of 40.66.

Tyldesley was a professional batsman, and the professionals were meant to be the less exciting ones to watch, dourly compiling scores to give the team an advantage, while the amateur batsmen, with their bright array of caps and blazers, played with flashing blades and a devil-may-care attitude to the bowling, the match conditions and their average. Tyldesley was by no means a devil-may-care batsman, but he was extraordinarily quick on his feet, and had an imaginative solution to most of the problems that bowlers put before him. He also had a very sound defence but rarely got bogged down by any bowler of any style. Neville Cardus, the writer who created legends when reality would not do, was a Lancashire man through and through, and he wrote that 'an innings by Tyldesley, though moving on wings and enrapturing the senses, was always attending to the utilitarian job of building the Lancashire nest'. But Cardus also wrote that Tyldesley once said to him that 'you couldn't play dull or crude cricket with Mr Spooner or Mr MacLaren at the other end'. Blythe was a man he liked to attack, sometimes with great success, and sometimes it was the bowler's turn.

Having scored over 3,000 runs in 1901, he was an obvious choice as a Cricketer Of The Year by *Wisden*, who said that he 'had a glorious season, and far surpassed everything he had done before'. They described his batting as 'brilliant as ever', but also noted that he could 'when the occasion demanded, play a steady, careful game with the utmost success'. The perfect professional batsman, in other words. Not a particularly tall man, he was known for his off side strokes, his cuts and his cover drives, but was also a fine hooker. He barely ever bowled (he took just three wickets in his long career) but was regarded as one of the country's top outfielders, with a strong throwing arm and a safe pair of hands. Three thousand runs on any wickets would have been remarkable, but to achieve this milestone when half of his innings were played at Old Trafford, often in uncertain weather and on pitches which were generally acknowledged to be among the poorest in England at the time, was a special achievement.

1906 was a summer of great personal success for Tyldesley, and Kent were one of his main victims. Tyldesley had first played against Kent in 1896, and in the match at Canterbury had scored 51 in partnership with Archie MacLaren, whose unbeaten double century helped Lancashire save the game. In subsequent games against Kent, he scored a couple of hundreds and several fifties and was averaging 56 in 19 games against them before the 1906 game at Canterbury. His big innings against them came on 7 June at Old Trafford, when he hit 295 not out, out of a Lancashire total of 531, made in five hours and 20 minutes. It was by no means a chanceless innings, with five catches going down from Tyldesley's bat alone, but he hit brilliantly and thoroughly destroyed the Kent attack, which was lacking the injured Blythe. Frank Woolley, whose first-class debut this was, dropped him twice, and told the story of how by the end of the innings, the Kent side wanted to see him reach his triple century. When the ninth wicket fell and the wicketkeeper Worsley (career batting average 6.03) strode to the middle, Tyldesley was on 290 and there was an on-field debate about how to avoid getting Worsley out until the 300 was reached. The solution, when five runs later it was seen that Worsley was going to have to face a complete over, was to put on Punter Humphreys, who at that point had taken no wickets for 101 runs in 19 overs. With strict instructions to bowl well outside off stump, Humphreys completed five balls successfully, but the sixth ball defied all predictions and swung in sharply to take

Worsley's leg stump. Tyldesley was thus left on 295 not out, the highest score of his career and still the highest score made against Kent in a championship match. Kent are the only county never to have conceded a triple century in a county game, a record that was so nearly given away in 1906. W.G. Grace – who else? – scored 344 against Kent when playing for MCC in 1876, but that is the only triple hundred that Kent's bowlers have ever conceded. No county or touring team player has ever reached 300 against Kent.

Lancashire went on to win that match by ten wickets, and so Kent were desperate for revenge in the return match during Canterbury Week. This was the seventh time in 11 years that Lancashire had been one of Kent's opponents during the Week, and Kent had never, since the start of the County Championship in 1890, beaten Lancashire at Canterbury. The six previous games had resulted in four draws and two losses for Kent, and it was time for the tables to be turned. Restricting Tyldesley, a player for whom Kent had the utmost respect and much affection, to just 19 and 4 was a major factor in Kent's win. It is possible that the batsman was affected by the previous game, against Yorkshire at Old Trafford over the August Bank Holiday weekend, which he had been given as his benefit. The match, which was rain-affected, resulted in a win for Yorkshire, and although Tyldesley scored more runs than any of his teammates in the game, the efforts involved in promoting his benefit – which raised over £3,000, a huge amount for the time – may have carried over into the Canterbury game.

Tyldesley played on after the war, for one season. He did well, hitting 272 against Derbyshire at Chesterfield among other big scores, but at the end of the season he retired. By that time, not only his brother Ernest, 15 years his junior, was playing for Lancashire and would go on to eclipse even his elder brother's statistics, but also his namesakes, the brothers Dick and James Tyldesley – no relation to John and Ernest – were in the Lancashire side. Against Derbyshire in 1919, they batted at numbers 3, 4, 5 and 8. Dick and James's other brothers, William and Harry, were not playing in that game, although in the 1914 season, all the Tyldesleys apart from Dick, who made his debut after the war, played for the county. There were never more than four Tyldesleys in any one Lancashire side, although that total was achieved at least a dozen times between 1914 and 1922.

Johnny Tyldesley did not have a long and peaceful retirement. He took up coaching and was much respected in his native Lancashire, working with the county team until the end of the 1930 season, when health issues forced him to retire. However, as he was getting ready to go out of his house in Salford in November that year, just five days after his 57th birthday, he collapsed and died, presumably from a heart attack. Pelham Warner described him as 'a rare fellow' and 'always welcome in any side because of his pleasant personality'.

The Imposter

Billy Findlay, the fresh-faced batsman backing up at the bowler's end, was not really there. As we have seen, his presence was a matter of artistic licence combined with Harry Makepeace's refusal to come to London and Chevallier Tayler's reluctance to go to Liverpool. Little did Billy Findlay realise that immortality would come his way because of a little logistical difficulty. William Findlay was born in Liverpool on 22 June 1880, and was sent to Eton College in 1893. He captained the Eton XI in his final year there, and went up to Oriel College, Oxford, where he gained his blue in three years from 1901. In 1901, the two Oxford openers were Slug Marsham and Ted Dillon, while playing for Cambridge were Dick Blaker and Sammy Day, and the five men all played again in the corresponding fixture the next year. The connections that played such a big part in amateur sport in late Victorian and Edwardian days were much in evidence. Findlay was secretary of Oxford University Cricket Club in 1902, and captain in 1903. In 1902 his captain was his old school friend Slug Marsham, and their lasting friendship which began at Eton was no doubt a factor in Findlay's decision to sit for Chevallier Tayler to allow the painting to be completed. In 1902, also, having played a handful of games for Lancashire after the end of Oxford's term, he was chosen to play for the Gentlemen against the Players at the Scarborough Festival, and there he played with Pinky Burnup, and incidentally against Johnny Tyldesley, further strengthening his links with the Kent players in the 1906 fixture in which he did not play.

The truth of the matter was that Findlay was not quite good enough as a cricketer. He played a total of 88 first-class matches, and was given all sorts of opportunities to show his skills, for Oxford, for MCC, for the Gentlemen and even for the Rest against the Champion County in 1902, but he finished with a batting average of under 20 and no centuries to his name. As a wicketkeeper, he took 138 catches and made 28 stumpings, respectable but not outstanding figures. 1906 was probably his best season: he played 21 matches, 19 of them in the championship, scored four fifties and finished with a batting average of 22, 17 runs better than the other keeper used by Lancashire, William Worsley. On top of that he dismissed 45 batsmen, his best tally for a season. We do not at this distance know why he was not available to play for Lancashire at Canterbury – he played in their previous match, Tyldesley's benefit match against Yorkshire, and in the match that followed their Canterbury defeat, against Sussex at Hove. All we can say in Chevallier Tayler's defence, and Lord Harris's for that matter, is that he should have been playing.

Early in 1907, he moved south, to take up the position of secretary to Surrey County Cricket Club at the Oval, following the death of Charles Alcock, who had been running things at the Oval since 1872. These were very large boots to fill, as the Old Harrovian Alcock virtually invented organised team sport in England in the latter part of the 19th century. Football was probably his first love, and he was secretary to the Football Association from 1870 to 1895, as well as proposing and organising the first FA Cup competition, which was won in the first FA Cup Final at Kennington Oval by The Wanderers, captained by Alcock. He also organised the first football international match, between England and Scotland in 1872, although he was injured at the time and thus did not play. In 1880, he organised the first ever Test match in England, again at Kennington Oval against Australia, and in his time at the helm of both football and cricket revolutionised both sports and encouraged other entrepreneurial sports lovers to do the same for other games. Findlay, a man 'of great charm with beautiful manners and a lovely and gentle nature', according to Pelham Warner, had to pick up the reins, obviously with no guidance from his now deceased predecessor, but he was extremely competent as an administrator and thus was immediately both popular and successful.

His appointment in the first place was something of a surprise. He was not on the short list of candidates which was given in the Surrey CCC committee meeting minutes at the time, although his name seems to have been pencilled in a little later. It seems he owed his appointment largely to Lord Harris, the man with fingers in every cricketing pie. Sir Henry Leveson-Gower, known to all as 'Shrimp', was a power in Surrey cricket for many years, and he wrote in his memoirs of remembering Harris telling him that 'your county would be very lucky indeed if a great friend of mine and yours, William Findlay, could be induced to take Alcock's place. He is one in a thousand. Don't forget I told you.'

His time at Surrey continued until 1920, when he moved to Lord's as assistant secretary to F.E. Lacey, later Sir Francis Lacey. In 1926 Sir Francis retired and Findlay took on the role of secretary of MCC, the top administrative job in cricket at the time. Findlay remained at Lord's for ten years, earning the somewhat condescending praise from Field Marshal Lord Plumer, president of MCC in 1929, that 'if Findlay had been a soldier, I should have liked to have had him on my staff'. During his time at Lord's, the Grandstand with the famous Father Time weather vane was constructed (it was replaced by the present Grandstand in 1996), and he had to cope with the Bodyline crisis of 1932/33, among many other issues of the day. Sir Pelham Warner, who served as deputy assistant secretary under Findlay at Lord's, said that he 'held all the threads in his hands, and the club were fortunate indeed to have so courteous and charming a man at the wheel'. In those days of empire, Findlay also knew, as Lord Harris did too, that cricket was a great asset in spreading British values around the globe. 'His charm of manner', said Warner, 'made him very popular with the members, the officials of the various counties, and with Dominion and Colonial visitors. He radiated a most pleasant atmosphere.'

Findlay had by this time moved to live in Kent, near Tenterden. He had married Eleanor Tylden of Milstead Manor, near Sittingbourne in 1907 – probably another reason for his move down south – and in 1937, on retiring from Lord's, he joined the Kent committee. He stayed on the committee until 1951, with a break of two years in 1946 and 1947, when he was president of Lancashire CCC. At one stage in those years he was reportedly a member of four county club committees, as well as being a trustee of MCC. A busy retirement indeed. He must have enjoyed coming into the pavilion at Canterbury and seeing his younger self from 30 or 40 years earlier portrayed in a painting of a match in which he had not taken part. Or perhaps he felt guilty at having been the unwitting cause of Harry Makepeace missing out on lasting renown. In 1951, he stepped down from the Kent committee after being appointed president of MCC, and if he had lived, would surely have been president of Kent CCC as well. He did take on the role, from 1946 until his death, of fourth Chief of the Band of Brothers, the Kent cricket club whose original members had also been at the heart of the establishment of Canterbury Week in the 1840s. All in all, looking back on his career after he stopped playing first-class cricket, he seems to have as much right as anybody else to be part of Kent v Lancashire 1906.

Findlay died in June 1953, of a heart attack after a long illness, at his home in Westwell, near Tenterden, three days before his 73rd birthday.

The Man In The White Coat

There is also an umpire in the painting, standing resplendent in his white coat and dark cap, holding Blythe's sweater and looking intently in the direction of the batsman. This is Alfred John

Atfield, who was born at Ightham, near Sevenoaks, on 3 March 1868. He was thus 38 years old when he stood in that Canterbury Week match, having had a very minor career as a first-class cricketer, firstly for Gloucestershire, for whom he played three matches in 1893. Atfield was a batsman, but not a particularly successful one at first-class level. A top score of 45 in a career of eight matches, finishing with an average of 12.45 is nothing to be particularly proud of, but this did not prevent him from being both a good coach and an excellent and highly respected umpire. As *The Star* newspaper pointed out in its sports pages in June 1920, 'The most competent umpires are not the greatest cricketers. To name a few: Archie White, Harry Bagshaw, Walter Richards, Jim Street, Alfred Atfield and W.A.J. West – none of these got above the ruck of ordinary cricketers, but they are top-notchers as umpires.' Atfield played plenty of minor cricket matches, mainly for his employer William Henry Laverton of Westbury, Wiltshire, who loved sports of all kinds and was keen to promote his own cricket ground as a first-class venue. He had the disadvantage of his county, Wiltshire, not being a first-class county, but between 1888 and 1908, around 70 good quality club matches were played at W.H. Laverton's Ground, as it was known, and Atfield played in at least 40 of them. Atfield was taken on to the MCC staff in 1901, and played a number of games for junior MCC sides, without ever making a breakthrough.

According to one report, his best innings, of 121 not out for Cross Arrows on the Nursery Ground at Lord's, came on the afternoon after he had got married at Hanover Square register office in the morning.

In the winter of 1897/98, when he was 29 years old, he first went to South Africa to coach, and played one game for

Natal while he was there. In 1900, he used his Gloucestershire connections to play one match for London County, led by W.G. Grace, at Edgbaston against Warwickshire. He batted at number ten, scoring 2 and 3, and did not bowl as Warwickshire came home easy winners, so it was a surprise when the next season he was chosen to play for MCC against London County at Crystal Palace, and invited to bowl for the first and only time in his first-class career. He bowled 28 overs, and among the three wickets he took was that of W.G. himself, but not until the great man had made 132. That was Atfield's final first-class game in England, although he did play once more in South Africa, for Transvaal in March 1907, seven months after having umpired at Canterbury.

Atfield began umpiring in first-class matches in England in 1902. Five of the seven first-class matches he umpired in before he was put on the official umpires' list in 1905 involved MCC, who thus had a chance of judging his abilities at close quarters. He established his reputation quickly, and became one of the busiest umpires on the circuit.

In 1909/10 and again in 1913/14, Atfield was in South Africa and stood as umpire in four Tests in each series. In the first series, in which England fared badly, Atfield would have stood once again with Charlie Blythe, and on the second tour, he would have had the best view of Sydney Barnes's amazing bowling, as the Staffordshire man took 49 wickets in only four Tests, and England gained full revenge for their poor showing on the previous tour. Even though Atfield never stood as umpire in Tests in England, he continued to umpire regularly until the late 1920s, when he was approaching his 60th birthday. His final first-class match as umpire was at Leyton, where Essex played and lost to Oxford University in June 1932. This was the match which began the day after Yorkshire beat Essex on the same ground, thanks to Percy Holmes and Herbert Sutcliffe putting on a world record 555 for the first wicket. Atfield was not umpiring that match, but he might have been watching.

There is an ironic footnote to Atfield's presence in the Tayler painting. In July 1923, Atfield was standing at square leg as umpire at Northampton in the county game against Lancashire, when he was unable to avoid a hard pull, which hit him on his side as he turned away and broke several of his ribs. The batsman who struck the ball was Lancashire's Harry Makepeace, the man who should have been standing next to him at the bowler's end in the Chevallier Tayler painting.

Alfred Atfield died on New Year's Day 1949, at his home in Caterham, aged 80.

The one other man who was standing on the playing area when Blythe bowled to Tyldesley on that clear August day was unlucky enough not to feature in the painting at all. He was Valentine Adolphus Titchmarsh, the splendidly named square leg umpire, who Tayler could not fit into his panorama. Titchmarsh was born on St Valentine's Day 1853, at Royston in Hertfordshire, making him 53 at the time of that Canterbury Week. He had been a minor cricketer, like Alfred Atfield, playing eight first-class games between 1880 and 1891, mainly for MCC, whose ground staff he had joined in 1885. In four of those games he played alongside W.G. Grace, but without much success. He was described in *Scores and Biographies* as 'an excellent batsman and a successful fast round-armed bowler, while in the field he takes no particular place'. Prophetic words, given that he was in the field but took no particular place in Tayler's painting. He played many Minor Counties matches for Hertfordshire between 1895 and 1897, and first stood as an umpire in a first-class game as early as 1882. Even when he was still playing for Hertfordshire, he was equally busy as an umpire, but it was not until he finished playing that his umpiring career reached its zenith. In 1898 he was umpiring at Blackheath, a match between Kent and Surrey, when Colin Blythe asked to have a bowl in the nets and a new star was discovered, but whether Titchmarsh noticed the slight lad bowling left-arm spin at the edge of the field is not recorded. In 1899 he umpired the first Test against Australia at Trent Bridge, a match that ended in a draw, with England definitely in the worse position when time was called. In all, Titchmarsh umpired in ten of the tourists' games that summer, so they must have thought he was a good umpire, at least. His next opportunity to umpire in a Test came with the second Test at Lord's in 1902, again against Australia, but this match was an almost complete washout, with England reaching 102 for 2 in their first innings before the weather intervened. In 1905 he umpired the third Test against Australia at Leeds, but again the match was drawn, but this time with England on top. Blythe and Tyldesley were both playing in this game.

1906 was his final season as an umpire, and the only time he umpired in Canterbury Week. He had umpired two games at the St Lawrence Ground in earlier seasons, but not in the Week, so perhaps it was a tribute to his umpiring skills that he was chosen to stand in both games, county cricket's social highlight of the summer, in his final season. Earlier in the year, the Whitsun weekend match between Middlesex and Somerset at Lord's had been set aside for Titchmarsh's benefit, a rare honour for an umpire but a mark of MCC's appreciation of his services over two decades. Unfortunately, although the sun shone and

George Beldam the photographer made a lot of runs, the match did not produce the financial result that Titchmarsh must have been hoping for. Just over a year later, at the age of 54, Valentine Adolphus Titchmarsh died, of what was described as locomotor ataxy, a disease of the nervous system which causes the sufferer to be unable to coordinate his movements and bodily functions, a key skill for an umpire. One of the commonest causes of this condition is tertiary syphilis.

These, then, were the men in the painting, and the one who wasn't.

What Happened Next

CANTERBURY Week 1906 had been the most successful one, on the field at least, in Kent's history. Never before had they won both matches in the Week by such crushing margins – in fact only twice before, in 1903, against Essex and Worcestershire, and in 1904 against Essex and Surrey, had they won both games in the Week, and very often they had come away from Canterbury smarting from two defeats. Both socially and financially, too, the Week had been successful, and when the season culminated in the County Championship for the first time, everybody at the club was understandably very content with how things had turned out.

But a year later, things were a little different. Kent had had a poor season on the field: as defending champions they should have finished higher in the table than eighth, and the symbol of the triumph of 1906, Chevallier Tayler's painting, was proving hard to make money from. The books recorded a loss on the work, despite the best efforts of Lord Harris and the entire committee to promote the sale of prints of the painting, and Tayler had no doubt by now resigned himself to the probability that there would be no more money coming to him as royalties on these sales. The extent to which this would have worried him is open to debate – most artists (and writers for that matter) work on the basis that the advance fee that has been agreed for the work will be all that he or she will earn from it, whatever the royalty clauses may be for sales over a certain amount. Anyway, this painting, although now considered Chevallier Tayler's masterpiece, was not as highly regarded at the time. As a private commission, it would not be shown in any major gallery, however much it was appreciated by cricket aficionados, and it was quite different from the mainstream of Tayler's work. For him, it was no doubt a pleasant diversion, a fairly well remunerated representation of his favourite pastime, but it is unlikely he ever considered that his reputation might hang on this one painting a century later.

People liked the painting, which was commonly known in those days as *The Kent County XI in the Field at Canterbury*. The name *Kent v Lancashire 1906* is something that has just evolved, probably because it is less of a mouthful than the original title. In an attempt to sell a few more prints of whatever you liked to call it, as well as in the spirit of showing the painting around the county, it was loaned to Blackheath Cricket Club for a few months in 1908. The club minutes record that 'a request had been received from Blackheath for the loan of the picture of the Kent Eleven of 1906 to be shown at a picture exhibition: also that MCC were willing to hang the picture in the pavilion at Lord's for a few months. These arrangements were approved.' It is not certain from when until when the picture was on show at Lord's, or indeed whether MCC ever did turn their willingness to hang the picture – quite probably prompted by Lord Harris – into reality, but it is certain that the painting was quickly gaining a reputation as a major work of cricket art.

Chevallier Tayler, largely on the basis of the excellent reception of his portraits of *The Empire's Cricketers* in 1905, was extremely busy with private commissions and creating new works for general exhibition. In 1906, he also completed a portrait of his friend E.W. Horning, the author and creator of Raffles, the gentleman thief and cricketer. Hornung and Tayler had played with and against each other several times on the cricket field, and were both equally obsessive cricket enthusiasts. From this time one can also note the change in Tayler's subject matter, away from his naturalist plein air works that he had devoted himself to in the first two decades of his professional life, and much more fully towards portraiture, which was probably a safer and more lucrative career for an artist, especially one who now had a wife and two sons to support. Among the eminent people he was asked to portray in the years before the First World War were Sir Thomas Stevenson, the toxicologist who was an expert witness in many notorious poisoning trials; Charles Wicksteed, an engineer and son of a notorious Unitarian minister who after the war turned his company into one specialising in playground equipment; Guglielmo Marconi, the radio pioneer; and John Howard, a Kent notable who was MP for North-East Kent from 1902 to 1908. Howard's portrait is today part of the Canterbury Museum collection.

The First World War was very cruel to the Chevallier Tayler family. Tayler's two sons, William and John, both died in the conflict, and both as the war was almost over. The younger son, Lieutenant John A. Chevallier Tayler RN RAF, was killed while flying in France on 7 August 1918, probably on a training flight, and was buried with full naval honours at Dunkirk. He was just 18 years and eight months old. His elder brother, Lieutenant William Ulric Chevallier Tayler of the West Kent Regiment, was wounded in France in 1917, but recovered to rejoin his regiment before the end of the hostilities. In 1918, he was taken prisoner, but when the war in Europe ended and he was liberated, he took up arms again. In 1919, he was attached to the Royal Engineers and sent out to eastern Russia to join the international force, known as the Entente, led by imperialist Russia, Britain and France, to fight on the side of the White Russian (anti-Bolshevik) forces in the civil war that broke out in Russia after the October Revolution. The whole operation, known as the North Russian Intervention, was not a success, partly because it was seriously underfunded and underequipped, and partly because the White Russian troops were corrupt and equally underequipped. On 10 August that year, 13 years to the day after Kent had been playing Lancashire at Canterbury, fierce fighting broke out along the River Dvina. This was a full four months after the Americans had decided to withdraw from this war, and at the same time as the British and French were planning their own withdrawal. In a letter dated 15 August 1919 to his mother, one officer described the scene. 'Lost my second in command in the attack. Awfully bad luck. He'd been wounded six times in France. I am the only officer in my company who hasn't been hit as I had one killed and one wounded in a raid a short time ago.' We cannot know for certain whether William Chevallier Tayler was the second in command mentioned, but the description and the dates fit. The official report of his death states that he was killed 'while gallantly leading his platoon into action in North Russia, on 10 August 1919'. He was 21 years old. On 11 August 1919, General Henry Rawlinson arrived in Murmansk to assume command of the British evacuation, one day too late for young William.

After the war, Tayler also painted portraits of both Admiral of the Fleet Earl Beatty and Field Marshal Earl Haig, which were unveiled in the Guildhall in London on 2 November 1920. He had some trouble in pinning Admiral Lord Beatty down for a sitting, and enlisted the help of Lord Harris to help him fix a date. There is a letter in Lord Harris's archive from Lord Beatty promising to write to 'your friend Mr Chevallier Tayler and say that I will do what I can to help him, but I am afraid … I am fully engaged for many weeks to come'. The fact that Tayler felt able to write to Lord Harris asking for this favour a dozen years after he had finished his Kent painting shows that there was a lasting bond of friendship between the two men. And in the end he got his man. Tayler insisted that £1 of the price of each print copy of these two portraits should be donated to a servicemen's charity, no doubt in memory of his two sons. He also created a triptych of three paintings as a memorial to the Dvina Relief Force, the unit which arrived just too late to save his son. Painting them was no doubt therapy for his loss in an age when therapy was almost entirely unknown.

Tayler, who had been a Roman Catholic for many years, turned more and more to religious themes and subjects in his final years, painting portraits of both Henry Southwell, the Anglican Bishop of Lewes, in 1922, and Cardinal Francis Bourne, Roman Catholic Archbishop of Westminster, in 1925. His subjects, if not directly connected with religion, tended to be very conservative and establishmentarian in his later years, but occasionally there would be reminders of the earlier lyricism in his painting.

Tayler died on 27 December 1925, at the comparatively young age of 63. As his obituary in *The Cornishman* noted, he had 'wonderful abilities in the portrayal of character'. It went on to say that 'there can be no doubt that he was always at his best on a crowded canvas. He above all preferred, and indeed concentrated on, figure painting, though he never dealt with the nude. There was a chastity, and in many cases a religious fervour in all his pictures that had to portray vice, which was most marked; and which surely few artists have shown better.' He was a prolific painter, and has left a large catalogue of paintings, which are now spread among many art galleries and private collections all around the world. The painting that he considered his best, or at least the one that gave him most satisfaction, was *The Last Blessing*, painted during his time at Newlyn and exhibited at the Paris Salon in 1891, where it won the gold medal. The painting was later bought by an art gallery in Buenos Aires, spreading the word of Tayler's artistic excellence across the globe. Other paintings are currently in galleries as far apart in distance and status as Folkestone and Tokyo, and many places in between. He was represented at the Royal Academy exhibitions for 40 years in succession, his final contribution being his portrait of Cardinal Bourne a few months before he died. Tayler warranted a brief obituary in *Wisden*, but it did not mention his great painting. It merely called him 'a well-known artist, he will be remembered by followers of the game on account of his series of drawings entitled *The Empire's Cricketers*, published in 1905'.

His great friend Stanhope Forbes wrote that 'Chevallier Tayler, besides his fine talent as an artist, possessed a character of extraordinary charm and a most delightful personality. His cheerful and bright disposition endeared him to all his confreres and sustained him in failing health, and through the trials of the Great War, in which he lost his two dear sons.' He was a good man buffeted by fate, but supported by his art and his friends. He will never rank among the great painters, but he was a very good one, and *Kent v Lancashire 1906* is a worthy memorial to his skill.

* * * *

As for the painting itself, apart from its brief foray to Blackheath, where the club failed to sell any significant number of prints, the painting spent most of its time on a wall in the pavilion at Canterbury. In May 1911, the Managing Committee of the club, still with stocks of the prints that they could not sell at the prices they had originally set, responded to an approach from Mr A.J. Baker, a member of a family closely connected to the club, by suggesting to him that 'the Committee would probably be able to let him have some copies of the picture The Kent Champion Eleven at 7/6d each'. This was well below the figure that earlier estimates of profitability had been based on, but beggars could not be choosers. How many copies were sold to Mr Baker is not recorded, but a month later, the same committee decided to make the remaining plain prints of the picture of the Kent Eleven of 1906 available to all at 7/6d each. But stocks remained, and reprints, which had been hoped for by Kent and by the artist, were no longer being thought of, and nor would they be for many years to come. Perhaps the problem was the size, because although the original painting is 7ft 6in wide and 3ft 9in tall (228.5cm x 114cm), and the prints are smaller, they are still about 4ft by 2ft in their frames, and that is a fairly large work of art to put up on a suburban wall. Not everyone owns a residence the size of Belmont House, the Harris home.

A year later, in June 1912, the Kent committee resolved 'to ask the advice of Mr Chevallier Tayler as to having the painting of the picture of the Eleven varnished'. It seems astonishing to imagine that the original painting had not been varnished, as varnishing an oil painting makes the colours much richer, and most artists would not consider their painting complete until it had been varnished. Possibly it needed to be cleaned and revarnished, although after only five years this would be unusual, unless it had been treated very roughly in the interim, which also seems very unlikely. What advice Mr Chevallier Tayler gave, and whether or not the painting was varnished, revarnished or cleaned is not recorded.

Lord Harris died in 1932. He had stepped down from the chairmanship of Kent CCC the previous year, yielding the position to his old friend William Patterson, who had captained Kent in the 1890s and who featured on Chevallier Tayler's panel portraits which accompanied the main painting. Patterson in turn held the chairmanship until he died in 1946. Lord Harris was very active, even into old age. In 1928, in his late seventies, he took part in an Old Stagers Canterbury Week production, and as one spectacularly obsequious reviewer noted, 'it was a great delight to his many admirers to see Lord Harris prove himself as great an actor off the field as he used to be on the field when he captained the Kent eleven. His charm of manner and self-confidence in his part, together with his natural actions and movements, were reminiscent of his great cricketing days.'

On his 80th birthday, in 1931, Lord Harris wrote his famous letter to *The Times*, in praise of cricket. This was not meant to be a valedictory letter – 'Cricket has been too good a friend to me for nearly seventy years for me to part with it one moment before I have to.' He then launched into an obviously sincere if somewhat stilted plea: 'You do well to love it, for it is more free from anything sordid, anything dishonourable, than any game in the world. To play it keenly, honourably, generously, self-sacrificingly is a moral lesson in itself, and the classroom is God's air and sunshine. Foster it, my brothers, so that it may attract all who can find the time to play it; protect it from anything that would sully it, so that it may grow in favour with all men.' His words are just as applicable almost 90 years later – but finding the time to play it is becoming increasingly difficult.

Harris, who had been widowed in 1930, developed influenza and was seriously ill throughout February 1932, with daily updates on his condition appearing in many newspapers. He seemed to be making a recovery, but he died suddenly at 2pm on 24 March; as one newspaper put it, he was 'sitting in an armchair in front of the fire, smoking a cigarette after lunch' when he had a heart attack and died. Never have the dangers of smoking been more clearly demonstrated.

The tributes were many and heartfelt. Even King George V sent his condolences to Lord Harris's son, now the 5th Baron Harris. Most of the cricketing tributes mentioned two things – his part in outlawing throwing in the 1880s, and his espousing of the cause of the professionals. Jack Hobbs, then in the evening of his great career, said that 'Lord Harris was a great friend to the professional cricketer. If ever I was in any trouble, I never had any hesitation in going to him. He always gave the professional player a square deal.' Pelham Warner, who in due course took over from Lord Harris as the *éminence grise* at Lord's, wrote in *The Cricketer* that 'his influence in the cricket world was immense. His word was almost law – what he said, went – but he always used his unsurpassed authority wisely and fairly; and if one had to sum him up in a single word, that word would be "just"'.

* * * *

Its artist and its author were now both dead, but the painting remained at Kent, hanging in the pavilion, until the 1990s, apart from the years of the Second World War, when it was taken down for its own protection, although there is no record of it being removed to another, safer, site. As it turned out, the St Lawrence Ground survived the war intact, with no fewer than 579 games of cricket being played there between 1940 and 1945. According to the club's official history, 'about 268 incendiaries fell on the property, 138 of them on the playing area. Luckily the damage was negligible: in fact their ingredients appeared to be good for the grass'. All the same, in retrospect it seems quite a risk to take with what was becoming one of the club's most valuable assets. In the end, it was the value of the painting that triggered the moves that took place in the 1990s.

In 1996, the Kent committee undertook a valuation for insurance purposes of all their assets, and they quickly realised that the insurance required to protect this painting was so great that something needed to be done, and quickly. The Kent committee minutes of 24 October 1996 show that 'a valuation had revealed that the 1906 painting by Chevallier Tayler was worth considerably more than had originally been thought, which had prompted debate concerning its future. The recommendation of the Management Board was that a copy of the painting be commissioned for display at the St Lawrence Ground and that the original be left in the care of MCC on a loan basis. This would obviate the necessity of producing an expensive security cabinet and substantially reduce the annual cost of insurance'. In the mid-nineties, all county cricket clubs were feeling the pinch, and the cost of providing security for the painting that would be acceptable to the insurers was too much to bear. Clearly it was highly unlikely that anybody would steal a painting of that size, but protecting it against accidental or deliberate damage, and against fire or water damage, would be a costly process. The committee endorsed the Management Board's proposal 'on the proviso that MCC display a plaque next to the painting stating that it was on loan from Kent County Cricket Club'. MCC were then approached, and accepted the loan with alacrity.

At the same time, E.W. Swanton, the noted cricket writer and former Kent president, was asked to find an artist who could make a good copy of the painting. Jim Swanton telephoned Henry Wyndham, then chairman of Sotheby's, to ask his advice. Wyndham suggested there was only one man who could do a good job, an artist called Barrington Bramley, who had gained a reputation as a copyist of major works in a wide range of styles. If an Arab sheikh or a Russian or Chinese billionaire wanted a copy of the Old Master or whatever other works of art he had just purchased at auction, perhaps so that he could put the original into a secure vault, or maybe so he could have what appeared to be the original both at his home and on his yacht, then Bramley had become the man to go to. This was not forgery, as every copy was clearly marked as being by Bramley, but the copies were so good that only an expert could tell the difference with any accuracy.

So Swanton telephoned Bramley at his studio in the New Forest on 30 September 1996. 'He said, "Could I speak to Barrington Bramley, please?" and I thought, "I know that voice."' Bramley himself had listened often enough to cricket commentary to

228

recognise what he called 'that calming, peaceful English voice', and by the time the phone conversation was done, the commission had been offered and accepted. At the next Kent committee meeting on 24 October, the deal was confirmed. According to the club minutes, the fee agreed with Mr Bramley was £8,500, some 40 times more than the club had paid Chevallier Tayler for the original 90 years earlier. However, after taking inflation over those 90 years into account, Tayler was still paid almost twice as much as Bramley, and his painting is now worth perhaps 40 times as much as the copy.

Barrington Bramley was born in Knaresborough, near Harrogate in North Yorkshire, in 1950. As a young art teacher at a school in Leeds, he conceived the idea late in 1973 of copying every one of the extant paintings of Johannes Vermeer, the 17th-century Dutch master. Word got round of this eccentric young art teacher's strange ambition, and the local newspaper and local BBC television both took up the story. This resulted in an exhibition of Bramley's Vermeers at a small gallery in Ilkley, opening in December 1975, the tricentenary of Vermeer's death. A number of reviews of the exhibition appeared in a range of newspapers and magazines, and the reviews were universally favourable. The exhibition was also written up in a Dutch newspaper, which led to Bramley being offered the chance to exhibit his Vermeers in the painter's home town, Delft. There, a wealthy Dutch businessman bought the entire collection, and Bramley's new career was decided.

Although he tried to make a living as a creator of original artworks, it was his copies of Old Masters that attracted attention, simply because he was so good at it. Over the years since his first success with Vermeer, he has been commissioned to copy around 400 other paintings, ranging from Hogarth to Manet, from Renoir to Stubbs and from Breughel to Rossetti, a wide and eclectic range of styles. He takes great pains to use a similar canvas, for example, by counting the number of threads per inch in the original, and he tries to use the same paints and techniques used by the artist whose work he is copying. The commissions come from a variety of sources and for a variety of reasons: the big auction houses are a strong source of work, as many sellers wish to retain a copy of the work they are selling, as do many museums, but his work is not usually publicised, simply because many owners of Bramley copies do not want the world to know that they are not the original. Kent CCC, who like so many others wanted to keep a copy of the painting they were about to sell, were quite happy for the world to know that the one they retained was a copy.

Bramley has made very few copies of sporting scenes, apart from one or two portraits of noblemen and their families with horses or guns, in the style of many 18th-century portraits, but one cricket painting he has made a copy of is Francis Cotes's famous painting dating from 1768 of *Master Lewis Cage, The Young Cricketer*. This remarkable portrait of a determined young boy holding a cricket bat, curved in the style of the time, was sold at Christie's in 1996 for over £700,000, and at the same time Bramley made his copy for 'an English gentleman', presumably the vendor.

Bramley's extraordinary talent has found a niche which may be very profitable, but perhaps in other ways rather unsatisfying. As he himself has said, 'The great disappointment with copying is that there is little creativity, like reading the same book over and over again and knowing the ending.' Those of us who have read our favourite books many times and still derive pleasure from the umpteenth read might dispute the use of the word 'disappointment', but the point is well made. The experience of copying a painting must be very different from the experience of creating an original, however carefully the copyist might recreate not only the painting but also the materials, traditions and techniques of the past.

For Bramley, the process begins with taking a photograph of the painting and blowing it up to full size. He also usually works with the original to hand, either at the site where it is housed or at some other studio convenient for all concerned. In the case of *Kent v Lancashire 1906*, the original painting was delivered to the studio where he had chosen to work, and throughout the process he was able to compare his copy with the original. Bramley, however, never came to the St Lawrence Ground to see where the original had hung, and nor has he been since. That is not to say he has no feel for Kent: over the course of his career he has painted two originals connected with Canterbury, one of the cathedral and one of Archbishop Donald Coggan, Archbishop of Canterbury from 1974 to 1980.

Bramley worked on creating his copy of the painting every morning from 7am until noon, seven days a week. It took him about six weeks to complete, and then early in 1997 it went to Canterbury, while the original went to Lord's. MCC were holding an exhibition in the spring of 1997 entitled *The Fine Art Of Cricket*, and the original was to be loaned to Lord's just for the duration of the exhibition, which ran from May to September. However, the Kent committee then decided that it would be better staying at Lord's and in September the then secretary of MCC, Roger Knight, was able to write to Kent saying, 'I understand that MCC will be keeping the painting for the time being. This is good news, since so many visitors have said how much they enjoyed seeing it.'

Bramley's copy, meanwhile, was very well received by the committee and members alike at Canterbury, even though it had proved to be quite a difficult commission, being very large and quite detailed. It was not the largest painting he had ever worked on – he once had to copy a painting which measured 13ftt by 12ft (about 4m x 3.65m), over five times the area of the Chevallier Tayler, and that required scaffolding and stepladders to complete. The Kent committee minutes for 7 January 1997 report that 'the copy of the Chevallier Tayler had now been completed and was remarkably similar to the original', a judgement that would have pleased Barrington Bramley. It was placed in the original frame, with MCC having agreed to reframe the original at their expense, for their exhibition.

In 1990, the club issued another edition of prints of the original painting, this time signed by Leslie Ames, Colin Cowdrey and Jim Swanton, as opposed to Lord Harris and Chevallier Tayler himself who had signed each copy of the original print edition. The new edition sold reasonably well, but did not sell out. In 2000, a Millennium Edition print was also produced, signed this time by Cowdrey, Swanton and Matthew Fleming, then captain of Kent. Again, sales were steady but not remarkable. By 2005, the finances of Kent County Cricket Club were in poor shape, in common with the finances of many other first-class counties. Plans to sell off some of the acreage of the St Lawrence Ground were discussed at committee, and there was general agreement that some of the land could be sold without impacting too much on the look of the ground or on the actual playing of cricket. Many other counties were facing the same issues, with some selling off part of their grounds for hotels, flats and other buildings just to survive the difficult times in the early part of the new millennium. But while these plans, which would eventually result in several houses and retirement flats being built around the ground, were still taking shape, the cash crisis would not go away. In August 2005, the committee took the decision to sell the painting the following year, the centenary of the match which inspired it. From a business point of view, the decision made perfect sense: the painting was not at Canterbury anyway, there was an excellent copy hanging in the pavilion (together with Chevallier Tayler's original extra panel portraits of the other players and officials of 1906) to delight those members who were interested, and the club needed the money urgently.

The decision was not greeted with unanimous delight. Many people thought this was selling off the family silver for the sake of a few bills being paid, and one descendant of Cloudesley Marsham felt that the decision to sell was not the club's to make, as in his opinion the painting was owned by the original subscribers and their heirs. This was not the case – the painting had from the outset been owned by the club itself – and although there was a great deal of regret from many of the older members that another link with Kent's greatest era was being lost, the sale went ahead. At the same time, the club was planning to sell some of its land and, to cap it all, the famous lime tree was blown down in a winter storm in January 2005. Canterbury was changing too fast for many people's taste, and the sale of the Chevallier Tayler was symptomatic of the change and an easy target for protest.

Kent chose Sotheby's to handle the sale. Henry Wyndham, the man who had recommended Barrington Bramley to Jim Swanton, took personal charge of the sale. The Proposal for Sale, for the Victorian and Edwardian Art Auction which Sotheby's were planning for 27 June 2006, described the painting as 'Albert Chevallier Tayler's great masterpiece' and talked of 'gentlemen with rolled up sleeves battling in the summer sun before the expectant eyes of an encouraging crowd, as the Union Jack flutters in the breeze'. Apart from the obvious error that not all the cricketers were gentlemen in the cricketing sense (some were professionals, after all), the sentence sums up what the picture was about. The pre-auction estimate was £300,000 to £500,000.

At the same time, the club issued a third edition of the print, a centenary print signed this time by Derek Underwood, that year's president of Kent CCC and the only left-arm bowler to rank with Colin Blythe in the pantheon of Kent cricketing greats, and Robert Key, then Kent captain, as this was the last chance to celebrate the painting before the reproduction rights passed to a new owner. The quality of both the 21st-century print editions was very good, but the market for them was soggy at best, and copies still remain.

At this point, I must declare an interest. In 2006, I was a member of both the Kent committee and MCC's Arts and Library Committee, and the sale of *Kent v Lancashire 1906* was on the agenda of both. I pointed out to the Arts and Library Committee that the reason for the sale was because the Kent committee could no longer see the point in holding on to an asset that we could not afford to keep or even see, unless we were also members of MCC. The valuation of the painting in 1996 had been £250,000 and Kent needed the money. According to the minutes of the meeting of 11 January 2006, I did also point out that 'the Kent committee would be delighted if MCC were to express an interest in purchasing the painting', although whether I used such a formal set of words I cannot quite remember. However, it emerged at the next meeting, in April 2006, that the MCC committee had set aside £1.5 million as an Acquisition Fund for the five years to 2010, and that the money to bid for this painting would have to come out of that fund. There was no extra money to be had. 'The Officers and Trustees of MCC did not feel that the painting represented a special case', and that therefore they advised against using perhaps one third of the Acquisitions Fund, which was meant to fund acquisitions over a five-year period, to bid for the painting. The then president of MCC, Robin Marlar, expressed the view that although it was 'a very attractive work of art, the painting was not one which the club had to acquire at any cost', even though the MCC collection was then, and still is, the most important collection of cricket art and memorabilia in the world, and this was quite possibly the most well-known (and expensive) cricket painting in the world. There were contrary views expressed at the meeting (I declared my conflict of interest and said nothing), with one committee member stating that the painting would provide more enjoyment than, for example, a collection of ceramics, a view with which the chairman thought 'many members would probably agree'. However, trustees' and MCC committee views trump the Arts and Library Committee, so although a representative of MCC would attend the auction, unless it sold at the very lower end of the estimate range, MCC were not going to buy it.

In the event, the painting was sold for £600,000, well over the estimate and equalling the record at the time for a painting of a cricket match, which had been set by a Lowry in 2004. The purchaser was The Andrew Brownsword Art Foundation, who immediately offered it to Lord's on a rolling long-term loan basis. So the painting went from a wall in the Lord's pavilion to the Sotheby's saleroom and then back to the wall in the Lord's pavilion, without MCC ever having ownership. This was a most satisfactory outcome for all concerned.

Andrew Brownsword was born in Wolverhampton but moved to Kent as a young boy and was educated at the Harvey Grammar School in Folkestone. He made his fortune in his publishing business and subsequently branched out into commercial property and hotels, owning the Abode Hotels chain, one of which is on the High Street in Canterbury. His lifelong interest in sport is reflected in the fact that for many seasons until 2010, he owned Bath Rugby Club. When the painting came up for sale, Brownsword was enthusiastic about trying to buy it, because, in his own words, it is 'a great action painting in the true Edwardian tradition, a picture of a bygone era'. In his view, Chevallier Tayler was a very good artist, not a great one but quite possibly underrated today, and this is his masterpiece. His foundation buys paintings which excite his personal interest, and the Edwardian era has long been an interest of his, but he also wants to buy paintings that otherwise might be lost to the nation, and then display them where people can enjoy them. It is, as Brownsword admits, 'an eclectic collection'.

And that is where the two *Kent v Lancashire 1906*s are now: the original is hanging in a prime position at Lord's where it is expected to remain indefinitely, and the copy dominates the back wall of the Long Room in the pavilion at Canterbury, where it will also stay. The panel of portraits that were part of the original commission by Chevallier Tayler but not part of the sale at Sotheby's, is also in the pavilion at Canterbury, on the wall next to Bramley's copy.

* * * *

The influence of Tayler's painting on cricket art that followed its unveiling was considerable. Tayler himself was by no means a revolutionary artist. He may have adopted new ways of going about his work – committing himself to plein air and the techniques of his friends and colleagues at Newlyn – but the results were not revolutionary. His entire *oeuvre*, which is a very broad one, is essentially familiar and readily accessible, even to those who, like Lord Harris, were by no means art connoisseurs. His later output, his portraits of solid members of the establishment and elegant and often elegiac compositions such as *Girl Looking Out To Sea* (1918), *The Club (*1921) or *The Escritoire* (1924), may be skilfully executed and thought-provoking, but they are not groundbreaking. It would be quite wrong to suggest that Chevallier Tayler wanted to change the world with his art, or even to imagine that any of his paintings might have an effect on other artists that would follow him. But even if he did not mean it or expect it, his *Kent v Lancashire 1906* did make a difference to the way artists looked at sport.

The development of photography, as shown in the work of George Beldam and others, allowed artists to gain a real insight into the way the human body moved when playing sport, and the popularity of photography challenged artists to match the action that cricket followers could see every day in their newspapers and magazines. The popular success of *Kent v Lancashire 1906* has not changed cricket art: most portrayals of cricketers in action are these days done with a camera, and many very brilliant photographers have taken their art form into areas that Beldam could not have imagined. But cricket art is now more than just the art of painting a landscape with a bit of cricket in the foreground, or maybe the background. Portraits of cricketers are no longer limited to the likeness of a cricketer standing rigidly, holding a bat or a ball. Chevallier Tayler's painting, which was influenced by Beldam's photographic pioneering, showed the way the cricketers work as a team, how they appreciate and respect each other, in a way that earlier cricket match scenes had not even attempted. Today the more formal portraits, like Andrew Festing's two superb *Conversation Piece* portraits of great cricketers together indoors at Lord's, show the relationship between the cricketers in the painting, rather than just a row of faces staring at the spectator, eyes following him around the room. A photograph can explain the physiological details of the human body, but it often cannot explain the person within that body. That's what a good artist should be able to do.

Sometimes it is hard to remember what impression a familiar painting made the first time you looked at it. Many people – indeed, most cricket lovers – have seen the painting in many different places and guises and have become so used to it in magazines, on biscuit tins or tea towels that it is hard to see it again through new eyes. We think we know the story, we think we know the colours, the textures, the atmosphere of the painting, and there is nothing more to learn by looking at it again. But there is always something new to discover in any great painting, just as there is on rereading a great book or seeing a wonderful film again. The *Mona Lisa* is the enigmatic smile, or at least the first impression for most people who have seen it is the smile, but what about, for instance, the road in the background? Where is that going to or coming from? What does that add to the portrait? We can all make up our own minds about that.

Tayler's use of light and shade is at its very best in *Kent v Lancashire 1906*; the colours of the grass on the wicket and in the outfield are brilliantly varied in each stroke of the brush, yet combine to give a clear impression of a lush greensward in the Garden of England. The trees in their full summer bloom, the flags fluttering in the breeze and the lively colours of the spectators all give a sense of movement which is curiously absent in the players on the field, apart from the bowler. All the players are stock still, in that brief moment before the bowler releases the ball and the action begins. Only Blythe, dancing on tiptoe as he prepares to bowl, is obviously moving: the imagined Billy Findlay is backing up well, but the fielders are all absolutely still, concentrating on the delivery that is about to bring any or many of them into sudden action. The way Tayler has composed his work steers the eye towards Blythe, the focus of the action and of the painting. The human action is elsewhere, among the crowd. There is a man towards the right-hand edge of the painting who is wearing what may well be an MCC blazer and who seems to be almost on one knee as he looks at the lady sitting next to him, rather than at the cricket. Is he proposing marriage to the young woman? Is he already so full of wine that he has slipped off his chair? There are several little cameos like this which Tayler has artfully introduced into his portrait, which is meant to be of the Festival Week, not just 11 triumphant cricketers.

Cricket is today one of the most popular sporting subjects for artists of all types. Horse racing has always inspired many great painters and paintings, from Stubbs onwards, but few others can match the wealth or depth of art that cricket has inspired. MCC, which is the spiritual home of cricketing art of all types, has commissioned many fine paintings (and some pretty dreadful ones, too) over the past decades, but most of their commissions are portraits of an individual cricketer, often head and shoulders, sometimes with a bat or ball in hand. Some of the best (Viv Richards, Inzamam, Keith Miller in his later years) are wonderful works that pull the viewer in to consider all that makes a great cricketer, but most of the artists who are painting cricket scenes today are not commissioned by MCC or anybody else. Noted artists like Lowry, Lawrence Toynbee and Ruskin Spear all have cricket subjects in their catalogue, and if you go to any county ground during the season, you will almost certainly see somebody on the boundary with paints and easel, or a sketchbook and pens, creating their own vision of what is going on within the boundary. Two distinguished artists of recent vintage, John Ward (*St Lawrence, Canterbury 1985*) and Hugh Cushing (*Field of Dreams*), have painted scenes of Canterbury Week, but unlike Chevallier Tayler, they concentrated on the crowds rather than the cricketers. Former cricketers such as Arthur Mailey, Jack Russell and Martin Speight have turned their hands to painting cricket scenes, with skilful and popular results. But in one way, Chevallier Tayler's painting remains unique. There has only ever been one painting of a real cricket match in progress in which all the players on the fielding side are portrayed and are clearly recognisable, and that is *Kent v Lancashire 1906*.

Type 'Cricket Art' into your search engine and see how many hundreds of images that throws up. Some are good, some are indifferent and some can command reasonable sums for their efforts. But they all, to some extent, owe their inspiration, and the artists owe their livelihoods, to what Albert Chevallier Tayler created, at Lord Harris's bidding, at the end of the 1906 season.

Cricket Then and Now

C HEVALLIER Tayler's painting tells us a great deal about how cricket was played, and how it was administered, in 1906. Canterbury Week has always been an exception to the rule, of course, a festival and a social highlight of the cricket season, and the scene depicted in the painting would not have been typical of a game in that golden Edwardian era at, say, Catford on a cold day in May. However, it is not just the weather or the size of the crowds that tells the story. Every aspect of the painting is familiar to cricket lovers, and yet it is nothing like how cricket is played today. The players, the ground and the sunshine are just the same as they could be over a century later, and yet they are completely different.

Let us begin with the ground. The St Lawrence Ground at Canterbury, like every county cricket ground in England, has changed a great deal since Kent first won the championship. There is still the pavilion, which has not changed externally all that much since 1906, but there are also many new buildings around the ground. Lord Harris would still recognise the Chiesman

Pavilion, at least until he went inside, although he would not know the man after whom it is now named. He would also recognise the stand that was not there in 1906, but which was built before Lord Harris died. This stand, to the left of the pavilion as we look at it, was built in 1927 and was originally called either the New Stand or the Concrete Stand – one name startlingly unoriginal and the other massively unromantic – but since 1973 it has been called the Frank Woolley Stand. There is also an annexe to the pavilion, completed in 1909 but with the construction work starting as Chevallier Tayler was completing his painting. It is now named after Derek Underwood and Alan Knott, and is on the other side to the Woolley Stand. A reporter from *The Times* was not particularly complimentary the first time he saw it, in the year it was opened. He described it as a 'red-tiled, two-storeyed annexe' which was, in his view, 'altogether not so satisfactory from an aesthetic point of view, though it will add greatly to the comfort of a fair number of the spectators'. It occupies a space which had for half a century been where I Zingari pitched their tent. Moving that tent further away from the pavilion ruffled a few aristocratic feathers. Next to it there is now a 21st-century building which houses the club's administrative staff, a Sainsbury's and the Lime Tree café. This building lacks a name.

Other buildings are less anonymous. Beyond the Woolley Stand is the Cowdrey Stand, which contains a Harris Room and a Cornwallis Room. Lord Harris just gets a room, while Stuart Chiesman, a former club chairman, and first father-in-law of Colin Cowdrey, gets a whole pavilion. That is mainly because he paid for a lot of the refurbishment in the 1960s. The Ames Levett building (named after two of Kent's many great wicketkeepers), which houses the indoor nets, the physio rooms and many other physical welfare projects, is beyond the Cowdrey Stand. Then there is the Leslie Ames Stand at the Nackington Road end of the ground, which would have been behind the artist as he planned his painting. This houses hospitality boxes, a thriving bar and one of the last remaining hand-operated scoreboards in county cricket. It was built before Leslie Ames was born in 1905, and was originally known as the Iron Stand until 1973. There are also floodlights, installed in 2011, which even when not in use tend to dominate the skyline. At least two of the five would have had to be included in Chevallier Tayler's painting if day-night cricket had been a reality then.

Outside the ground there is development too. In 1906, the Nackington Road led across farmland to the villages to the south of Canterbury and then on to the old Roman road, Stone Street, which leads down to Folkestone and Hythe on the south coast. The road still exists, but has become far more built up. Where once the St Lawrence Ground was on the very edge of the city, about a mile beyond the city walls, now it is rather more a part of the city, with two secondary schools and the Kent and Canterbury Hospital within a few hundred yards. There are new residential streets, named after the likes of Cowdrey, Underwood and Woolmer. Private houses have sprung up there too, and there are plans to develop the whole eastern part of Canterbury, which would bring the ground much more into the heart of the city. This is not necessarily to everybody's taste, and county cricket lovers are on the whole a conservative bunch, but a similar process is going on all over the country, and no county cricket ground is immune from these pressures. The population of Britain is at least double what it was in 1906, and no part of our society can be untouched by progress, in whichever direction it takes us.

This quick tour of the ground shows how the place has changed since 1906. Not all of these changes have been made without attracting some opposition. Even in 1909, there was a strongly held view that, as *The Times* correspondent said, 'one does not want to see the St Lawrence Ground converted into a sort of Lord's, with an unsightly Mound Stand taking up one quarter of the circle around the ground. However, so far no great harm has been done.' Some present-day followers of Kent, and those who yearn for the old days at St Lawrence, might argue that much harm has been done. It is not necessary to revisit all the arguments and discussions that took place from around 2005 regarding the redevelopment of the ground, developments which have upset many members in recent years and which at one stage threatened to bankrupt the club. However, the end result – significant parcels of land sold to developers to build houses and retirement apartments – makes the St Lawrence Ground a very different, and rather smaller, place from the one Lord Harris knew. What's more, the ancient lime tree, which was once the quirky symbol of cricket at Canterbury, blew down in a winter gale in January 2005, and has been replaced by a new sapling, which no longer stands quite within the playing area as its predecessor did. The Lime Tree is now more familiar to Kent supporters as the name of the café on the other side of the ground.

Since 1906, some county cricket clubs have simply uprooted themselves and found somewhere else to play, and all county clubs have reduced significantly the number of outgrounds they play at. In 1906, Kent played their home county games at Blackheath, Catford, Gravesend, Maidstone, Tonbridge and Tunbridge Wells, as well as at Canterbury, and in the first 70 years of the last century also played regularly at Beckenham, Dover, Folkestone and

Gillingham, as well as occasional matches at other grounds. It was considered, in those less commercial days, a good way to spread the word of county cricket around the county, but nobody ever really worked out the costs involved. Today, the cost of moving around the county to play is very great, and any county has to be assured of a healthy crowd and a good financial return before they entertain the idea of moving lock, stock and advertising hoardings to another part of the county for a few days.

Today, only a handful of counties such as Gloucestershire, who move from Bristol to use Cheltenham College for their Cheltenham Festival, and Yorkshire, who use Scarborough, play cricket on a regular basis outside their headquarters ground. Most other counties have second grounds where their first team may play sporadically given special circumstances, but they all tend to stick to their headquarters for as many games as they can. Kent still use Beckenham, which is a newly developed ground in the most densely populated part of Kent and which they lease on a long-term agreement for a peppercorn rent, and they also play at the Nevill Ground at Tunbridge Wells. Hampshire have moved to a purpose-built ground in another part of Southampton, and have been rewarded with the granting of Test match status, and Durham, the new boys to the County Championship, also have a purpose-built ground at Chester-le-Street. Middlesex play at Lord's and occasionally have to move out to Uxbridge or Radlett, mainly for limited overs games, and Surrey, after a few seasons of experimenting with school grounds, are limiting themselves to playing virtually all games at the Oval, with occasional forays to Guildford. Essex, who used to be almost as peripatetic as Kent, now only rarely leave Chelmsford for Colchester, and Worcester and Derbyshire have both in recent years had bad experiences with outgrounds. The days of Glamorgan playing at Abergavenny or Sussex at Horsham and Hastings are long gone. Warwickshire do not even have a second ground, and have been forced in 2019 to play home games at Worcester while Edgbaston is requisitioned for the World Cup. Professional cricket is now a big city game; its rural roots have disappeared under a rampant growth of television rights and the game becoming a profession rather than an amusement. Canterbury is, after Chester-le-Street, the least populated centre for any county cricket team in England or Wales, but it is no longer a bucolic idyll. It's just another venue.

It's a venue not just for cricket. What began as farmland, with sheep grazing on the outfield to keep the grass short before the invention of the gang mower, is now a multi-purpose venue, hosting all sorts of entertainment besides games of cricket. Like very many sports grounds and stadia (and the St Lawrence Ground is certainly not a 'stadium'), the important thing is to be able to use the asset – the ground itself – to make money even when no sport is being played. Canterbury has hosted several pop concerts, so they can now boast that not only W.G. Grace but also Elton John has played there, and the annual fireworks display now attracts several thousand people, so it is reasonable to guess that more people come to the ground for non-cricketing reasons than for cricketing ones. But that's as it should be. Cricket is played at the ground for no more than about 60 days a year, even counting all the extra games like the Kent women's games and the match between the University of Kent and Canterbury Christ Church University, so that leaves a lot of time to make the most of the facilities in other money-making ways. This is how county cricket works these days. Those clubs that can make money out of their non-cricketing activities are the ones that will survive. The cricketing business model has long been broken, to be replaced by handouts from the ECB based on the sale of television rights, a way of running a cricket club that would have been completely alien to Lord Harris and his contemporaries.

In 1906, Kent CCC boasted a committee of 23 people representing the heritage of both East and West Kent, plus the chairman, Lord Harris, not to mention the club secretary, A.J. Lancaster, the general manager, Tom Pawley, and the president, Lord Henry Nevill. Such a large committee could well have made for fractious committee meetings, and the need for a large room in which to hold them. In reality, the club was run by Lord Harris, who instructed Lancaster and Pawley what to do, and who occasionally deferred to Lord Henry Nevill when there was some ceremonial club business to be done. The other committee men (and they were, inevitably, all men) had little to do except rubber-stamp Lord Harris's decisions and see if they could serve long enough to be in the running to be president themselves one year. There were past cricketers among the number, including Lord Darnley who, as Hon. Ivo Bligh, had led the England team to Australia in 1882/83 that won the series and gave rise to the creation of the Ashes urn. Jack Mason was on the committee, too, as was Captain McCanlis, the coach, George Marsham, Slug's cousin, and plenty of others with old Kent names such as Sondes, Cornwallis, Weigall, Tufton and Mackeson. The club ran well, doing very little apart from the business of putting on cricket matches and making sure that the players were fit and well trained, and the spectators had a good time at the match. There was little or no other business for the club. There may occasionally have been events at the ground in the winter, but it was still the custom in those days to hold club functions in the banqueting halls of Canterbury, Maidstone and Tunbridge Wells rather than in the rather less elegant buildings at the St Lawrence Ground.

Fast forward a century or more, and things have changed, but they have also stayed the same. The Kent committee still runs the club, but executive decisions rest as ever with the chairman, the chief executive and the treasurer. The chief executive used to be called the secretary or the general manager or a combination of both, but the change in title has not massively altered the job description. The committee consists of fewer elected members, and the mathematically precise split between East and West Kent has long gone by the board, but when you add in the top management team – finance director, director of cricket, marketing director, community cricket director and others who may be invited to attend meetings from time to time – the club still needs a big room for its meetings. Kent is not unusual in this: most county clubs are still run on the same basis. They may be incorporated as limited companies, but still run as though they are members' clubs. Membership subscriptions are no longer the main source of income – far from it – but a thriving membership is still one of the ways in which the success of a county club can be assessed. Some counties, such as Durham and Hampshire, are now run entirely as commercial companies, without a membership as such, but they still need and actively encourage regular support, even if those supporters have no direct say in who runs the club. It seems probable that the Durham and Hampshire model is the way of the future, assuming that county cricket in England survives in any form against the many slings and arrows that are currently being hurled at it. Professional football clubs may be called clubs but they are all limited companies these days, with season ticket holders rather than members, and that is a structure that works well for most of the clubs most of the time. It does, however, leave them open to takeover and sudden changes, which may not suit cricket quite so well. However, cricket in its present economic state is unlikely to attract Arab sheikhs or Chinese billionaires as potential buyers of county clubs, even if they were for sale. Franchises are a different kettle of fish.

One of the biggest differences between 1906 and now is in the competitions that cricketers play, which in turn are decided by the game's governing bodies. In 1906 the game's governing body was the Marylebone Cricket Club. Self-appointed and over-aware of their own importance they may have been, but the club ran the domestic game impartially, even though most of their most influential members, from the president down, had allegiances to one county or another. In 1906, the president of MCC was an exception to the rule. The Rt Hon. Walter Hume Long, a Conservative and Unionist member of parliament for South County Dublin, was a man without obvious cricketing allegiances, although he was in the Harrow XI as a schoolboy, and played occasionally for both Devon and Wiltshire. The secretary was Francis Lacey, who had played for Hampshire and among the committee men were two Kent men, Jack Mason and William Patterson, along with men from Middlesex, Essex, Surrey, Lancashire and Yorkshire. Between them they ran the County Championship and England's Test matches, and nobody felt that there was any other way of doing things.

In 1906 there was only the County Championship for cricket followers to focus on. There were no Test matches and no other competitions, apart from the Second-Class Counties Championship, which still exists today, although in a revised form. For many years it was known as the Second-Class Counties Championship, and then the Minor Counties Championship, but in 2019 a new name was given to the competition – the National Counties Cricket Association Championship. It just trips off the tongue.

In 1906 the Second-Class Counties title was won by Staffordshire, who had the huge advantage of having the great bowler Sydney Barnes, the man who shared the Test match winning partnership with Arthur Fielder in Australia, in their side. Barnes was a grumpy chap, always a law unto himself, never wanting to play for a first-class county. Although he did make a few appearances for Warwickshire and Lancashire, he always felt his worth was undervalued and as a result he never played any championship cricket after 1903, and no first-class cricket at all between 1904 and 1907. His medium-pace bowling (which varied from slow-medium to fast-medium as the wickets and the opposition demanded) was extraordinarily good, and he became the only man since the beginning of the 20th century to be picked for England when not playing regular first-class cricket. For Staffordshire in 1906, he took 119 wickets at 7.83 each. No batsman could cope with him, and it could easily be argued that if Lancashire, for whom he was qualified, could have afforded to pay him what he felt he was worth and play him throughout the season, they would have been far tougher opposition and quite possibly could have won not only the match at Canterbury but the title as well. And then there would have been no painting of the game, and Chevallier Tayler would have been 200 guineas the poorer. The whole season was full of ifs and buts, but then so is every season.

MCC's control of cricket was on the whole benign. They were, then as now, in control of the laws of the game and were in particular at the time on the lookout for illegal bowling actions. However, it was the way that MCC made sure the game was played that set cricket apart from other sports. 'It's not cricket' was a mantra that really meant something, and if cricket was not played in the Corinthian way, hard but fair, then it was not worth playing at all. In maintaining this code, it was felt that the role of the amateur was crucial.

The distinction between amateur and professional was for many years central to many sports in Britain. Rugby union was amateur, rugby league was professional; football was largely professional, but until the 1950s amateurs occasionally played for professional teams, and the amateur game was followed by almost as many as the professional game. The Amateur Cup Final used to fill Wembley Stadium as easily as the FA Cup Final, and in the 1950s the great amateur players, like Bob Hardisty of Bishop Auckland, were almost as well known as Stanley Matthews or Tom Finney.

Tennis, athletics and swimming were all amateur sports until the 1960s or later, and of course the Olympic Games were a bastion of the amateur ideal – that was their whole point. The top golfers were professional (Bobby Jones of the United States always excepted), but in most sports amateur and professional mixed easily. In cricket, the distinction was always more clearly defined. As Neville Cardus put it, 'The amateurs went into the field, and came back from it, through the pavilion entrance; the professionals used another and smaller gate, a sort of "servants' entrance."'

It was Lord Hawke, the Yorkshire counterpart and friend of Lord Harris, who expressed the view that no professional should ever captain England. Not until almost two decades after both noble lords had died did Lord Hawke's nightmare come true, when Len Hutton was appointed England's captain, and promptly won back the Ashes. But even before then, in the 1930s, Wally Hammond had switched his status from professional to amateur so that he could captain England. In this, the cricket hierarchy conspired to help him so that he could afford to play as an amateur. In 1906, the game was ruled by amateurs, who were men deemed to be obviously more capable leaders than the professionals. The theory was that they could be impartial because cricket was not their living. They did not earn any money from cricket, apart from their expenses, which were often at least as much as the professionals' salaries, and in the case of W.G. Grace, very much more. Most amateurs were batsmen, because bowling was what professionals did in the nets for the amusement of amateur batsmen, and most amateurs had other jobs which limited the times they could play for a county each season. August – the holiday month – was the time when most amateurs came out to play, and the month when even the best professionals knew there was a chance they would have to stand down for a game or two. There was nothing fair about it, but who said life, or cricket, was meant to be fair? Many of the amateurs – schoolmasters, lawyers, stockbrokers or gentlemen of private means with no need to demean themselves with a paid job – were very fine cricketers, and that was most certainly the case with Kent in their triumphant years between 1906 and the Great War. Most professionals earnt very little, and would be on contracts that only paid them during the season. In the winter they would have to find other ways of earning money, whether by coaching or some other cricket-related job, or else by taking a manual labouring job to keep fit during the long winter months.

The very best would possibly be picked for an MCC tour, which would give them a pleasant few months in a warm climate, but the opportunities would be few and far between. England cricket tours did not happen every winter, and those that did take place were under the control of MCC, who often picked on personal character as much as cricketing skills. This did not change until the 1960s, and even at the end of the period of MCC control and the distinction between amateurs and professionals, players could miss out on lucrative and enjoyable tours on the basis of whether or not they were the right sort of fellow to wear an MCC touring blazer. Fred Trueman, Brian Close and Johnny Wardle, three Yorkshire professionals, were among those who were not picked for MCC tours in the 1950s for disciplinary rather than cricketing reasons, and in the first half of the 20th century there were probably several more.

The distinction between amateurs and professionals was dropped at the end of 1962. Before then there had been many examples of county sides being led by a professional – Horace Dollery of Warwickshire was the first to be appointed on an annual basis and his county won the championship in 1951, his first season in charge – but there was still the view that somehow amateurs did it better. After all, a professional could not be as impartial with his fellow professionals, and be as willing to select or drop them, as an amateur could. An amateur had no financial stake in the game and therefore would allow no outside pressures to bear on him in making crucial decisions, both on and off the field. Wouldn't he?

There were, of course, hundreds of anecdotes and statistics to prove this theory wrong, or at least to have too many exceptions to prove the rule. At Kent, the amateur captains routinely asked their senior professionals for 'advice', as Slug Marsham readily admitted he did in 1906, and the same was true at every other county. Yorkshire, the other great bastion of amateurism, relied on players like George Hirst, Wilfred Rhodes and in later years, Herbert Sutcliffe, Hedley Verity and Len Hutton to give the captain strong support on the field, even if that captain might be a bit of a martinet off the field. As late as 1958 Yorkshire drafted in their second XI captain, the 39-year-old Ronnie Burnet, to take over as club captain when Billy Sutcliffe, son of Herbert, stepped down, rather than to entrust the leadership to a professional. Given that they had players who would become two of England's best post-war captains on their books at the time, Brian Close and Ray Illingworth, it may seem a perverse decision in retrospect, but it worked. In his second season in charge, Burnet led Yorkshire to the title in 1959. Billy Sutcliffe, by the way, was the son of one of Yorkshire's greatest ever professionals, but his father's success for Yorkshire and England had enabled him to give his son a leg up the social scale and become a privately educated amateur.

In many ways, that winter of 1962 was one of the most important turning points in English cricket, and not just because several counties spent the winter refurbishing their pavilions to knock down the walls between the amateur and professional changing rooms. It was also because the 1963 season saw the first limited over competition played by the first-class counties, which that season was called the Knockout Competition for the Gillette Cup, later simplified to just plain Gillette Cup. The first competition was won by Sussex, led by one of the last of the true amateurs, Ted Dexter, who was by now just a 'cricketer', and it proved to be a huge success with the public.

The reasons for its popularity were not hard to find. It fitted the time frame that in the 1960s suited the casual cricket watcher, in that it was all over in just one day – a day of 130 overs, though – and it encouraged 'brighter cricket', whatever that was. The players enjoyed it, because it was a piece of relaxation from the hard grind of county cricket, and the spectators and the broadcasters, who had in recent seasons got used to the Rothman's Cavaliers on Sundays on television. The Cavaliers, sponsored by a tobacco company, were almost a cricketing circus featuring famous names from around the world, from the present and the immediate past, and their obvious enjoyment of the games they played quickly endeared them to the public. The counties, however, were less enthusiastic about letting their players risk injury by playing in light-hearted games every weekend, and so the Knockout Competition was born as a way of controlling a form of the game that might otherwise have slipped away from them.

The success of limited overs cricket was bound to change the game. The extent to which the game has been changed, however, is beyond what the originators of the Knockout Competition could possibly have imagined. This form of cricket attracted the crowds, the crowds attracted sponsors and the sponsors gave money to the game. The whole thing then became a self-fulfilling circle: as long as the game attracted the crowds, the money would be there, although at first nobody realised how much money there could be if there was some clever negotiation. The 65 over game, which is what the Knockout Competition was, quickly became a 60-over game, and when that was no longer exciting enough, 50-over and 40-over variants were introduced, until somebody had the bright idea of asking the professionals to play the game that every club and village cricketer had been playing on summer evenings since – well, probably since Lord Harris's time, a 20-over-a-side match. The success of the 20/20 format worldwide has changed the game entirely, and not in a way that traditionalists necessarily enjoy.

Throughout this evolution of cricket over the past 50 years, county cricket has been at the bottom of the pecking order. In 1906, there was only county cricket, and the Gentlemen v Players matches, to entertain spectators, but these matches still brought in the crowds. The decline in county cricket gates over the past hundred-plus years has been precipitous, but this has happened not just because the cricket has got more boring. In many ways it has become more interesting, with fielding skills, for example, way above what they were in Lord Harris's day. The main reasons for the decline of county cricket are three – the rise of other forms of summer entertainment, the emphasis that cricket's governing bodies have put on all other forms of cricket, and the way that all cricket has sold itself to the media. All three of these factors have militated against the survival of County Championship cricket.

We should remember that before the County Championship was instituted in the 1870s (and officially recognised from 1890) the big matches were controlled by impresarios who owned and managed touring teams with names like the All-England XI and the United All-England XI, the use of the word 'United' only showing that, like Orwellian ministries, the words reflected the opposite of what they should have meant. Their very disunity did nothing to enhance the reputation of professional players as organisers and leaders of cricket, a reputation that encouraged people to believe the myth of amateur leadership in sport, and thus facilitated the rise of the county structure of cricket. The counties, by recruiting the major landowners to their cause, were able to create a more stable form of cricket entertainment for the masses, but now there is the prospect of big cricket turning full circle and slipping back once again into the hands of the backers and promoters of private teams.

In 1906, when August came around, those people lucky enough to be able to take holidays from their workplaces would catch a train to the nearest bit of coast. For east Londoners, this meant Kent – north coast resorts like Whitstable, Herne Bay, Margate and Ramsgate, or south coast resorts like Folkestone, Dymchurch and Dover. Many more would come to Kent to help pick the hops for the local breweries like Mackeson and Shepherd Neame, and a good percentage of this flood of holidaymakers would want to see some cricket at Canterbury as part of their holiday. So Canterbury Week was assured of good crowds whoever was playing and almost regardless of the weather. Even half a century later, in the mid-fifties, the Canterbury Week Ball attracted 450 guests, from the High Sheriff down. In the 21st century, on the other hand, there is no Canterbury Week Ball at all. There are so many other ways of spending leisure time, even though most of us have far more of it to spend than our grandparents and great-grandparents ever had. Yet the trend was there, even in 1906. As holidays abroad began to become more commonplace, around 70,000 people passed through Dover that August on their way to, or back from, the continent. Nowadays holidaying in Britain is only for those who either have a peculiarly British hobby – walking in the Lake District or brass rubbing or collecting manhole covers – or who have no money to spare to go abroad, while the rest of the population heads to Florida or Ibiza or the Maldives for a two-week dose of sunshine and alcohol, an option which is probably cheaper than spending the same time holidaying in Britain. Very few people still come down from London to pick hops, and those that do are these days most probably Poles, Serbs or Lithuanians, who may be willing hop-pickers but who have no interest in cricket. Towns like Margate, Folkestone and Dover have long since given up the pretence of being fashionable resorts, and if you spread the net to other counties, you will find the same story at Scarborough, Blackpool and Hastings, among many other towns that used to host cricket festivals.

Even aside from the holiday weeks in August, there is little to attract anybody with only a casual interest in cricket to a county game. Most of the matches are played midweek, during working hours, and they probably won't finish on the day you choose to watch. One-day matches, by definition, finish on the day they start, thus guaranteeing the spectator a result (unless rain intervenes). The cricketers enjoy the freedom that limited overs cricket gives them, even if in their hearts they may believe that it does not matter as much as what is now known as 'red ball cricket'. It is no wonder that the game has become less subtle and that the money has followed that less subtle route. Many players can now earn many times their county salaries over a six-week stint in the IPL, and if that clashes with domestic tournaments, too bad. You cannot blame the players: all professional sportsmen have a limited time in which to earn as much money as they can, before age or injury reduces their effectiveness and their box office power, so quite naturally they wish to build up their bank balances while they can. You are a long time retired, as the saying goes.

The effect on county cricket and other first-class domestic competitions around the world is obvious. Fewer and fewer people come to watch the games, media interest becomes almost negligible and thus fewer and fewer people know about the games and interest dies away. County Championship cricket may be, to hardcore cricket followers, the only true form of cricket outside the Test arena, but it is dying. It is not quite dead yet, but it is hard to see how even the kiss of life, several seasons in intensive care and a whole bank of life-support machines can give the patient more than a very limited life span. It does not help that the cricket authorities of the world, lured by the riches promised by broadcasters, do their best to shove it on to the sidelines, while raking in the money available for broadcasting limited overs cricket, most notably T20 in all its guises. Even Test cricket in almost every country except England has limited appeal for local spectators. It is easy for a visiting Brit to get tickets for Test matches almost anywhere outside the UK, and at short notice, even though in England most Test matches are near sellouts, and Lord's Tests always so. On the other hand, T20 cricket is still a powerful attraction to the man in the street, and the woman and child in the street. The games may only last three hours, but those three hours are packed with all the razzmatazz of a baseball or American football game. It's clearly the format that appeals to the people that the ECB have defined as 'people who don't know they like cricket yet'. Whether or not a diehard cricket lover would describe it as cricket is another question, but it's played on the same grounds by the same people, so on the principle that if it quacks like a duck and swims like a duck, then it must be a duck, T20 must be cricket, and county and Test match cricket are the ugly ducklings.

It seems there can only be one of two outcomes. The two forms of cricket could split completely, creating two related but different sports with different ruling bodies, in the manner of rugby union and rugby league, leaving red ball cricket to work out ways to survive as a viable sport without having merely to hang on to the coat-tails of the white ball game. The other option, if the two games stay united under one ruling body, is that the white ball game will eventually – and in the not too distant future – come to take over the whole game, and county and Test cricket will be as obsolete as underarm bowling and curved bats. The long form of the game just cannot survive as a charity case looked after by the brash youngster that is white ball cricket. The brash youngster will get fed up soon enough, wondering why so much money that it earns has to go to supporting this elderly relative in a nursing home. Can't we just smother it with a pillow or send it off to Dignitas? That's what will happen unless the two forms of cricket split completely and red ball cricket is given the chance to work out how to carve its own niche in the sporting public's affections.

The players enjoy both formats, but switching from one to the other on an almost daily basis at the height of the season is hard, and it affects the ability of the players to perform at their best in either format. Of course, there are many players around the world who can be world beaters in all formats, but you could say the same of many rugby players who have shown that they can be top performers in both union and league. But not if they switch codes every other Thursday. To be the best, you have to concentrate on one thing. Very few people can get to the top of two greasy poles at the same time, whatever their skills may be. In cricket, players like Chris Gayle and Carlos Brathwaite, Eoin Morgan and Tymal Mills have chosen the shorter form of the game to become world beaters, and have all but given up any pretence of playing the longer game. They have made a very good living for themselves and do not worry about the fact that *Wisden* will not remember them as great Test cricketers. Other players, such as Alastair Cook and James Anderson, have played comparatively little limited overs cricket, and although it is possible that this has adversely affected their bank balances, it has meant that their astonishing careers in red ball cricket will guarantee them a place in imaginary all-time elevens for many generations to come. Which route is right and which is wrong? Answer: both and neither. But there must come a time, and it will be soon, when every professional cricketer must decide whether he or she wishes to be a white ball or a red ball player.

There is a similar situation in tennis, though not quite as pronounced. Originally, all games were played on grass – hence the name lawn tennis. Now, however, the four major championships are played on four different surfaces, and some players are far stronger on one surface than another. Rafael Nadal is virtually unbeatable on the clay at Roland Garros, while others virtually skip the clay court tournaments altogether. In an earlier generation Ivan Lendl won the French and US Opens three times each, but never won on Wimbledon's grass. The different varieties of tennis are unlikely to split entirely, but very different sets of skills are needed as players switch from one surface to another.

The limited overs format in cricket has one major advantage over any longer form of the game in that it is the way that school, club and village cricketers play the game. Since childhood, everybody who has played cricket on a social level has played a one-innings, one-day match, most often with a limitation on the number of overs each innings will last. It is therefore much easier for the casual observer to relate to the white ball game (although clubs and villages play with a red ball, of course) than the two-innings, four- or five-day matches which comprise the County Championship and Test matches. Social footballers play the same 90-minute game to the same rules that the professionals play each weekend; so do rugby, tennis, bowls, hockey – any team sport you care to mention – but only cricket historically has expected people to watch the professionals play a different game from the one the amateurs enjoy. No wonder the limited over game, played by professionals, caught on so quickly. People could understand it, and relate to it, and compare their own performances more easily with what the pros were up to.

What does all this mean for the county clubs? What should the club committees, largely made up of cricket-loving amateurs, be doing about it? Already county cricket is completely subsidised by ECB handouts from the television pot, which will only get bigger with the new television deal that runs from 2020. If that money disappeared, there is not one county that could continue to support its cricket team, unless a very wealthy and rather stupid benefactor came along, and there are precious few of those around – I know, I've looked for them.

The first thing that all county committees are doing is to continue to become more professional. Committee members these days have to bring some particular skill to the table, rather than just memories of a distinguished playing career or friendship with the chairman, which is largely how the committees of 1906 were made up. Increasingly, a triumvirate of chairman, chief executive and chief financial officer are running county clubs, and the rest of the committee act in non-executive roles, making sure that every decision taken is in the best interests of the club, rather than merely letting the chairman have his way because he is the chairman. And it is always a 'he', or it has been so far. There is a sad lack of diversity across all county committees, with only a handful of women even elected on to committees, and only two who have become chief executive of any county and perhaps three who have been elected to the role of president over the years. The president is a purely ceremonial position anyway, with some counties involving their president in club affairs more than others, but it is an opportunity for all county clubs to show that cricket is not purely a man's game – or indeed a white Anglo-Saxon game. Where is the diversity on committees which is shown on the cricket pitch itself, especially at levels immediately below the first-class game?

We can't blame the county committees for the state of cricket in England today, but perhaps they have their share of the guilt, because the component parts of the England and Wales Cricket Board (ECB) are the counties, first-class and minor counties, and MCC. So in theory the actions of the ECB are the actions of the counties. We can also criticise them for not realising quickly enough that the economic model on which county cricket was established in the 19th century – wealthy patrons subsidising a popular sport – has long since fallen into disrepair. However, the main issue remains that cricket has not got just one villain who is the cause of its current woes: this is not *Who Killed Cock Robin*, where we can all blame the Sparrow. We are in *Murder On The Orient Express* territory here (spoiler alert!) – everybody did it.

There are a number of factors that have changed the shape of cricket totally over the past 60 or so years. There's the complete professionalisation of the sport; Kerry Packer's revolution in the late 1970s; apartheid in South Africa; India winning the T20

World Cup in 2007; and the lure of television money, just to name a few of the more important ones. There is plenty of overlap between these five issues, as each affects the others to a greater or lesser extent.

Until the 1960s, probably the majority of first-class cricketers around the world did not see cricket as their sole source of income. There were plenty of amateurs in all cricketing countries, as well as professionals, and as with every sport in those days, even the greatest players did not earn very much. In the off-season, those who were not touring with a national team would have to supplement their incomes in other ways, because the county would not be paying them all year round. Perhaps the tipping point from amateur to professional came from Jimmy Hill, then chairman of the Professional Footballers' Association, who in January 1961 persuaded the Football League to abolish the maximum wage for professional footballers, and his Fulham clubmate Johnny Haynes became the first £100-a-week footballer. Today wages in football clubs have ballooned so that the highest earners may be taking home 500 times that amount or more, but once footballers were able to earn a decent wage, then professional cricketers would not be far behind. At the end of the 1962 season, when the distinction between amateurs and professionals in cricket was abolished, cricketers' pay packets could in theory expand to the size of their footballing counterparts. Certainly, those cricketers who also played professional football at the time were quick to appreciate the difference, and pass on the information to their cricketing colleagues. However, if Football League clubs and county cricket clubs were going to have to pay more money to their players, they in turn demanded a greater loyalty. This meant that the sportsmen had increasingly to choose one or the other: no more

Makepeaces and Burnups playing at the top level in both sports. Most chose football because the rewards were greater, even then. The county clubs did their best to keep wages down, despite the competition from other sports, for the very good reason that they could not afford to pay very much, given that the crowds who came to the games were as small and rapidly diminishing as they were in the 1950s. Cricket lost a good number of fine players when that choice had to be made, the last double international at cricket and football being Arthur Milton, of Gloucestershire and Arsenal, in the 1950s, before the football maximum wage was abolished.

Possibly spurred on by the need to make more money to be able to pay their stars a little more, in 1963 the first one-day tournament was launched in England, and the spread of this form of cricket around the world was pretty rapid. However, the creation of World Series Cricket in 1977 by the Australian Kerry Packer, while not specifically aimed at providing one-day cricket for his television channel, did focus the minds of administrators everywhere on the amounts of money cricketers were paid. Packer broke all the rules, and the players he recruited benefited significantly. By the end of the 1970s, the world's best players were beginning to earn the sort of money that their skills and dedication deserved, and counties were definitely feeling the pinch. Packer also broke the bond of loyalty between the players and their countries' governing bodies, a bond that has never been firmly re-established. The court case between the TCCB, as it then was, and the Packer organisation in the High Court in London was won by Packer, and the TCCB had to swallow its pride and make the best of what they had left. The knock-on effect was that the other national bodies whose players were converts to Packer, notably Australia and West Indies, also had to accept defeat, and their patrician assumption of the right to hold power within the sport was broken forever.

Almost a decade earlier, cricket, which had always considered itself above politics (despite the fact that men like Lord Harris had been active politicians all their adult lives), was embroiled in the D'Oliveira Affair, which eventually resulted in South Africa being banned from all international sport for two decades. This may not have had a direct influence on county cricket, but it created a market for expatriate South Africans with British connections to come to Britain to play in England, and in many cases, for England too. English crowds, who were just getting used to overseas stars who had been allowed to play in the County Championship for a year or two before the crisis year of 1970, loved it. To watch people like Allan Lamb and the Smith brothers was exhilarating, and county players learned from playing with them too. Players from all over the world began not only to become county stalwarts; men like Richard Hadlee and Clive Rice at Nottinghamshire, Barry Richards and Malcolm Marshall at Hampshire, John Shepherd and Asif Iqbal at Kent, or Courtney Walsh at Gloucestershire all became as familiar on the county circuit as the English-born players in the elevens. Even Yorkshire eventually dipped their toes in the waters of internationalism by contracting the teenage Sachin Tendulkar to play for them, and by the early years of the 21st century, the Australian Darren Lehmann was establishing himself as an all-time Yorkshire great. Loyalty to the county or country of one's birth was becoming a thing of the past. Many South Africans who could not play Test cricket in the 1970s and 1980s tried their luck elsewhere and nowadays all pretence at birth or other old-fashioned qualifications for the County Championship seem to have been dispensed with. The counties are working with something not far short of football's transfer system, but without the tens of millions of pounds. Yet.

As far as national qualifications are concerned, something certainly needs to be done. It seems amazing that somebody who has played for his country's under-19 team can a year or two later play for another country, basing their new allegiance on a residential qualification or a grandmother's passport or the like, but that is what is happening. Players are chasing international recognition wherever they can find it, and nobody seems to think this is wrong. There is a strong risk of a drain of talent from poorer nations to the richer ones, if something is not done to limit the freedom with which people can switch their national allegiance; well, we call it allegiance, but it is more just a preference, a pay cheque rather than a sense of belonging. The rule should be that if you play for a country at under-19 level, then that is the only country you can ever represent. There may be necessary exceptions to this rule, perhaps one every decade for overwhelmingly good reasons (such as when a country gains Test status for the first time), but otherwise that is how all countries in cricket should make it work. I fear that is wishful thinking, and the poorer countries will continue to lose their top talent to the richer ones.

In county cricket the same thing is happening. Even as late as the 1960s, players had to qualify to play for a county by date of birth or residence, and as great a player as Tom Graveney had to spend time out of the championship when he moved from Gloucestershire to Worcestershire, until he qualified by residence. In 2018, players moved from county to county in mid-season, with no pretence at any form of qualification apart from the right to work in Britain. The rich counties are picking the cream of the poorer counties' talent, until we can expect the lesser clubs, mainly the non-Test match clubs, will simply become feeders for the big boys. The dangerous precedent created by 'The Hundred', due to start in 2020, which will be built around eight 'franchises' based at Test match grounds, will only serve to speed up this process. Enjoy your cricket in Worcester, Leicester, Derby and Canterbury while you can.

When cricket professionalised, its management needed to get professional too. But like every other sport which up until then had been run by well-meaning and honest patrician amateurs, the lure of large sums of money brought many undesirable people into the game, as well as a few with all the right motives. It was not just cricket that attracted the less scrupulous: football and athletics and the Olympic Games, which was created to be the perfect stage for amateur sport for sport's sake, have all had to weather major scandals in their international governing bodies, and cricket has not been far behind them. At first, in all these sports, there were too many well-intentioned but naïve administrators who were just too easy to dupe. It has taken years for all these sports to begin to put their houses in order, and it would be a brave man who suggested that there was not more corruption still bubbling under the surface, waiting for some little scandal to expose it all again. Most sports administrators in the past were idealists, doing what they could for the love of their sport, but idealists are easy meat for those who just want a slice of the money. There is a great danger that before long the unscrupulous will be the power in all sport, including cricket, but only after they have installed a well-meaning figurehead to hide behind. Good governance has not been the rule in professional sport around the world for many years.

When India won the T20 World Cup in 2007, the structure of cricket changed completely. Until that moment, the Indians had been fairly cool towards the new format, but from that time on, they embraced it in a bear hug that has not weakened in the years since then. Indian broadcasters and the executives of the Board of Control for Cricket in India (BCCI), realising that the wish of the Indian people was to have a surfeit of T20 cricket, invented the Indian Premier League (IPL), in which the best players from all over the world, as well as many Indian cricketers, play about six weeks of T20 cricket, mainly under floodlights and to huge crowds inside the grounds and even larger ones on television and online. And they earn a lot of money, sums that were unimaginable only a few years ago, let alone to men like James Seymour who had to make do with a benefit of less than £2,000 after a career lasting over two decades. The auction system, which allows the franchises to bid against each other for players, means that the most sought-after players can make life-changing amounts of money: for somebody like Tymal Mills, who may be fast but who is so susceptible to injury that he cannot trust his body not to break down in longer forms of cricket, to be bought for around $1 million changes his immediate prospects, and if he is well advised, it changes his life forever. Many cricketers have therefore decided that there is little point in playing red ball cricket, or striving for a place in their country's Test team, because they can earn all they need in a couple of months of jet-set living in India.

The success of the IPL has spawned many imitators, and a canny cricketer can spend the northern hemisphere winter months moving between India, Australia, Bangladesh, Pakistan and West Indies picking up hefty pay cheques for less difficult playing hours than a summer in county cricket. The big innovation of the IPL was not the money per se, it was the fact that the teams are franchises, owned by the rich and famous. They may in theory be part of the BCCI competition structure, but the success of the tournament has transferred power away from the national ruling body and towards the franchises, so that, just as in professional football in Europe, the power lies with the clubs, not the national governing bodies. In football, players earn their income from club football; playing for the national side is an honour, yes, but it is done for love rather than money. Until now, in cricket, the money has been generated by the national game – Test matches and one-day internationals – rather than by the counties or their equivalents in other countries. The best-paid England cricketers are those on an ECB central contract: the cap for county clubs on the combined annual salaries of all the playing staff is about what a top footballer could expect to make in about four months' work. That is to say, one man in football can earn in a third of a year what an entire squad of perhaps 18 county players will earn in a full year. How long will county loyalty last? As *The Economist* put it in the week after the West Indies had beaten England 2-1 in the Test series early in 2019, the IPL and its imitators have 'put huge pressure on the culture of international competition that has underpinned cricket since the late 19th century. Attracted by million-dollar salaries in India, some of the best Caribbean players have abandoned their international side to become globe-trotting freelancers. No wonder the West Indies has struggled.' The article accuses India, England and Australia of doing little to stop this happening.

'They are mainly concerned to maximise their revenues from the shorter formats the franchises play.' Their conclusion, having seen that the crowds in Antigua, Barbados and St Lucia for the Tests were predominantly made up of holidaying Brits, was that 'these changes, the downgrading of international and Test cricket, will be seismic. They augur a game almost unrecognisable from its current form, and less loved by its devotees'.

Extrapolating from this, it could be argued that cricket could eventually go full circle and go back to a form of the game that was very popular in the 18th and 19th centuries – single wicket cricket. Then there's Five-a-Side cricket, One Man and his Dog against The Rest, One-Armed v One-Legged, Left-Handers v Right-Handers, Married v Unmarried, Smokers v Non-Smokers ... Who knows where the cricket authorities will look for popularity and money?

The ECB's creation of The Hundred is an attempt to repeat the money-spinning IPL formula in Britain, and we must wait to see how successful it will be. It will consist of eight franchises, carefully controlled by the ECB but with only a nod to the geographical loyalty that has been the basis of county cricket for a century and a half. It seems that the thought processes behind the invention of The Hundred (or whatever it might finally be called) are threefold. Firstly, the ECB needed a slightly different format so that they could patent and/or copyright it and make up for the millions they lost in not copyrighting 20/20, which was their original idea. The Hundred could perhaps be the format that is successfully sold to the Olympic Games or the Commonwealth Games, so the owners of the format could make millions, and become the Bernie Ecclestones of cricket. Secondly, the broadcasters need something that can be finished within three hours, so that it can be easily scheduled into the evening's viewing. T20 is meant to be over within three hours, but needless to say, with so much money now riding on the results in the IPL and other matches, they rarely do finish on time. Ludicrously, The Hundred is planned to have two built-in 'time outs', for strategic and/or advertising purposes, which means that the time saved by not bowling an extra 20 balls is largely frittered away on messages from the sponsors – but they of course add to the broadcasters' income. The third reason is that the tournament will break the power of the county set-up, by setting up the eight franchises – not really franchises at all as they will be tightly controlled from the centre, at least at first – with little connection to the traditional county structure. In a fit of collective madness, brought on no doubt by the lure of £1.4 billion over five years, the counties voted in favour. Some turkeys do vote for Christmas, and The Hundred could well be the butcher's knife to county cricket.

Will the crowds turn up to support a side with whom they have no obvious close connection? Does it matter? We have to remember that even though the ECB's money is coming from the broadcasters, with the gate receipts a comparatively incidental source of income, the television channels will want to show big crowds on screen, of the type that used to be the norm in Canterbury Week all those years ago, to prove they made the right decision in wanting to televise it. Expect a lot of very cheap tickets to become available if the tournament does not kick off with a bang. The broadcasters with the money and the facilities to show all these games in their entirety are not the free-to-air channels – they are all subscription channels. They do an excellent job, both technically and artistically, but they do it to a limited audience, and one of cricket's major problems in Britain is that it is not available to watch from the sofa unless you are willing to pay the subscription charges. As a result, public awareness of cricket has slipped dramatically, which in turn depresses interest in the game and thus depresses attendance at games as well. To take just one example: at the end of the 2018 cricket season, both Kent and Sussex were playing key championship matches which would decide whether or not either side would gain promotion to the First Division for 2019. It was also the first weekend of the football season when even a win or a loss by 20 goals would decide nothing over the season, but BBC SouthEast local television news did not even mention cricket that evening, preferring to spend several minutes assessing the chances of Gillingham FC in the lower reaches of the Football League. I don't blame Gillingham or their supporters, I blame the ECB who have over the past decade or so let cricket slip out of sight of the average sports follower. It is a huge mistake that no amount of money can make up for.

And what if The Hundred is not the success its promoters want it to be? What if after the first few years of televising the tournament, Sky or BT or the BBC or whoever decide that the viewing figures do not justify continuing to support it? If the TV money tap is turned off, professional cricket as it currently exists in Britain will die, and it will be a sudden and violent death. Scenarios don't get much more doomsday than this. There's a lot riding on this eccentric competition, and you will be hard put to find many people who are confident it will work. This is not a cricketing version of Project Fear, it is a realistic look at the risks and opportunities involved.

If you watch any cricket on a subscriber channel for longer than about three overs, you will come across an advertising break, and without any doubt the main subject of these advertisements will be gambling. Cricket grew from a rural pastime of shepherds into a hugely popular game in the 18th century because landowners and aristocrats saw it as a means of satisfying their urge to gamble. The first laws of the game include a section on betting, and one of Kent's great landowners, Sir Horatio Mann, was at the forefront of this. He managed to ruin himself by betting on the games he was trying to fix, but left behind him a sport that was much more fixed in the minds of the English public than it had been before he began promoting matches on his ground in Bishopsbourne, near Canterbury. That does not mean that gambling should be an intrinsic part of the game today, although of course it is. Cricket is a simple game to bet on, because there are so many uncertain factors in any game, especially in a five-day Test match, which people can take a punt on. It is therefore extremely tempting to try to make a gamble a sure thing, because asking a bowler to overstep the line on the fourth ball of his second over is not likely to change the result of the game, so where's the harm? Many people have given in to the temptation. The best attempted fix that I have come across is of the wicketkeeper who was asked to break the stumps every time the ball was returned to him, whether or not a run out might be possible, because the gambler making the request had placed a spread bet on the number of times the wicket would be broken during the day. Apart from wasting a bit of time, the actions of the wicketkeeper would have no effect on the game, so why not? Fortunately, the keeper in question was not interested.

So many fixes have been tried and exposed, and no doubt even more have gone ahead, that we should worry for the honesty of the game. Every country's board professes allegiance to their determination to stamp out corruption, and they may well all be entirely honest in their efforts, but as long as betting is encouraged on cricket, and as long as people in India, say, can watch an unimportant league game televised from the West Indies, for instance, people will gamble on the outcome and the details, and the temptation to cheat will be there. Please gamble responsibly, as the advertisements implore us, as if gambling in itself could ever be anything other than an irresponsible act.

Not that fixing matches or parts of them in order to win large sums of money are the only sources of corruption in cricket. As the sandpaper-in-Bancroft's-jockstrap scandal, when Australia played South Africa early in 2018, shows, trying to gain an unfair advantage by sailing close to the edge of the rules, or indeed far beyond the edge, is common enough these days. Umpires seem to spend as much time inspecting the shape and surface of the ball as they do counting the number of balls in the over. Sharp practice of all kinds has been part of the game since before the age of W.G. Grace, one of the canniest practitioners of ploys at the edge of morality that the game has ever known. The Laws of Cricket even include an opening section on The Spirit of Cricket, first published in 2000, suggesting that in the 21st century cricketers need to be reminded of the fact that cricket is just a game. 'Cricket owes much of its appeal and enjoyment to the fact that it should be played not only according to the Laws, but also within the Spirit of Cricket' is how this section begins. What the Edwardian amateurs took as read, the late Elizabethan professionals actually have to read. It's no good saying 'it's not cricket' as activities on the playing area show that, these days, anything is cricket, good and bad. Can we imagine Pinky Burnup with sandpaper down his trousers, or Arthur Fielder deliberately bowling a no-ball?

All these problems might lead us to believe that there is no hope for cricket as a professional game. But many of these issues are not new ones; the only problem is that the old ones are still there and nobody has come up with a solution to those yet, let alone the more modern problems like the fact that only 22 per cent of state schools today have facilities for cricket. How can cricket compete with other ways of spending our leisure hours and our leisure pounds? How can the game survive another 200 years?

For professional cricket to flourish, there must of course be a strong underpinning of amateur clubs and amateur players in towns and villages around the country. Here things are not looking healthy. Although Kent is, after Yorkshire, the county with the most active cricketers, every year there are clubs which fold through lack of players, never to restart. The pressure on land is something that has been increasing since cricket began. In the 18th century, there was plenty of space to fit in all of Britain's population of around seven million people, and only 15 per cent of them lived in towns and cities. Today, Britain's population is around 66 million, and the vast majority live in towns and cities, mainly because the towns and cities have had to expand to house this almost tenfold increase. This in turn puts great pressure on cricket pitches, which once were merely underused parts of the rural landscape but which now can be profitably converted into housing, supermarkets, car parks or motorways. That's a lot simpler than preparing and maintaining a cricket pitch to a decent standard, and trying to encourage 11 people to turn out on a Saturday or Sunday afternoon. And with the decreasing number of clubs and pitches, there is a corresponding decrease in players. In 2008 there were 428,000 registered cricketers in

Britain (exactly what a 'registered' cricketer is, I cannot be sure), but by 2016, just eight years later, this number had tumbled to 278,000, a drop of 150,000 players. At this rate, there will be nobody left playing cricket by the year 2030. To give them their due, the ECB and all the county clubs are well aware of this and are taking steps to halt the decline. But the economic pressure on land will not get less; a few acres of greensward can be put to far more profitable use than hosting a gathering of men in white flannels about 20 times a year.

One part of cricket's heritage that has survived to the early 21st century, but which must now be on life support, is Canterbury Cricket Week. In 2017, Canterbury Week did not include a county game for the first time in very many years, the only first-class game being a match against the touring West Indians. In 2018, the 167th Cricket Week took place at Canterbury, with mixed fortunes. Firstly, it had to break with tradition and be held in mid-July rather than early August, because the fixture list gave Kent no home first-class games in August. There were two T20 evening matches at either end of the Week, both of which had to be abandoned partway through when the rains came down, and a four-day game against Leicestershire, which Kent managed to lose in two blisteringly hot days. There was no Ladies' Day, no military bands playing, and only a smattering of tents – the president shared a marquee with the Band of Brothers, while the Buffs, the Kent Supporters' Club and CAMRA made up the numbers. The days of the mayor of Canterbury, the Canterbury Club, I Zingari and several private individuals hosting a tent are long gone. It was hardly a Festival Week at all. In 2020, with the arrival of The Hundred, it seems quite likely that there will be no possibility of a Canterbury Week at any time in high summer.

This collapse of Canterbury Week has been both insidiously slow and, in the end, calamitously sudden.

To read the newspaper reports in Kent's golden years before the First World War is to be reminded that the past is another country. 'Clubman' in the *Sketch* wrote in August 1912, 'The first week of my holiday is being spent at Canterbury where last week was the County Cricket week with its usual accompaniment of illuminations and arches of flags down the main streets, and band concerts in the Dane John, the little park tucked snugly away in a bend in the city walls, and The Old Stagers' performances at the Theatre, and balls in the Rink, and much entertainment in the tents which half-encircle the cricket ground. I know of no other week in which good cricket and all the other joys of life are so pleasantly mingled.' He goes on to say that 'the flags of a dozen clubs fly before the tents on the St Lawrence Ground, and many of the county magnates who have secured the coveted sites for tents – for it is easier to buy a thousand acres of farmland in Kent than to obtain the right to a few square yards of turf at the edge of the field during Canterbury Week – also fly their private colours'.

In 1914, Canterbury Week ploughed on despite the outbreak of war. Although some members of the Kent committee, notably Major the Hon. J.S.R. Tufton, advocated ceasing cricket immediately and encouraging all Kent players to join up at once, Lord Harris was more relaxed. Pelham Warner, then captain of Middlesex but already working his way up the administrative hierarchy of cricket, telegraphed Lord Harris on Monday, 3 August, the first day of Canterbury Week and the day before war was declared, saying, 'Think cricket should stop when war declared kindly send your advice. Warner'. Harris, no doubt aghast at the prospect of a minor European skirmish upsetting his beloved Festival Week, sent back the message, 'The committee will not at present cancel fixtures. They dislike the idea of their employees having to suffer. Harris'. Kent duly played both games that week, losing to Sussex but beating Northamptonshire, but the two Canterbury Week Balls, scheduled for the Wednesday and the Friday at the skating rink (from 9.30pm, tickets 17/6d each) were cancelled. Only 40 tickets had been sold in advance and the Austrian Ambassador's Band, which had been booked to play, was unsurprisingly no longer available. Attendance at the cricket on the Thursday was much smaller than usual, but the game continued, and when Canterbury Week was able to reappear after the war, it seemed stronger than ever.

In 1923, Pelham Warner, writing in *The Cricketer*, described the Week as 'that festival that stands for all that is most pleasant and charming and delightful in cricket'. This was the Week in which Frank Woolley scored 270 against Middlesex, the highest score by a Kent batsman on the ground until it was beaten by Matt Walker against Somerset 73 years later, and the ground and the spectators were looking at their very best. 'The parades on the Thursday, when there seemed to be more ladies on the ground than men during the intervals, were worthy of an Eton and Harrow match,' as Warner went on to note. 'The members' tents can seldom have contained more noted county families.' Warner was, of course, an outrageous snob to our modern eyes, and his definition of 'pleasant and charming and delightful' included only those of sufficient social standing to be noticed by him.

Five years later, the cricket writer G.D. Martineau commented on 'the Blythe memorial and the rough, natural grass around the tall trees, under which grey sheep were strolling. I cannot imagine that any first-class ground in England keeps the rural origin of the greatest game more closely within memory.' Sheep strolling under the trees by the Blythe memorial? During Cricket Week? This was Canterbury playing up to Kent's 'Garden of England' soubriquet to the full.

Even in 1931 there were 17 tents around the boundary edge during the Week, of which seven were private tents taken by wealthy Kent families, and the other ten were taken by organisations such as the Band of Brothers, The Old Stagers, I Zingari, the Buffs, and the Royal East Kent Yeomanry. The president had his own tent, too, of course. Seventeen was perhaps the largest number of tents that Canterbury Week saw – details are sketchy – but throughout the 1920s and 30s, the numbers were always at least 15. Even after the Second World War, Canterbury was a beacon in the gradually less glorious world of county cricket.

For a few years after the war, cricket made a strong comeback in the public's affections. Gerald Hough, then Kent's manager and secretary, stated that in 1939 attendances at Kent home matches were just short of 100,000, but in 1946 they were 125,611 and in the gloriously hot summer of 1947 they rose 45 per cent to 182,452, of whom roughly a quarter were 'juveniles'. Canterbury Cricket Week reflected this growth, with 13,267 people paying for admission on the first day of the Week, a figure that had only been beaten when the touring Australians played at Canterbury in the 1930s, and for the whole Week the paying attendance was 46,756, about double the average paying attendance for Weeks in the 1930s. It looked as though cricket as a popular spectator sport was safe for generations to come, at least in Kent.

In that year, 1947, there were several other cricket festivals going on around the country. Kent had weeks, on a less grand scale than Canterbury, but weeks nonetheless, at Tunbridge Wells, Gravesend, Maidstone and Dover, while Gloucestershire enjoyed a record crowd of 14,500 for the first day's play of their Cheltenham Festival game against Middlesex. Yorkshire held their usual festival at Scarborough (Yorkshire v MCC and North v South), and a quick flick through *Wisden* reveals a Harrogate Festival in late August (North v South again and M. Leyland's XI v The Rest), a Hastings Festival (South of England v South Africans and South of England v Sir Pelham Warner's XI) and a Kingston Festival in early September (North v South yet again, and Middlesex and Essex v Surrey and Kent). By 2018, Harrogate and Kingston-upon-Thames were no longer used as first-class grounds, and nor were Gravesend, Maidstone and Dover, while Hastings had become a supermarket car park. Only Cheltenham and Scarborough battle on, but crowds have dwindled. The high hopes of 70 years ago have been dashed.

In 1960, Colin Cowdrey, then captain of Kent, wrote a foreword to *The Story of Canterbury Week*, by H.W. Warner, in which he wished that 'I could have been Lord Harris's guest at one of the famous Weeks. Arriving along the narrow streets, decorated with bunting …. We would alight behind the tents, a busy scene, with his Lordship's minions by the score …. In a few moments we would be at ease, seated with good conversation all round, a feast of cricket before us and an air of festivity to warm our heart. Maybe it has changed a certain amount today, but we must not lose it all. It is our privilege and responsibility to remember with awe and gratitude and do our utmost to guard our heritage.' Even in 1992, in a book celebrating 150 years of

Canterbury Cricket Week, Christopher Taylor, a former curator and librarian of Kent CCC, was able to write that 'visitors will see little change when they arrive today at the St Lawrence Ground … They will still see the huge semi-circle of colourful tents and marquees sweeping away to the left' occupied by all the old favourites of a century before – the Buffs, I Zingari, Band of Brothers, the East Kent Club and so on. But how quickly it has changed, in only a quarter of a century or so.

There are so many other things to occupy people's time and minds in August each year. Canterbury City Council, encouraged by the low profile that professional cricket has given itself and perhaps not encouraged by the comparatively poor performances on the field by the Kent elevens of the 90s and the 21st century, have all but forgotten the fact that cricket brings in something like £10 million to the local economy each year, and thus do little to join in with Canterbury Week. Individuals no longer see entertaining at the cricket ground as a good thing to do, and most organisations now think that hiring a tent for a week would be difficult to justify to their members, shareholders or accountants. To add to the general trend away from entertaining at cricket festivals, the way that Kent CCC, like many other county clubs, has organised its commercial contracts means that, for example, there are strict rules governing the supply of food and drink to the ground. One company has bought the ground catering rights – a profitable deal for the county club – which means that tent holders cannot bring in their own supplies without paying fairly hefty corkage charges (and whatever the food equivalent of corkage is).

Then there's the British summer weather, fickle at best. Even though the great families of Kent risked it at the end of the 19th century and still booked tents through rain or shine, these days everybody has the option of heading off to Greece or the south of France or Florida rather than sticking around in England and taking pot luck with the climate. And you can still follow the game on the internet from your deckchair on the beach. What's more, the quality of the cricket on show at county grounds these days, inevitably stripped of the centrally contracted England stars, is not always as great as can be found at a Test match. Why would anybody, apart from extremely sociable county cricket fanatics with money to spare, want to take a tent at Canterbury or any other county ground?

We may be able to blame the fixture list for finally killing Canterbury Week, but in truth, if it dies it will be because it no longer serves its purpose, it makes no money and it goes almost unnoticed by the local population anyway. We are a very long way from Lord Harris, or even Colin Cowdrey, in our commitment to the Week.

If all this sounds much too gloomy, far from the triumphant optimism of Chevallier Tayler's painting of sunshine on a beautiful cricket ground, it is only because there is little concrete evidence that all the fine words that are brought out in mission statement after mission statement by cricket's governing bodies are turning into reality. We can only hope that they do mean what they say, that they really are trying to put things right, to recreate an exciting and vibrant sport that very many people will enjoy watching, playing and hearing about. It is possible if the will is there. There is a huge amount of goodwill for cricket, but unless it can fight back to its central place in British sports lovers' consciousness, it will fade away, and become just a memory, a sport of the past like stool ball and knur and spell.

Cricket has always changed to survive. From the third stump and round-arm bowling to helmets and the front foot no-ball law, there have been changes almost every season, and the cricket we watch now is quite different from the cricket that Lord Harris would have seen from his tent at Canterbury, however much the basic principles remain the same. The only way the game can readily survive in this asset-rich time-poor era is to concentrate on the version of the game that fits in with people's lifestyles, and with the experiences of those who play the game at whatever level. That means limited overs cricket – the white ball game. It means floodlit matches and further tinkering with the playing conditions. It means the eventual death of red ball cricket, of two innings, four- and five-day matches, with the possible exception of one or two Test matches each year to keep the tradition going. The yelps of pain from those who would hold back this progression should be heard, but not heeded. The money is riding on white ball cricket in its several formats, and money will always beat tradition when they clash.

The women's game, which is currently enjoying a thoroughly deserved surge in popularity, is centred on the white ball game, with only England and Australia indulging in the longer form of the game. There can be few who were there who would not put the Women's World Cup Final of 2017 into the select category of Thrilling Games of Cricket I Have Seen, so it would be foolish to imagine that cricket cannot survive without red ball cricket. It can and I think of necessity it will. In 20 years' time, if Kent and other county cricket clubs still exist, and if the St Lawrence Ground has not been sold for housing and a new stadium built somewhere else in Kent, and if therefore Canterbury Week is still going strong, it will consist of several white ball games, played by both men and women. Whether there are marquees and flags fluttering in the breeze, marching bands or landed gentry in all their finery is much harder to say. And whether or not there is much of a crowd watching the cricket live at the ground, it will be streamed to thousands – perhaps millions – of people in Kent, in other parts of Britain and around the world who will be able to follow the game from wherever they are. You can bet on that.

The future can be bright for cricket if we understand that the game has always changed and must continue to adapt to fit in with the times. Darwin's principle of the survival of the fittest applies to sports just as much as it does to Galapagos penguins. Cricket must adapt or die. It can, it must, it will adapt.

1906 was not the beginning of county cricket, or even of modern cricket, and it was certainly not the end, but Lord Harris and Albert Chevallier Tayler, two good men who loved cricket and who had its best interests at heart, captured forever a moment when the sport, Britain and its empire were at their very peaks of power, excitement and public involvement. Britain has changed completely since then, and is changing still; its empire has crumbled and its influence in the world has shrunk, but that does not stop us looking back with affection to those days when life may not have been easier for most people, but it was certainly simpler. Cricket may have grown since then, bats have got bigger, fielders more athletic and records of all kinds may have tumbled, but it would be hard to argue that it is any better than it was on that August day in 1906, when Blythe bowled to Tyldesley and the sun shone on the crowds at the St Lawrence Ground in Canterbury.

Bibliography

An incomplete list of the books and magazines that I have consulted in the writing of this book should include:

Barclay's World of Cricket, edited by E.W. Swanton (Collins, 1980)

The Canterbury Cricket Week – Volume First (William Davey, 1865)

Cardus Uncovered, by Christopher O'Brien (Whitethorn Range, 2018)

Cricket – The Golden Age, by Duncan Steer (Cassell, 2003)

Cricket's Golden Summer, by Gerry Wright & David Frith (Pavilion, 1985)

Cricketers of Vanity Fair, by Russell March (Webb & Bower, 1982)

The Father of Modern Sport, by Keith Booth (Parrs Wood Press, 2002)

For Kent And Country, by Paul Lewis (Reveille Press, 2014)

The Golden Dream – Biography of Thomas Cooper Gotch, by Pamela Lomax (Sansom, 2004)

Great Characters From Cricket's Golden Age, by Jeremy Malies (Robson Books, 2000)

A Half Forgotten Triumph, by Martin Moseling & Tony Quarrington (Sportsbooks, 2013)

Bibliography

A History of County Cricket – Kent, by R.L. Arrowsmith (Arthur Baker, 1971)

The History of Kent County Cricket, Volume I, edited by Lord Harris (Eyre and Spottiswoode, 1907)

The History of Kent County Cricket, Volume II (Kent CCC, 1997)

The History of Kent County Cricket Club, by Dudley Moore (Christopher Helm, 1988)

Kent County Cricket Club Annual, several editions (Kent CCC)

Kent, Cricket Champions 1906, by Clive Porter (Limlow Books, 2000)

Lord's, 1787–1945, by Pelham Warner (Harrap, 1946)

More Than A Game, by John Major (Harper Collins, 2007)

The Noblest Game, by Neville Cardus and John Arlott (Harrap, 1969)

Pageant of Cricket, by David Frith (Macmillan, 1987)

Pageantry of Sport, by John Arlott & Arthur Daley (Paul Elek, 1968)

Presidents of M.C.C., by Jonathan Rice (Methuen, 2006)

A Social History of English Cricket, by Derek Birley (Aurum, 1999)

Start Of Play, by David Underdown (Allen Lane, 2000)

The Story of Canterbury Cricket Week, by H.W. Warner (J.A. Jennings, 1960)

Stroke of Genius, by Gideon Haigh (Simon & Schuster, 2016)

Swinging Away, by Beth Hise (Scala, 2010)

Treasures of Lord's, by Tim Rice (Collins Willow, 1989)

The Way To Lord's, edited by Marcus Williams (Collins Willow, 1983)

Wisden Cricketers' Almanack, many editions from 1865 to 2018 (Bloomsbury Publishing)

Wisden on The Great War, edited by Andrew Renshaw (Bloomsbury, 2014)

Wisden Collector's Guide, by Andrew Renshaw & Jonathan Rice (Bloomsbury, 2011)

Newspapers and magazines, current and extinct, including:

Athletic News; The Cornishman; The Cricketer; The Daily Telegraph; The Economist; The Globe; The Graphic; Illustrated London News; Kent & Sussex Courier; Kent Messenger; Leeds Mercury; Liverpool Echo; Morning Post; The Pall Mall Gazette; The Sketch; The Sphere; Sporting Life; The Star; The Tatler; The Times; Vanity Fair; Western Daily Press; Whitstable Times

Websites

Cricket Archive – cricketarchive.com

ESPNcricinfo – www.espncricinfo.com

Kent CCC – kentcricket.co.uk

National Portrait Gallery – npg.org.uk

Penlee House – www.penleehouse.org.uk

Wikipedia – en.wikipedia.org

Other sources:

Belmont House archives

Kent CCC archives

MCC archives